THE PENTECOSTAL MINISTER

SERMON RESOURCE MANUAL

THE PENTECOSTAL MINISTER

SERMON RESOURCE MANUAL

VOLUME 3

Floyd D. Carey and Hoyt E. Stone, Editors

P·R·E·S·S

CLEVELAND, TENNESSEE 37311

Library of Congress Catalog Card Number: 87-72041
ISBN: 0-87148-951-1

CONTENTS

Section 1, Manuscript Sermons

Section 2, Outline Sermons

INTRODUCTION

Pathway Press is pleased to present this third volume in our annual series of sermons and outlines gleaned from Pentecostal ministers of all denominations.

These sermons have been selected, edited, and designed exclusively for Pentecostal ministers. The book divides conveniently into two sections: **Manuscript Sermons**, which offer a total message with appropriate illustrations and guidelines, and **Outline Sermons**, designed to provide seed thoughts so that one can include personal illustrations and significant points.

By and large, these sermons have been purposefully solicited from people actively involved in the pastoral ministry. The primary exceptions are sermons from denominational leaders, but these too are men and women known for their spiritual zeal and continuing involvement with pastoral responsibility. Our writers represent congregations of different sizes and from varying social and geographical backgrounds. All contributors are Pentecostal. We believe the strength of *The Pentecostal Minister Sermon Resource Manual* lies in the variety of preaching styles and the wide range of subjects covered.

Though beleaguered by demands from many publics, the pastor in today's world knows that first and foremost he must minister the Word. In order to do this with power and effectiveness, the minister must prayerfully cultivate his personal relationship with Christ in the private sanctuary, and he must enter the pulpit with a true message etched on his heart of the Holy Spirit. We as editors in no wise offer these sermons and outlines as a substitute for that intimate and absolutely necessary contact with God; but we do offer them as a sample of the type preaching being done in Pentecostal pulpits across our nation and as food for thought, perhaps seed thoughts, from which a busy pastor may occasionally sip and find inspiration.

Since the sermons are arranged primarily to express variety, rather than by subject or author, we suggest ready use of the contents pages. Also, each chapter heading is boldfaced, making it easy to flip to the numbered chapter or the designated page. Sermons are listed alphabetically in the reference section.

Note too that in this volume we have listed our contributors in alphabetical order, with names, addresses, and position held at the time of contribution (see author index).

The editors appreciate the warm reception given to Volumes 1 and 2 of this series. We owe a special note of thanks also to James Humbertson, Daniel Black, Lance Colkmire, Nancy Neal, and David Willingham, associate editors at Pathway, for their editorial assistance.

Pathway Press welcomes your comments and suggestions in terms of how you relate to these sermons and would appreciate any suggestions, comments or contributions toward volumes to follow.

Floyd D. Carey and Hoyt E. Stone

The Editors

JESUS, THE HOLY SPIRIT BAPTIZER

Ray H. Hughes

SCRIPTURE: Matthew 3:11

INTRODUCTION

Out of 400 years of silence, John the Baptist announced that Jesus Christ is "the Lamb of God, which taketh away the sin of the world" (John 1:29). But his message was twofold. He preached not only that Christ takes away sin but also that He shall baptize men with the Holy Ghost and with fire. The Gospels bear a fourfold record of this prophecy of John the Baptist. It might seem strange to some that the first promise of Pentecost in the New Testament was made by a "Baptist."

THE ANNOUNCEMENT OF THE BAPTIZER

Matthew recorded the prophecy: "I indeed baptize you with water unto repentance: but he that cometh after me is mightier than I, whose shoes I am not worthy to bear: he shall baptize you with the Holy Ghost, and with fire" (Matthew 3:11).

Mark recorded an abbreviated version: "I indeed have baptized you with water: but he shall baptize you with the Holy Ghost" (Mark 1:8).

Luke recorded it in a similar manner as Matthew: "John answered, saying unto them all, I indeed baptize you with water; but one mightier than I cometh, the latchet of whose shoes I am not worthy to unloose: he shall baptize you with the Holy Ghost and with fire" (Luke 3:16).

John expanded the prophecy by including the baptism of Jesus: "And I knew him not: but he that sent me to baptize with water, the same said unto me, Upon whom thou shalt see the Spirit descending, and remaining on him, the same is he which baptizeth with the Holy Ghost" (John 1:33).

In all four of the Gospels, Jesus Christ is set forth as the Holy Spirit baptizer. The fact that the Holy Spirit has taken such care to record this passage in each of the Gospels is evidence of the importance of the experience. It is not only by the Evangelists that the baptism with the Holy Ghost was foretold but by the Lord Jesus himself. When the earthly ministry of Christ was coming to an end and the Cross and the Resurrection were behind Him, Jesus announced to His disciples, "For John truly baptized with water; but ye shall be baptized with the Holy Ghost not many days hence" (Acts 1:5).

Jesus Christ spoke with the same definiteness with which John the Baptist spoke. He said, "Ye shall be baptized." Without a doubt, Jesus and John were talking about the promise of the Holy Ghost that was fulfilled on the Day of Pentecost and that was accompanied by the outward physical evidence of speaking with other tongues as the Spirit gave the utterance.

The apostle Peter confirmed that the baptism with the Holy Ghost was the outpouring of the Spirit which fell on him at Pentecost. "And as I began to speak, the Holy Ghost fell on them, as on us at the beginning. Then remembered I the word of the Lord, how that he said, John indeed baptized with water; but ye shall be baptized with the Holy Ghost. Forasmuch then as God gave them the like gift as he did unto us, who believed on the Lord Jesus Christ; what was I, that I could withstand God?" (Acts 11:15-17).

Peter said that John the Baptist had prophesied that Jesus would baptize with the Holy Ghost. Peter was expressing that it was this experience that he had received at Pentecost and that was now poured out upon the household of Cornelius.

THE MEANING OF BAPTISM

John baptized with water, but Jesus baptized with the Holy Ghost and with fire. It has been said that individuals came dripping from the hands of John but they came burning from the hands of Christ. The baptism with fire is not something separate and distinct from the baptism with the Spirit. The fire expresses the intensity and the power of the divine baptism. It means that a soul baptized with the Holy Ghost is a soul on fire—a soul consumed by the flames of Pentecost.

Lord, as of old at Pentecost
Thou didst Thy pow'r display;
With cleansing, purifying flame,
Descend on us today.

The word *baptize* ordinarily means "to dip"; therefore, the believer is dipped in the Spirit. The word is sometimes used with reference to dipping garments to dye them. So the baptized man is one who is dyed through and through with the Spirit. The color and texture of his life have been changed by being immersed in the Spirit. He is Spirit-dipped, Spirit-saturated, Spirit-soaked, and Spirit-drenched.

At the outset of this message, let us understand that this baptism with the Holy Spirit, which is the crown and glory of Jesus' ministry, is not just a historical experience or a memorial of past glory; it is a continuing ministry of Jesus Christ for believers today. In John 1:33 the word *baptizeth* is used. This word of linear force indicates that baptizing with the Spirit is a continuing ministry of Jesus Christ; He continues to baptize believers today. For those who say that the baptism with the Spirit is an experience for the past, notice that our Lord said, "that he may *abide with you for ever*" (John 14:16).

Forty-six years ago when I attended my first Pentecostal service, they were singing a song titled "He Abides":

He abides, He abides,
Hallelujah, He abides with me!
I'm rejoicing night and day,
As I walk the narrow way,
For the Comforter abides with me.

Praise God! The Comforter abides in this 20th century.

THE RELATIONSHIP OF THE BAPTIZER

Jesus and the Fullness of the Spirit

Christ received the fullness of the Spirit. According to Luke 4:1, He was full of the Holy Ghost. "For God giveth not the Spirit by measure unto him" (John 3:34). There was a concentration of the Spirit in the person of Christ.

At the baptism of Jesus, the Spirit descended upon Him and abode with Him. This was His anointing for the ministry. And it was by the power of the Spirit that Jesus carried out His ministry. Every phase of Jesus' earthly life was intimately connected with the Spirit. C.K. Barrett said, "Jesus has the Spirit in order that He may confer it. And it is the gift of the Spirit which preeminently distinguishes the new dispensation from the old."

Jesus and the Guidance of the Spirit

The Spirit is evident in the ministry of Christ from His baptism to His ascension. No part of His life, ministry, or miracles can be divorced from the leadership of the Holy Spirit. He was led by the Spirit into the wilderness. After His wilderness temptation "Jesus returned [into Galilee] in the power of the Spirit" (Luke 4:14), who equipped Him for His work. No man can be an effective minister without the Spirit. No matter how brilliant or talented and no matter how polished or magnetic, no one can do God's service effectively without the empowerment of the Spirit. All of the human equipment that a workman has is useless without the equipment of the Spirit.

Jesus and the Anointing of the Spirit

In Acts 10:38 we read, "God anointed Jesus of Nazareth with the Holy Ghost and with power: who went about doing good, and healing all that were oppressed of the devil; for God was with him." When Christ was anointed with power, He went about doing good. The anointing motivated, actuated, and propelled Him to do good. Likewise, when the anointing comes upon us, we will be constrained to go.

He acknowledged that the Spirit of the Lord was upon Him and provided the anointing for Him to preach the gospel, to heal the sick, and to bring deliverance to the captives. He was anointed by His fellows. It was through the power of the Spirit that He wrought miracles and cast out devils (Matthew 12:28).

It was the Holy Spirit that raised Christ from the dead. "But if the Spirit of him that raised up Jesus from the dead dwell in you, he that raised up Christ from the dead shall also quicken your mortal bodies by his Spirit that dwelleth in you" (Romans 8:11).

The Spirit that is to quicken our mortal bodies and to raise us up in the last days is the Spirit that raised up Jesus. So then, in every sense of the word, the life of Jesus was a life in the Spirit. He was by Him promised, by Him conceived, by Him begotten, by Him indwelt, by Him empowered, by Him taken to Calvary, and by Him raised from the dead. He was "justified in the Spirit . . . [and afterward] received up into glory" (1 Timothy 3:16).

Although Christ performed His ministry in the power of the Spirit and the Spirit was given without measure unto Him, He could not baptize anyone in the Holy Ghost until He, through the eternal Spirit, offered Himself a sacrifice unto God. Only then would He receive the promise of the Holy Ghost with power to baptize believers.

During His ministry upon the earth, He had baptized no one with the Holy Ghost. According to John's testimony, "The Holy Ghost was not yet *given*" (John 7:39). Notice that the word given is italicized. The scripture literally reads, "The Holy Ghost was not yet" (John 7:39).

The Holy Ghost had been at work in the world since Creation. It was the Spirit of God that moved upon the face of the waters (see Genesis 1:2); it was by the Spirit that the heavens were garnished (Job 26:13). The psalmist said, "Thou sendest forth thy spirit, they are created" (Psalm 104:30). The work of the Spirit was evident throughout the life of Israel and the prophets of old. What then did John when he said that the Holy Ghost was not yet given? He meant simply that Jesus had not yet given the baptism of the Holy Ghost and that the Spirit had not come in the Pentecostal fullness.

THE ASCENSION OF THE BAPTIZER

The coming of the Spirit was dependent upon the ascension, the exaltation, and the glorification of Jesus Christ. For this reason Jesus said, "Nevertheless I tell you the truth; It is expedient for you that I go away: for if I go not away, the Comforter will not come unto you; but if I depart, I will send him unto you" (John 16:7).

His departure prepared the way for the coming of the Spirit. He could not be with them in the fullest sense unless He departed from them. The choice lay between Christ in a bodily fashion or the divine Spirit capable of being universally present at all times. In the days of His flesh, He was limited by space and time. But His departure made possible the coming of the Spirit, who could be with the disciples constantly, everywhere, at all times. The Comforter, unbound by flesh, could be in an unlimited number of places at once, working miracles and doing the work of Christ. By His departure His local presence was changed into a universal presence. Therefore, He said, "It is . . . [better] for you that I go away [it is to your advantage; it is profitable for you]: for if I go not away, the Comforter will not come unto you" (John 16:7).

THE EXALTATION OF THE BAPTIZER

In His humiliation, Christ longed for His original glory. He prayed, "And now, O Father, glorify thou me with thine own self with the glory which I had with thee before the world was" (John 17:5). This was not a selfish desire, because He knew what it would mean to His disciples. He said, "And, behold, I send the promise of my Father upon you" (Luke 24:49) and "If I depart, I will send him unto you" (John 16:7). He spoke of praying for and giving the Spirit (John 14:16) and of sending the Spirit (John 15:26).

The culmination of Christ's exaltation was the authority or power of baptizing with the Holy Ghost as was foretold by John the Baptist and announced by the Lord himself. When He ascended on high, He gave gifts unto men. The Spirit was Christ's ascension gift to the church. It was this point that Peter drove home to the multitudes on the Day of Pentecost. "Therefore being by the right hand of God exalted, and having received of the Father the promise of the Holy

Ghost, he hath shed forth this, which ye now see and hear" (Acts 2:33).

Christ is now ascended and is at the right hand of God, above all principality and power and above every name that is named. We know He is ascended on high, because He promised to pour out the Spirit from on high (see Luke 24:49; Isaiah 32:15). He is not among the patriarchs; He is higher up. He is not among the prophets; He is higher up. He is at the right hand of God. He is at the right hand of power—the right hand of Majesty on high—in the midst of the throne, which is the throne of God and of the Lamb. It is from this lofty position that He sheds forth, or pours forth, the promise of the Father. It is from this exalted seat that He dispenses the Holy Ghost. In response to the outpouring of the Spirit, Peter said, "He hath shed forth this, which ye now see and hear" (Acts 2:33). Literally, He was saying, "All that you see flows from Him." This is the communication of the Holy Ghost from the hands of the exalted Redeemer. He is the unique dispenser of the Spirit. He is the bearer of the Spirit. The whole fountain of the Spirit is His to pour forth upon His followers. He is the Holy Ghost baptizer, whom everybody ought to know. You cannot receive the Spirit except through Him.

The outpouring of the Spirit was direct evidence that Jesus was with the Father. It was a witness of the Resurrection consummated in crowned glory. It was a testimony of the lordship of Christ. It was the divine fulfillment of the promise that could not find its accomplishment until the Son of Man had been glorified.

THE BAPTISM AND THE BAPTIZER

The purpose of the advent of the Spirit was to empower believers to continue the ministry and works of Jesus Christ. The Spirit, who equipped Jesus for His mission equips, His disciples to carry on.

"Verily, verily, I say unto you, He that believeth on me, the works that I do shall he do also; and greater works than these shall he do; because I go unto my Father" (John 14:12).

The baptism of the Spirit is a glorious baptism of divine energy. The Holy Spirit is to be to each of us what Christ would have been if He had remained among us and had been our personal companion and guide.

On the day of His ascension shortly before His departure, Christ said, "But ye shall receive power, after that the Holy Ghost is come upon you: and ye shall be witnesses unto me both in Jerusalem, and in all Judaea, and in Samaria, and unto the uttermost part of the earth" (Acts 1:8). This power (*dunamis*) is the ability to accomplish. It is divine empowerment.

The Spirit is come to give not a new revelation but an interpretation of the old revelation of the mystery of Christ's birth, the wonder of His life, the glory of His cross, the miracle of His resurrection, the truth of His ascension, and the reality of His return.

CONCLUSION

There are some who are looking for a new revelation of Pentecost; however, it is not a new revelation that we need but a reaffirmation of the old revelation of Jesus Christ, which is ever new. There is a great deal of talk today about relevancy. My friend, Christ is relevant to our times. He has transcended every age and has become the ideal of this age. The Scriptures say that the heavens will wax old like a garment and like a vesture they will be folded up, but "thou remainest . . . thou art the same" (Hebrews 1:10-12). The theme of the Spirit is Jesus Christ. The Spirit has come to glorify Christ and to take the Christ and show Him unto us that we in turn might glorify Christ and show Christ to the world.

The Spirit is the Lord of the harvest, and He is in the world, calling out a people for His own and gathering them together for the last day. Jesus is God's last word to man, and He is the answer to all human ills. The Spirit that you feel drawing you and convincing you of Jesus Christ is the Holy Spirit, for "no man can say that Jesus is the Lord, but by the Holy Ghost" (1 Corinthians 12:3).

WHEN SELF-WILL CHALLENGES DIVINE AUTHORITY

R. Lamar Vest

SCRIPTURE: Jeremiah 5:1-5, 12, 23, 24, 30, 31

INTRODUCTION

This is one of the most startling messages in the entire Bible. It is part of a message which was to be declared in the house of Jacob and published throughout all of Israel. It shows to all generations the inevitable results when self-will challenges the rule of God. The prevailing issue of our time is, Who is going to be god? Humanism and materialism call for self to be in charge. The Bible declares that the Lord is God. We ultimately decide this question by our faith and action.

The prophet Jeremiah is one of the most colorful figures to walk across the pages of the Bible. His very name evokes in us the idea of trouble and lamentation. He is so very human that most of us can readily identify with him. We watch him go from periods of great elation to deep depression in a very short period of time. He was overwhelmed by the lingering agony of an exhausted nation that had come to disregard God in its daily affairs. The priests were ruling by their own authority, and the people had forgotten God, hewed

21

cisterns in the sand, and spurned the forgiveness of God. Perhaps worst of all, they seemed to love the condition they were in. By their actions, they were saying, "Stand back, God, we are capable of running this show by ourselves."

When self-will challenges divine authority, there will always be some terrible corresponding effects.

A LACK OF REVERENTIAL AWE OF GOD

Jeremiah 5:12-14 (*TEV*) sums up the attitude of the people: "The Lord's people have denied Him and said, 'He won't do anything. We won't have hard times; we won't have war or famine.' They have said that the prophets are but windbags and that they have no message from the Lord. The Lord God Almighty said to me, 'Jeremiah, because these people have said such things, I will make my words like a fire in your mouth. The people will be like wood, and the fire will burn them up.'"

The people did not deny the existence of God. They were too smart for that. They simply denied God's authority and His right to work in their lives. Like spoiled children they said, "He won't do anything about the way we're living." The battle for the soul is fought at this point: "What rights does God have in my life?"

Our self-willed society does not want to dump God altogether. We just want to keep Him at a comfortable distance. We want enough of God to keep our guilt above the threshold of pain but not enough to disturb our prejudices. We want enough of God to fulfill our personal ambitions but not enough to change our plans. We want enough of God to live respectable lives but not enough to alter our lifestyles. We want enough of God to say grace over our meals but not enough to help feed the starving people of this world. We want enough to escape the flames of hell but not enough to get nervous over the fact that most of the people of this world are on their way to hell.

There is a great gulf between the God of the Bible and the god of modern folk religion. The god of folk religion is seen as a god of sentimental love rather than holy love. He is viewed as "the man upstairs" who is approached as an indulgent, permissive father who demands nothing and expects nothing.

In Jeremiah 5:22, God literally said to the people, "Go and stand by the sea. Its fury cannot prevail against the limits I have set." He asked, "Can you beat back the waves? Can you divert the paths of the sea?" The message was clear: Stand by the sea and understand that there is a higher power than yours. If you cannot control the creation, how can you control the Creator?

A LOSS OF A RIGHTEOUS CONSCIOUSNESS

When self-will challenges divine authority, there is always a loss of righteous consciousness. People shut up their hearts of compassion for others and start looking out for number one.

In Jeremiah 5:1 the prophet was challenged to find one man who executed justice and sought for truth. Literally, he was challenged to find one man who had a right relationship with God and cared about his fellowman. He sought among the poor, but he found none. He sought among the rich, and he found none. He found none among the priests nor the pagans. No class has a monopoly on elevating self-will above the rule of God.

There is evidence today of a great loss of a righteous consciousness:

- Human life is disregarded by abortion on demand.
- Child abuse and child pornography are rampant.
- Sin is winked at by religious leaders.
- Thousands of people die each year because of drunk drivers.

Until God is given His rightful place in our society, we will continue seeing a disregard for truth and justice.

A DISASSOCIATION OF THE GIFT FROM THE GIVER

Jeremiah 5:24 says, "Neither say they in their heart, Let us now fear the Lord our God, that giveth rain, both the former and the latter, in his season." This is a natural process. When God is pushed back and self-will takes over, it is necessary that God be excluded from any involvement in supplying our needs. There is more of a tendency to say, "Look what I have done" or "I did it my way" than to say, "Look what God has done or I did it His way."

There are many scriptural warnings regarding our self-dependency. Paul tells us in 2 Timothy 3:2, "Men shall be lovers of their own selves, covetous, boasters, proud" Galatians 3:3 warns, "Are ye so foolish? having begun in the Spirit, are ye now made perfect by the flesh?"

Most people like to feel that they are totally in charge. The last thing they want is for some preacher to disturb them. They had much rather someone confirm the way they are living. They want someone to tell them how good things are and that they are going to get even better. May God never let us forget what we were without Him. May we never cease to remember that we are nothing without Him. All good and perfect gifts come from Him.

CONCLUSION

Jeremiah's solemn warning is this: You can deny God's right in your life. You can close Him out if you choose. You can hold Him at arm's length if you wish. But what will you do in the end

—when all that you have accumulated falls down around you?

—when your family disintegrates and your sons and daughters defiantly shake their fists in God's face?

—when all hell breaks loose and the devil and his imps run rampant over this earth?

—when you stand in the presence of the Almighty God?

What will you do when you finally see that the Word of God is true, that Satan is the deceiver, that God is the sovereign ruler of the universe?

Holy, holy, holy! The Lord God omnipotent reigneth!

ARE WE BETTER THAN THEY?

H. Lynn Stone

SCRIPTURE: Romans 3:1-26

INTRODUCTION

This is an awesome question posed by Paul. The intent of this message, centered around Paul's penetrating question and straightforward answer in Romans 3:9, is not to condemn. Rather, it is to enable us to realize that the same Word that brings us to the humble realization that we are not better than they also assures us that they are not better than we. Acceptance of this simple truth can be transforming.

We will examine this question under three headings: (1) What did this question mean for the apostle Paul? (2) What does this question mean for us today? (3) What are the implications of this question for us?

WHAT DID THIS QUESTION MEAN FOR THE APOSTLE PAUL?

Let's carefully note Paul's question, "Are we better than they?" In Paul's everyday language this question was one word: *Proexometha*? The word means "to jut out, excel, be first" (Arndt & Gingrich) or "to excel to one's advantage, to surpass in excellences which can be passed to one's credit"

(Thayer). It is also translated "Are we any better?" (*NIV*), or "Do we excel?" (Marshall).

To fully understand what Paul was asking in verse 9, we must also examine his earlier question in verse 1: "What advantage then hath the Jew?" In this first question Paul used the word *perisson* from the Greek preposition *peri* (translated "advantage"), which means "all the way through, across, around" (Thayer). It is from this word we get the English word *perimeter* which literally means "the number of meters around."

Therefore, while Paul was dealing with quantity or area or size in Romans 3:1, in Romans 3:9 he was dealing with equality or character. The Jews do have an advantage. The area or size of their understanding has been enlarged through the Scriptures. "Chiefly, because that unto them were committed the oracles of God" (Romans 3:2). However, they are no better. The *quality* of their individual lives is no better before the righteous God. The broad expanse of their learning has not and cannot make the quality of their *being* any "better."

But how did Paul describe those Gentiles to whom he was comparing the Jews? His words are quite descriptive in Romans 1:28-31:

Furthermore, since they did not think it worthwhile to retain the knowledge of God, he gave them over to a depraved mind, to do what ought not to be done. They have become filled with every kind of wickedness, evil, greed and depravity. They are full of envy, murder, strife, deceit and malice. They are gossips, slanderers, God-haters, insolent, arrogant and boastful; they invent ways of doing evil; they disobey their parents; they are senseless, faithless, heartless, ruthless (NIV).

It is in comparison with these Gentiles that Paul asked, "What then? are we better than they?" Do we excel these awfully wicked and sinful Gentiles? His answer is unflinching: "In no wise." Knowing that such an indictment against the Jews would be rejected by many, Paul immediately appealed to the Old Testament Scriptures, quoting from both the Book of Psalms and the prophet Isaiah:

What then? are we better than they? No, in no wise: for we have before proved both Jews and Gentiles, that they are all under sin; as it is written, There is none righteous, no, not one: there is none that understandeth, there is none that seeketh after God. They are all gone out of the way, they are together become unprofitable; there is none that doeth good, no, not one. Their throat is an open sepulchre; with their tongues they have used deceit; the poison of asps is under their lips: whose mouth is full of cursing and bitterness: their feet are swift to shed blood: destruction and misery are in their ways: and the way of peace have they not known: there is no fear of God before their eyes (Romans 3:9-18).

Thus Paul showed from the Scriptures themselves that the Jew in his own nature was no better than the most wicked Gentile. The Jew did have an advantage. He had the covenant of circumcision and the inspired Scriptures. But neither the covenant with the patriarchs nor the law from Sinai nor the words of the prophets can save a man from the wretchedness of sin. While the Jew had an advantage, he was no better.

WHAT DOES THIS QUESTION MEAN FOR US TODAY?

If the Jews were no better than the Gentiles, then surely there is significance to the question we pose to ourselves today, "Are we better than they?"

Let the significance of Paul's words sink in. The Jews were the sons of David, Abraham, Adam; the Jews had the covenant of circumcision; the Jews were delivered from Egypt through the Red Sea; the Jews were led by the pillar of fire by night and the cloud by day; the Jews celebrated Passover, Pentecost, and the Feast of Trumpets; the Jews had built the tabernacle in the wilderness and the Temple at Jerusalem; the Jews gave to us the Old Testament Scriptures; and the Jews brought forth the incarnate Messiah to a lost and dying world.

Yet Paul said, "We are in no way better than they!"

If Paul, speaking of the Jews and Gentiles in his day, could emphatically say, "We are in no way better than they," then we today also must continue emphatically to say, "We are in no way better than they."

There are many different ways to frame the question, but the answer must continue to be "We are in no way better than they."

Are whites better than blacks? "No, we are in no way better than they." Are Americans better than Russians? Are middle-class homeowners better than the homeless? Are well-fed consumers better than starving beggars? Are healthy bodies better than the handicapped, the sick, or those with AIDS? Are those with good minds better than the mentally ill? Are males better than females? Are the delivered better than those in bondage to alcohol, tobacco, or drugs? Is the heterosexual better than the homosexual or lesbian? Is the married better than the single? Is one with a faithful companion better than the divorced? Are those who live by the law better than criminals who transgress the law? Are those with Harvard degrees better than illiterate mothers on the streets of Haiti? Are we in the Church of God better than they who are in the Assemblies of God, or Baptists or Catholics? Are Bible-believing Christians better in themselves than the Muslims who are incensed about the novel *Satanic Verses*, which suggests that Muhammad wrote the *Koran* and his wives were prostitutes? Are we who preach love and forgiveness any better than the Ayatollah Khomeini, who said, "Even if Salman Rushdie repents and becomes the most pious man of all time, it is incumbent on every Muslim to send him to hell"?

The answer must always be "We are in no way better than they." It is true that some white people have an advantage over some black people, but neither is better than the other. It is true that God made mankind male and female, but neither is better than the other. It is true that there is an advantage in today's world in having an education, but that does not make a person better. There is an advantage to living a sexual lifestyle according to the truths of Scripture, but that does not make the heterosexual better than the homosexual.

In fact, even after being born again, *we* are still no better. As Paul explained the goodness of the Christian life, it is no longer *I* that really lives. Rather, "I am crucified with Christ: nevertheless I live; yet not I, but Christ liveth in me: and the life which I now live in the flesh I live by the faith of the Son of God, who loved me, and gave himself for me" (Galatians 2:20). The only holiness of the saint is the holiness of the perfect Son of God.

WHAT ARE THE IMPLICATIONS OF THIS QUESTION FOR US?

Three significant implications surface when we truly come to realize we are no better than they: (1) The righteousness of God is revealed to the world; (2) the true gracious work of salvation is manifested through justification, redemption, and propitiation; and (3) we are enabled to truly come to believe that all people are equal. I am no better than any other. No other is better than I.

The Righteousness of God Is Revealed

Paul expressly made this statement in Romans 1:16, 17: "For I am not ashamed of the gospel of Christ: for it is the power of God unto salvation to every one that believeth; to the Jew first, and also to the Greek. For therein is the righteousness of God revealed from faith to faith: as it is written, The just shall live by faith."

As long as the Christian displays the attitude that he or she is better than the nonbeliever, it takes away from the glory of the righteousness of God and displays a type of self-righteousness. But as Paul explained, the glorious gospel is the "power of God unto salvation." To be saved requires God's power, not ours. We simply believe Him. Furthermore, it works the same way for both the Jew and the Gentile, for both the churched and the unchurched, for both the morally good and the rank sinner.

Paul explained again that the purpose of salvation is to declare God's righteousness and not ours, "that he might be just, and the justifier of him which believeth in Jesus" (Romans 3:24-26). Concerning any type of boasting on our part, he said, "Where is boasting then? It is excluded" (v. 27).

Therefore, the first implication for us today in understanding the question "Are we better than they?" is that God is the righteous One of both heaven and earth. Let us show forth His righteousness as Christ lives within us. To the rankest sinner let me have grace to proclaim, "I am no better than you. But there is a righteous God, and there is an advantage in believing that His Son died for our sins."

There Are Advantages in Accepting Christ as Savior

Paul pointed out that even though within ourselves we are no better than others, there are tremendous advantages for those who accept the gospel of Jesus Christ. These advantages are summed up by three words, *justification, redemption,* and *propitiation,* which the apostle used in Romans 3:21-26:

But now the righteousness of God without the law is manifested, being witnessed by the law and the prophets; even the righteousness of God which is by faith of Jesus Christ unto all and upon all them that believe: for there is no difference: for all have sinned, and come short of the glory of God; being justified freely by his grace through the redemption that is in Christ Jesus: whom God hath set forth to be a propitiation through faith in his blood, to declare his righteousness for the remission of sins that are past, through the forbearance of God; to declare, I say, at this time his righteousness: that he might be just, and the justifier of him which believeth in Jesus.

The first advantage mentioned is *justification.* "To be justified" is a legal term. It means that all charges have been satisfied in the courtroom. The fine has been paid. Now, instead of being criminals fleeing from the wrath of the law, we are upright citizens of a heavenly kingdom. Furthermore, we have an advocate, a mediator, a lawyer, in the person of Jesus Christ who eternally represents us before the throne and pleads our case. He himself reminds the Father Judge that all the debt for every crime has been paid and we who believe in Him have no further fine to face.

The second advantage is *redemption.* The word used by Paul was the common word used for the purchasing of the freedom of a slave. It means literally "to buy out the marketplace," because the slave auction blocks of most Oriental cities were near the center of the market area or town square. Through His Spirit, Jesus today goes into the spiritual marketplaces of this world, looking for men and women enslaved to sin, being auctioned to the highest bidder. However, none can outbid the price Christ has paid for each soul. To those who accept His offer, the soul is set free from the slavery of sin.

The third advantage is *propitiation.* Paul used the same word here as that which describes the mercy seat in the tabernacle. After Moses built the ark of the covenant and placed the Ten Commandments within, he then made a golden cover that was placed on top of the ark and called the mercy seat. It was there before the mercy seat that God said He would meet with His people. Christ is our covering of the law, our mercy seat before the Almighty God, where we now are able to come into His presence before the throne of grace.

Therefore, while believers are no better than they, believers certainly have a threefold advantage. Instead of the disadvantage of a criminal life, there is the advantage of citizenship. Instead of the disadvantage of enslavement, there is the advantage of freedom. And instead of the disadvantage of broken fellowship with God because of broken commandments, there is grace and mercy at the throne of grace.

All Are Equal

The final implication in understanding Paul's question, "Are we better than they?" is the affirmation within us that all men and women are equal. This has two meanings: first, we are no better than they, and second, they are no better than we.

One of the great needs of the Christian world is for each individual to have the humility to be able to sincerely say, "I am no better than you." Regardless of what advantages one may have, they are not sufficient for the salvation of the soul. Only in Christ is salvation come to the world. He treats us all differently according to our own individual needs and advantages. Yet in love He treats us all exactly the same. He died for the most wretched of sinners just as much as He died for the most pious saint.

However, once you have been able to honestly believe that you are no better than they, then (and then only) you can also believe that they are no better than you. If you think you're better than Judas, then you will always think that John was better than you. But if you can honestly see through God's Word that you are no better than the betrayer of the Lord (besides, have you never betrayed Him?), then you can also come to understand that John the Beloved was no better than you. God loves you just as much as He loved the Beloved Disciple. In fact, when you believe, you are His beloved disciple. Are we any better than they? No, in no way! Are they any better than we? No, in no way!

THE LORD'S PRAYER

G. Raymond Carlson

SCRIPTURE: John 17:1-26

INTRODUCTION

The prayer the Lord Jesus taught His disciples (Matthew 6:9-13) is commonly called the Lord's Prayer. Without arguing needlessly about terms, one can say that while this prayer is a pattern our Lord gave His disciples to follow, He did not offer it Himself. John 17 records what really is the Lord's prayer, the prayer Jesus offered to His Father.

The portion of the Gospel of John that relates the public ministry of our Lord may be compared to the court of the Old Testament tabernacle. His private ministry to the disciples (recorded in chapters 13-16) may be likened to the first room of the tabernacle—the Holy Place. In the tabernacle was another room, the Holy of Holies, into which only the high priest might enter once a year on the Day of Atonement. To follow the analogy, we are given in John 17 a glimpse into the holiest of all as we hear what the Lord Jesus says to the Father.

To share the true sense of the awesome scene of Christ in intercession before the Father causes us to stand with bowed heads and hearts. The greatest battle in history was about to culminate.

Early in His ministry Jesus stated that His hour had not yet come (John 2:4). In John 12:23 He declared the arrival of that hour. Now He opened this solemn prayer with the words "Father, the hour is come" (John 17:1).

THE THREEFOLD INTERCESSION

The prayer of our Lord can be divided into three parts: (1) Christ's prayer for Himself (vv. 1-5); (2) His prayer for His apostles (vv. 6-19); (3) His prayer for His church (vv. 20-26).

Christ addressed God in simple intimacy. Repeatedly He said, "Father." In verse 3 He called the Father the "only true God." In two places He added adjectives, calling Him "Holy Father" (v. 11) and "righteous Father" (v. 25).

Our Lord referred to His disciples 46 times in the prayer, using such terms as *they, them, these, thine,* and *mine.* He referred to the *world* 17 times. Twice the word is used in a sense of creation, six times it refers to man's abode, four times to the inhabitants of the world, and five times in the sense of antagonistic hostility to Christ.

Seven marks of discipleship are recorded in verses 2-8:
1. The believer is given to the Son by the Father (v. 2).
2. The believer has eternal life (v. 2).
3. The believer knows the Father through the Son (v. 3).
4. God's name is manifested to the believer (v. 6).
5. The believer keeps the Word of God (v. 6).
6. The believer knows the godhead or deity of the Son (v. 8).
7. He believes that the Father sent the Son (v. 8).

Seven times the Son expressed the thought that the disciples were given to Him by the Father (vv. 2, 6 [twice], 9, 11, 12, 24). How wonderful! God gave believers to His Son. The Son has given gifts to believers—eternal life (v. 2), the Father's words (vv. 8, 14), and His glory received from the Father (v. 22).

We, however, have given nothing; we have only received. There is nothing that we can give until we accept Him and become His. Then we can—and must—give ourselves wholly to Him in loving devotion and service.

TAKEN OUT OF THE WORLD

"The men which thou gavest me out of the world . . ." (v. 6). The word *world* here is used in the sense of the communion and fellowship of the world. The world lies in the lap of the Wicked One. It is unconcerned in mind, hostile in heart, and contrary in will to the things of God. The Bible tells us that the worldling—the unbeliever—is

1. **Dead in sin.** "Verily, verily, I say unto you, He that heareth my word, and believeth on him that sent me, hath everlasting life, and shall not come into condemnation; but is passed from death unto life" (John 5:24). "And you, being dead in your sins . . . hath he quickened together with him, having forgiven you all trespasses" (Colossians 2:13).

2. **Diseased.** "And as Moses lifted up the serpent in the wilderness, even so must the Son of man be lifted up" (John 3:14).

3. **Darkened.** "For ye were sometimes darkness, but now are ye light in the Lord: walk as children of light" (Ephesians 5:8).

4. **Doomed.** "But the heavens and the earth, which are now, by the same word are kept in store, reserved unto fire against the day of judgment and perdition of ungodly men" (2 Peter 3:7).

But a change comes. The dead are made alive. The diseased are made whole. The darkened are brought to light. The doomed are delivered.

This change comes through the new birth. The new birth is wrought by means of four instruments: (1) the Word of God (John 5:24; 1 Peter 1:23), (2) the blood of Christ (1 Peter 1:18, 19), (3) the Spirit of God (John 3:5), and (4) faith (Romans 10:9, 10). The Word illuminates, the Blood purges, the Spirit performs, and faith partakes.

Those who believe are given to Christ by the Father "out of the world."

DIFFERENT THAN THE WORLD

"I pray for them . . . not for the world, but for them which thou hast given me; for they are thine" (v. 9). "They are not of the world, even as I am not of the world" (v. 16).

34

Although the believer is in the world, he is not to love the world (1 John 2:15-17). The evil, unbelieving world is the whole system that is governed by Satan, the god of this world (2 Corinthians 4:4). It represents all that is opposed by the Lord Jesus Christ and all that is not of the Father. Worldliness is human activity with God left out. It is what we are, not just what we do—"for as . . . [a man] thinketh in his heart, so is he" (Proverbs 23:7).

The believer, though different from the world, still lives in the midst of worldlings. There is connection, but no real communion. The Bible says, "Ye adulterers and adulteresses, know ye not that the friendship of the world is enmity with God? whosoever therefore will be a friend of the world is the enemy of God" (James 4:4).

IN THE WORLD

"I am no more in the world, but these are in the world" (v. 11).

To some there may seem to be contradictions in these verses: "out of the world" in verse 6 and "in the world" in verse 11. Believers are saved *from* the world but left *in* the world. We are here for a purpose.

In the Dark Ages, man thought that to be saintly he must isolate himself from the world. Piety and monastic living came to be considered synonymous. But it must be remembered that sin and temptation abound everywhere in this world. Sin began in solitude. Eve was alone when she yielded to Satan's wiles. The Savior was alone in the wilderness temptation and battled alone in the Garden of Gethsemane.

We cannot isolate ourselves from the world; but thank God, He has given us the provision of insulation. It is a matter of state and not of place.

HATED BY THE WORLD

"And the world hated them, because they are not of the world, even as I am not of the world" (v. 14).

The world hated Jesus because His life and teachings condemned worldly living. He had chosen His apostles out of the world and had given His Word to them; therefore, the world hated them because they were not of the world. There is mortal combat between the kingdom of light and the kingdom of darkness.

LEFT IN THE WORLD—KEPT FROM THE EVIL

"I pray not that thou shouldest take them out of the world, but that thou shouldest keep them from the evil" (v. 15).

God wants us in this world. We are to be the "salt of the earth" and the "light of the world" (Matthew 5:13, 14). As salt we are to preserve by penetration; as light we are to guide by illumination.

The apostle Peter said, "Your adversary the devil, as a roaring lion, walketh about, seeking whom he may devour" (1 Peter 5:8). Satan did his best to destroy the apostles but was unsuccessful. They went forth into the world doing the will of the Father and spreading the glorious message of salvation through the Lord Jesus Christ. In like manner, Satan is pursuing after Christians today, but Jesus prayed for us that we should be kept "from the evil"—literally, "from the Evil One" (v. 15). We are "kept by the power of God" (1 Peter 1:5) as we place ourselves where we can be kept; or as Jude 21 says, "Keep yourselves in the love of God, looking for the mercy of our Lord Jesus Christ unto eternal life."

Satan is a defeated foe. Christ conquered him at Calvary, and we can claim that victory. As we meet the devil on the battlefield of life, we can win through the power of God.

SENT INTO THE WORLD

"As thou hast sent me into the world, even so have I also sent them into the world" (v. 18).

Now we come to the crux of the matter. This is the place of our relationship to the world. We are "sent . . . into the world."

HOW ARE WE SENT?

Take special note of the word as. "As my Father hath sent me . . ." (John 20:21). How was He sent?

Christ was sent (1) as One who didn't belong here, (2) in love, (3) in the fullness of time, (4) to declare the Word of

God, (5) to reveal the character of God, (6) equipped with the power of God, (7) to give His life a ransom, and then (8) to be called back to the Sender.

In like manner—"as"—Christ sends us into the world. We do not belong to the world; our citizenship is in heaven. We are pilgrims and strangers on earth. But we are sent here.

And we are sent in love. Who can measure the love that sent Christ from heaven's glory to Bethlehem's manger, to Gethsemane's battle, to Calvary's cruelty, and to the borrowed tomb? It begs for description. That love wants to grip our hearts and motivate us.

Nobody could know the truth of God, the holiness of God, and the greatness of God's compassion. But God chose to reveal this, and He revealed it in the person of Jesus Christ. Learn to know Him, and you will see God—His truth, His holiness, and His loving compassion.

As Christ was sent, He now sends us and works through us. Our Christian testimony by life and lip will show the outworking of God's character in our lives.

And as Christ was endued with power for His task, He has provided an enduement for us through the baptism in the Holy Spirit. He has given us the Holy Spirit to empower us for witnessing.

WHY ARE WE SENT?

"That they all may be one . . . that the world may believe . . . that the world may know . . . " (vv. 21, 23).

There is a unique oneness existing between God the Father and God the Son. They are one in essence, nature, and substance; and one in plan, purpose, and cooperation.

As the Father sent the Son, the Son sends us that the world may believe and know and experience the love of God. God has a great delight in His Son and in believers, for they are "accepted in the beloved" (Ephesians 1:6). And He has a deep yearning for the unbeliever. He wants His yearning love for the unbeliever to be turned into a love of delight. This He will do through human channels.

As the Father sent the Son in the "fulness of the time" (Galatians 4:4), the Son is sending us.

Our primary objective is basically a twofold task: (1) to evangelize individuals—"preach the gospel to every creature" (Mark 16:15) and (2) to disciple peoples—"teach all nations, baptizing them . . . teaching them" (Matthew 28:19, 20). This is our sacred assignment.

God has chosen men—you and me—to do this job. It is impossible to separate this task from men—*sent* men. God calls for men who are committed, involved, and endued—men who know God, believe God, trust God, and prove God.

God's purpose in this age is to establish a church (Acts 15:13-17). When this has been done, our Lord shall "see of the travail of his soul, and shall be satisfied" (Isaiah 53:11), and that church shall be "to the praise of the [Father's] glory" (Ephesians 1:6), "that in the ages to come he might shew the exceeding riches of his grace in his kindness toward us through Christ Jesus" (Ephesians 2:7). Then we shall "be with . . . [Him]" and "behold . . . [His] glory" (John 17:24).

DESIGN FOR DISCIPLESHIP

Sandra Goodwin Clopine

SCRIPTURE: Luke 9:23; John 8:31; Philippians 2:5-8; 3:17-19; Mark 8:34-36; 2 Timothy 4:7

INTRODUCTION

Jesus had a design for the evangelization of the world. His plan was a good one. He expected His sons and daughters to be followers, learners, and reproducers of Himself. But somewhere along the line human understanding has caused gaps in carrying out this plan. To fill the design, God's people must recognize and reemphasize their role as disciples. Whether man or woman, single or married, hourly worker or professional, teenager or senior citizen, my identity is in my being a disciple of the Lord Jesus Christ.

Discipleship is not based upon where I am, what I do, or what position I hold but upon who He is, what He does, and what He wills for my life. While serving as Nebraska Ladies Ministries director, I worked up a slogan using the letters L-A-D-I-E-S to stand for "Living As Disciples In Everyday Service." My thought was that as we go about our tasks, however mundane they might be, we are disciples of the Lord Jesus Christ. We're not only disciples when we dress up and go to church or teach a Sunday school class, but we're also disciples around the house when we view life from behind a vacuum cleaner or when we manage an office in a high rise. Whatever our status, we should be living as disciples in everyday service.

Someone has prayed, "In a world of casual inquirers, Lord, I would be a seeker." True Christians are seeking God today —not just casually interested in spiritual strokes but seeking for God to move and have His way in their lives.

In Luke 9:23 Jesus said, "If any man will come after me, let him deny himself, and take up his cross daily, and follow me." John 8:31 tells us, "If ye continue in my word, then are ye my disciples indeed." And in Philippians 2:5-8 Paul wrote, "Let this mind be in you, which was also in Christ Jesus: who, being in the form of God, thought it not robbery to be equal with God: but made himself of no reputation, and took upon him the form of a servant, and was made in the likeness of men: and being found in fashion as a man, he humbled himself, and became obedient unto death, even the death of the cross."

To be the kind of disciples God wants us to be, we must follow Christ, feel His concern, and finish our course.

FOLLOW CHRIST

Mark 8:34-36 proclaims, "And when he had called the people unto him with his disciples also, he said unto them, *Whosoever* will come after me, let him deny himself, and take up his cross, and follow me. For *whosoever* will save his life shall lose it; but whosoever shall lose his life for my sake and the gospel's, the same shall save it. For what shall it profit a man, if he shall gain the whole world, and lose his own soul?"

We must understand that those who took up their cross and became disciples of the Lord Jesus Christ, as the 12 who followed him intimately for three to three and one-half years of His life, were ordinary people like you and me. Remember also that beyond those 12 were many other men and women who followed the Lord and ministered to Him as He went from place to place. They were the "whosoever" of Mark 8. Jesus called people from all walks of life, pouring into them His vision and goals for the evangelization of the world.

They watched Him when He ate, saw Him when He ministered, and knew the times He slept. Because they observed that Christ was One who knew how to pray, the time came that the disciples inquired concerning prayer. He didn't have to draw all kinds of diagrams, create formulas, or say to them, "Now I'm going to teach you to pray." But they saw His life in action and desired to be like Him.

The early disciples were ordinary people, but the thing that made them special was their willingness to follow Jesus. These were people who couldn't understand all that God had planned. They tried to figure out what Jesus was talking about concerning the Temple being destroyed and raised up again in three days. They couldn't get it straight in their minds. When Christ began to speak about it Peter reacted. He didn't want to hear that. Because of Peter's response, Jesus had to rebuke him one of His own disciple who had been so close to Him (Mark 8:31-33).

Peter was just an ordinary person and was trying to put the message in a human framework. He may have been saying, "We don't want that to happen, Master; we're going to protect You. It will never take place like that." But Jesus let his disciples know this was not thinking as God but as man. He knew His followers were ordinary people, caught up in the mind-set of human activity, but He also knew they were willing to follow.

When God spoke to Moses to be the leader of His people, Moses was so taken back that the first thing he said was, "Who am I, that I should go?" (Exodus 3:11). Finally he expressed the real thing that was bothering him and said, " 'O Lord, please send someone else to do it' " (4:13, NIV).

We can *act* so humble, can't we! "O Lord, someone else can do a much better job." Really what we're saying is, "I don't want to be bothered. Let me do my own thing." But God spoke to Moses and in essence said, "You don't have to worry about your inabilities or weaknesses. I AM qualifies you for the task."

God was not looking for some perfect human specimen that had everything together, but He was looking for one that could prove through his life that God was the great I AM. He would give the directions, and Moses would carry them out. Together they would be a team in ministry.

Notice that *to follow* is to answer God's call, but it is not merely following along like a little puppy dog. There's a commitment involved, an acknowledgment of identity. We must not be ashamed of Him or of His words. We must be able to identify ourselves with Him and say, "Yes, I know Him. He's my Lord and Savior."

Peter had some problems with following the Lord and had to learn a lesson the hard way. Sometime later he was filled with the Holy Spirit and received the boldness to proclaim the truth as a true disciple of the Lord.

I think about so many people, ordinary folks, who are disciples of Jesus Christ. I remember a little lady from my missionary past in Ghana. Everyone called her Toothless Mary. She had nothing. She lived in a little mud hut with a straw roof and had only a little charcoal stove and a few tin utensils. Maybe she had one change of clothes in her meager possessions. But Mary had a burden on her heart for young people who wanted to go to Bible school. She went about her task of scrubbing floors and cleaning houses, keeping only a few coins for herself. She sent more than a dozen young men through Bible school. Mary chose to follow her Lord in discipleship.

We too must make the choice, take up our cross, and follow Christ.

FEEL HIS CONCERN

Christ's concern is opposite from the concern of the world. Our society has really sold us a bill of goods. We get the idea that if we don't have certain commodities on our hair, in our mouth, or around our home, we're not going to make it socially. The business world demands that we constantly seek for more.

You've probably read about Jolt Cola. It's being promoted as more classic than Coca-Cola. They brag that Jolt offers all the sugar and twice the caffeine of mainstream colas. "We're definitely going to have a lot of fun," said C.J. Rapp, who developed Jolt Cola with his father. "Our product is naughty and bold, and we don't mind that image." That's our society, the *me* generation—concerned only with self, regardless of the effect on others.

The disciples were to go out and win the world. Their task was to teach others who would come to be what they were

—disciples of Jesus Christ. They not only followed, they also led others to follow.

The Word tells us to go and make disciples of all nations. We must be as eager to share our lives as we are to demand our rights.

One author wrote, "To love the whole world, for me is no chore; my only real problem is my neighbor next door."

This is so often the true feeling we shelter. We are conditioned for comfort and convenience. Relief is only a swallow away. We want love without commitment. Pain, sacrifice, and effort are unacceptable. We want the American dream because we're so special. And we want it now!

Our instant society enforces that we should be able to speak and something will immediately happen. We look for the shortcut even in spiritual matters. What a tragedy when the mentality of the marketplace comes into the church. But there are no shortcuts when it comes to being a disciple of the Lord Jesus Christ. We have to do it His way.

In Philippians 3:17-19 Paul said, "Brethren, be followers together of me, and mark them which walk so as ye have us for an ensample. (For many walk, of whom I have told you often, and now tell you even weeping, that they are the enemies of the cross of Christ: whose end is destruction, whose God is their belly, and whose glory is in their shame, who mind earthly things.)" Paraphrased in *The Living Bible*, verses 18 and 19 say, "I have told you often before, and I say it again now with tears in my eyes, there are many who walk along the Christian road who are really enemies of the cross of Christ. Their future is eternal loss, for their god is their appetite: they are proud of what they should be ashamed of; and all they think about is this life here on earth."

Oh, what smashing words! That it could be possible to walk the Christian road and be enemies of the cross of Christ is a disturbing thought. But Paul reminds us that we're to have the mind of Christ.

Probably the greatest danger we face as Christians is the potential for the breakup of our homes, for homes impact the church. Look at parental ministry and service to our families. How necessary for us to realize the investment we make in the lives that have been placed around us—just like the 12 were positioned near Jesus. God didn't give us our children to hassle us and to mess up the house. He gave them to us to disciple, to win for Him.

If we separate the Great Commission from our role of discipleship, it won't matter what great goals we set for our family. We'll miss them by a thousand miles.

Long before I ever received ministerial credentials, I was a minister to my family. I had those around me who needed me and needed to see a godly example in the home. That's a hard assignment—to be a godly example with family and friends who see us day after day. That's why we must have those times alone with God and let Him develop in us the kind of concern for others that Christ displayed. "Let this mind be in you, which was also in Christ Jesus" (Philippians 2:5).

FINISH YOUR COURSE

Paul said, "I have fought a good fight, I have finished my course, I have kept the faith" (2 Timothy 4:7). I'm glad I wasn't called upon to run your course, because I don't know if I could do it. Neither have you been called to run my course. But God expects of you and me our very best—not *the* very best, but *our* very best. And He knows the difference. He does not want us to be clones of one another or a carbon copy of another ministry. We are unique individuals He has invested in and to whom He is saying, "Finish your course. Follow Me, feel what I feel, and then finish your own course."

An often-used word in the East African language, Swahili, is *bado* (pronounced *bah-do*). It simply means, "Not yet; later, maybe; no big deal." "Have you fed the dog yet?" "*Bado.*" "Have you cooked the evening meal?" "*Bado.*" That's a stock answer.

Sometimes our attitude is like that. Are you growing in the Lord, finding adequate time for waiting in His presence? *Bado.* Did you gather your children around you after the evening news to pray with them concerning the horrible situations they viewed? *Bado.* We live so far beneath our privilege in Jesus Christ. Many start out to follow and to feel, but the goal is to finish. We need to watch our use of *bado.*

Jesus promised His disciples that they would always have what they needed and be absurdly happy. But they would be in constant trouble. Life's courses are like that. One makes big mistake by assuming that everything changes when he comes to a special meeting and says, "Yes, Lord, I want to be Yours." If you expect to return home and find the house different, the family different, and everything glorious, forget it. It's not going to be that way. But you can go back home, look at the situation, and know Jesus has given you this course to travel and that you can do it in the name of Jesus.

I don't know what your course is. I know there may be sorrows, hardships, and problems. Paul said, "I bear in my body the marks of the Lord Jesus" (Galatians 6:17). *Moffat* translates this verse, "I bear branded on my body the owner's stamp of the Lord Jesus." My commitment charters my course.

There was a woman, an Anglican minister's wife, who changed the world through her leadership. This woman prayed one hour each week for each of her 19 children. That totaled 19 hours a week, or nearly half of a 40-hour week. Oh, it's true she didn't car pool her children or attend PTA meetings, nor did she taxi them to sporting events. But she *was* busy. This mother didn't have a dishwasher, washing machine, or clothes dryer; no refrigerator, sewing machine, or vacuum cleaner. She certainly couldn't afford a maid. Since preservatives were not yet added to foods, she had to buy provisions for making everything from scratch. Add up her hours of doing laundry with a washboard, sewing and darning by hand, washing and drying dishes, cleaning the house with broom and mop, and cooking for 21 mouths without a microwave, and the sum equals *busy.*

Through her children, however, many things were accomplished: a bill was passed by Parliament in 1805 outlawing slavery, the charity hospital movement for people too poor to pay was initiated, prison reforms were instituted, the prototype for the orphanage movement was created, the Salvation Army was organized, more than 6,500 hymns of the church were composed, 371 Christian books were published, and the Methodist church was born.

This 18th-century mother, Susanna Wesley, sustained powerful leadership through the course of her life. She didn't read books on success, nor did she attend seminars in self-assertiveness, but she knew the leadership of the Lord Jesus Christ in her life.

CONCLUSION

It has become acceptable to be religious. It's classy to be "born again." In fact, this term is thrown around so loosely that a lot of people equate it with something like a new television series. George Gallup has said that never before in the history of the United States has the gospel of Jesus Christ made such inroads while at the same time making so little difference as to how people live.

Truly, we need to return to God's design for discipleship. We need to reflect often on what salvation means and why we have been chosen for this privilege.

We've been saved to serve. What more can we do for Him? How much closer can we get to Him? How can we serve Him today through our family, our neighbor, our community? God's Word gives clear direction. Follow Christ, feel His concern, and finish your course.

THERE IS A DIFFERENCE

Gene Jackson

SCRIPTURE: Acts 19:1-20

INTRODUCTION

When Paul came to Ephesus, he began immediately to look for a church. It must have taken quite a search, but he finally found a wonderful little "Baptist" church of approximately 25 to 30 people.

The church was isolated and unnoticed. It was making little or no impact on the city. Now that is not a criticism, for in all honesty Ephesus was a tough place for a new church evangelism effort, and they had no "mother church plan" to help with the load. Ephesus was a thriving city, proud of its education, sophistication, and prosperity. The task of the little church was made even more difficult by the rampant idolatry.

The great Temple of Diana, one of the seven wonders of the ancient world, was a showplace of the city. It was a marvel of architectural and engineering genius. It was 425 feet long, 220 feet wide, 60 feet high, and supported by 127 massive pillars. It also housed the giant statue of Diana.

Silversmiths became fabulously wealthy making statuettes in the likeness of their idol.

So, admittedly, it was a tough place to start a church. It's pretty hard to convince a crowd of "know-it-alls" and "have-it-alls" that they have need of anything. As a rule, the gospel has a difficult time making an impact in such a place. It was the voice of experience talking when Paul wrote, "Not many wise men after the flesh, not many mighty, not many noble, are called" (1 Corinthians 1:26).

Be that as it may, this little church was virtually unnoticed in the bustling, prosperous city.

Actually, Paul may have been the first real, live visitor who had ever dropped in on that little congregation. When he showed up, they were so thrilled that they asked him to preach.

Now, we expect our preachers to exercise "diplomacy" and get the "lay of the land" before they come out too strong on any subject. He certainly should not introduce anything controversial on his very first visit. In any case, we want him to make sure the "climate" is right before openly preaching the baptism in the Holy Ghost, especially with the initial, physical evidence of speaking in other tongues. It's all right to talk about the Spirit-filled life, but don't come out too strong on "tongues."

But Paul was always more concerned with spiritual victory than with convention. He sensed a need in this little church. Probably the song service tipped him off. He didn't waste a second in asking a probing question, "Have ye received the Holy Ghost since ye believed?" (Acts 19:2).

Why did he ask such a question?

He knew this city needed a Holy Ghost-filled church if it was to be stirred. And there *is* a difference! Not every church is a Holy Ghost church.

These questions need to be burned into our hearts: "Have ye received?" and "Are you full of the Holy Ghost?" This generation desperately needs Holy Ghost-filled, Holy Ghost-directed, and Holy Ghost-motivated churches.

The church at Ephesus answered, "We have not so much as heard whether there be any Holy Ghost" (v. 2). Paul said, "Tell me about your experience."

They responded, "Oh, we can trace our roots all the way back to John the Baptist!"

Paul had great news for that little church. He rebaptized them under a new authority (v. 5), laid his hands on them, and "the Holy Ghost came on them."

From that beginning, spiritual revolution and revival came to Ephesus! The apostle Paul would be first to disclaim any personal credit. He only delivered the message. The people unhesitatingly accepted it. From that moment the power of God began to fall.

BAPTISM IN THE HOLY GHOST MAKES A DIFFERENCE IN POWER

It gives the believer power in prayer.

"For he that speaketh in an unknown tongue speaketh not unto men, but unto God: for no man understandeth him; howbeit in the spirit he speaketh mysteries" (1 Corinthians 14:2). He who speaks in an unknown tongue edifies (builds up, empowers) himself.

Some seem to feel that speaking in tongues requires a language which would be understandable somewhere in the world. Not at all. This verse makes very clear that "no man understandeth him."

There is a marvelous mystery in praying in the Spirit. You are on a direct "hot line" to heaven. There may be demons standing by, but they don't know what is going on. Strength pours into your soul. The bells of heaven begin to ring; your voice takes on a note of authority. God's power flows in. Victory comes.

This kind of prayer gives you access to the very heart of God. There is a difference in Holy Ghost praying.

Holy Ghost praying gives the believer access to divine wisdom. "Likewise the Spirit also helpeth our infirmities: for we know not what we should pray for as we ought: but the Spirit . . . maketh intercession for us with groanings which cannot be uttered. And he that searcheth the hearts knoweth what is the mind of the Spirit, because he maketh intercession for the saints according to the will of God" (Romans 8:26, 27).

There are times when the believer approaches the throne of grace with a burden to pray but the need is unknown. In a matter of moments, the Holy Spirit begins to pray through him in a gushing torrent of petition in other tongues. He is lifted on wings of power to fly above the frailties of human communications. He bypasses the human intellect and keys in on heaven's language. The Spirit makes possible a victory in prayer that would have otherwise been impossible.

The real impact of a church is not based upon its political influence, no matter how morally upright, nor upon its prestigious membership, no matter how socially acceptable, but upon its power in prayer.

"And when they had prayed, the place was shaken where they were assembled together; *and they were all filled with the Holy Ghost*, and they spake the word of God with boldness" (Acts 4:31).

In this wildly wicked time, we need some prayer-powered prophets who will speak the Word of God with unflinching boldness. We're in danger of turning out a generation of smiling, social diplomats who are very skilled in the art of *almost* saying something.

There is no redeeming purpose in sweet rivers of spiritual syrup flowing across the pulpit to a congregation that is already in a spiritual diabetic coma.

Preacher, pray through; let the fire touch your heart once again. Deacon, pray through; let God give you a fresh zeal of service. Sunday school teacher, pray through; let God give you a burden for your students and the wisdom to win them. There is power in true Pentecostal prayer.

The baptism in the Holy Ghost gives the believer power in evangelism.

Jesus said, "But ye shall receive power, after that the Holy Ghost is come upon you: and ye shall be witnesses unto me both in Jerusalem, and in all Judaea, and in Samaria, and unto the uttermost part of the earth" (Acts 1:8).

The impact of Jesus' words is this: There is a difference in a Spirit-filled, prayer-backed, power-packed witness.

This Movement started with plowboys in overalls and country women in calico who, when they were baptized in the Holy Ghost with the initial, physical evidence of speaking in other tongues, turned their backs on the farm to pursue a mission.

They were seized with a passion from the heart of God for souls. Those Pentecostal pioneers fearlessly invaded their generation. Their first question had nothing, absolutely nothing, to do with monetary costs or personal financial security. They disregarded sacrifice. Only one thing mattered: souls.

Men and women came to those meetings and felt stirrings in their heart. Conviction seized them, and they cried aloud, "What must I do to be saved?"

There was a high sense of a holy God brooding near. Sinners would grip the back of the old-fashioned benches to keep from falling under the Spirit of conviction. Altars would fill with men and women who were hungry to be free from the burden of sin.

If this generation is to be reached, we must have that same unflinching fervency and prevailing power. If the decade of harvest is to be successful (and there is absolutely no reason for it not to be), it's going to require that the church in this generation experience that same passionate love of Jesus Christ for a lost race. Our forefathers were a throwback to first-century saints.

When persecution arose in Jerusalem, the first-century saints simply packed their meager belongings, gathered their little families, and moved on. "Therefore they that were scattered abroad went every where preaching the word" (Acts 8:4).

But they did not move in quiet acquiescence to the Pharisees who hated them—not for one second. They refused to be intimidated. Their philosophy seemed to be, "All the devil can do is kill us, and what's so bad about going to heaven?" The only missions board behind them was God the Father, God the Son, and God the Holy Ghost.

They had one message: "Jesus Christ is the hope of the world, and He can set you free from any power sin may have over you." He dominated their horizon. Their method leaped from hearts afire with twin passions—love for their Lord and love for a lost race. The Holy Ghost convinced them that without Christ this world is lost.

No memorized routine with its clever leading questions would have ever sufficed for these evangelists and soulwinners. They knew that when one made a decision for Christ, it also meant conversion from sin. Impressive statistics on the annual report had no attraction. The cry of their heart was to rescue men and women from certain hell.

When the Holy Ghost comes in proportions of Pentecostal fullness, congratulatory comments of our fellow ministers are entirely unnecessary. The great motivating influence is to be approved by the King of Kings. No denominational official needs to keep us constantly stroked.

There is none of this "If I don't get a raise in pay, I'm going to quit" business, either. This crowd knows that the real reward comes at the end of the road. The experience of Pentecost literally and effectively provides enabling power for us to become mighty evangelists.

The baptism in the Holy Ghost gives power (and faith) to pray for the sick (Acts 19:11, 12).

Divine healing has become one of the most controversial subjects in the Evangelical church today. There is no doubt that we have bought more goldbricks, followed more spiritual quacks, and believed more tricksters on this subject than almost anything else in Pentecost.

But counterfeits always prove the genuine. Nobody is counterfeiting Confederate money today. Where could they spend it? Only the genuine can be counterfeited.

Whatever gave Paul the idea that special miracles could follow his ministry? The indwelling Spirit of God enveloping him in baptismal proportion enabled him to believe God for the impossible. It is simply "not possible" for a cloth to transmit healing virtue. And yet, "from his body were brought unto the sick handkerchiefs or aprons, *and the diseases departed* from them."

The Holy Ghost-filled church has the authority and power such as no other church has to pray for the sick. There is not only enough faith to believe God for the healing but also enough faith to trust God if, in His sovereignty, He withholds the healing.

The Holy Ghost-baptized believer keeps right on shouting the victory, whether the healing comes here or in heaven.

The baptism in the Holy Ghost gives power over demonic forces (vv. 12, 15).

If there ever was a generation that needed a church with miracle power, it was the one of Paul's day. Romans 1 sounds like a catalog of social evils from the daily news. Paul didn't mince any words when he wrote this passage:

God gave them over to shameful lusts. Even their women exchanged natural relations for unnatural ones. In the same way the men also abandoned natural relations with women and were inflamed with lust for one another. Men committed indecent acts with other men, and received in themselves the due penalty for their perversion. . . . They have become filled with every kind of wickedness, evil, greed and depravity. They are full of envy, murder, strife, deceit and malice. They are gossips, slanderers, God-haters, insolent, arrogant and boastful; they invent ways of doing evil; they disobey their parents; they are senseless, faithless, heartless, ruthless (Romans 1:26, 27, *NIV*).

The 20th-century crowd, so eloquently described in Romans, doesn't need counseling or psychoanalysis—they need deliverance. Today we have 17 million homosexuals, 20 million alcoholics, 40 million problem drinkers, an indescribable narcotics epidemic, and $8-$10 billion per year is spent on pornography.

While the world tries to figure out what happened in Junior's childhood to make him so mindlessly addicted to the self-destructive forces today, the Holy Ghost church can just cast the demon out of him.

It is simpler just to write them off. We can easily allow pushers, punks, and pimps to develop. But Jesus insisted that it is the responsibility of gospel believers to "preach *deliverance* to the captives . . . to *set at liberty* them that are bruised" (Luke 4:18).

Where can we find such power? You'll find it in the very same spot where the early church found it, lingering at an altar of prayer until the Holy Ghost comes down.

Playing little games of religious charades will never, not in a 9thousand years, produce the power we need to combat today's evils. Legislative bodies will enact restrictive laws to no avail. The generation that is bound must be delivered.

It takes more than the recitation of a superficial formula. Anyone can learn a few verses of Scripture and a certain incantation and then set forth to cast out devils. We've got a lot of look-alikes today. They want to get in on the excitement.

There is plenty of synthetic excitement today. When the shields of gold have been captured by the enemy, we are quick to substitute the shields of brass. While a lost generation speeds toward an eternal hell, we're trying to substitute the lost gold of the power of the Holy Ghost with the gleaming brass of motivational techniques or phony spirituality.

Well, brother, if you try to tackle the devil without the power of God in your life, you're going to get plenty of excitement all right, but you won't like it.

Seven young men who thought they were qualified because they grew up in the parsonage learned it the hard way. Being raised in a cracker box won't make a mouse become a cracker, and being raised in church will not automatically give you power with God.

These young men may have been deeply sincere, but sincerity alone is no substitute for the power of the Holy Ghost. They found a genuine candidate for exorcism, a man who was really demon-possessed. The formula was pretty good: "We adjure you by Jesus whom Paul preacheth . . . " (Acts 19:13). The evil spirit talked back to them. He said, "Jesus I know, and Paul I know; but who are ye?" (v. 15). And then follows quite a graphic description.

The man in whom the demon lived *leaped on* them, *overcame* them, and *prevailed* against them. They had to leave running, wounded, and naked.

If you don't know there is a difference, you can be assured the devil does.

There is a difference in a church or a believer who is *full* of the Holy Ghost. Have you received the Holy Ghost since you believed? Are you currently *full* of the Holy Ghost?

BAPTISM IN THE HOLY GHOST MAKES A DIFFERENCE IN PURPOSE

The initial, physical evidence of the baptism in the Holy Ghost is speaking in tongues, but the great overriding purpose of the experience is the exaltation of Jesus Christ. The Spirit does not come so we can "get in and have a good time as we enter into our worship service," as I heard one pastor begin a meeting.

In the first place, it's not *our* worship service, although in many instances, *we* are the worshiped; *it is His worship service*. The object is *not* to "have a good time." The entire purpose is for the glory of Almighty God and the exaltation of our Lord Jesus Christ.

The apostle Paul did not send out a monthly magazine with his picture in a variety of poses on every page. The inspired historian was careful to record, "The name of the Lord Jesus was magnified" (Acts 19:17).

The Holy Ghost *always* exalts Jesus Christ exclusively. Praises for the Lamb of God instinctively roll from the lips of the Pentecostal saint.

It is more than habits of phraseology.

It is more than spiritual cliches.

It is more than a Hebrew hoedown or a Jewish jig.

It is more than uniformed, carefully rehearsed, and choreographed dance troupes.

These praises spring from hearts that are vitally in love with the Crown Prince of glory.

He lives. We know He lives. We love Him. And without intimidation or inhibition, we praise Him.

HOLY GHOST BAPTISM MAKES A DIFFERENCE IN PURITY

The baptism in the Holy Ghost produces holiness. Revival fires began to burn at Ephesus. People were being delivered, saved, and baptized in the Holy Ghost.

And another fire was kindled. They started discarding those things that were ungodly and impure (Acts 19:19). We might say they had a bonfire for their ungodly VCR movies. They burned their horoscopes and zodiac charts. The filthy rock records went into the flames. Dirty magazines were consumed in the fire. In fact, a few of them even tossed in the television set, testifying that it led them to all sorts of ungodly fantasies.

The Holy Ghost may come upon a person who has some questionable habits and practices, *but He soon cleans house.*

The church cannot hobnob with Sodom and be chummy with Gomorrah and retain the sweetness of the Holy Ghost or the dynamic of the power of God.

God's people cannot hang out with the world's celebrity crowd and keep the touch of God.

You cannot be addicted to alcohol and drugs and still be filled with the Holy Ghost.

The church cannot live in immorality and maintain a consistent walk with Christ.

Our youth pastors cannot rent ungodly videos and have home movie parties for their young people and still be pleasing to God. You cannot feed your mind on garbage and reap wholesomeness.

As a general rule, Pentecostals can shout loud and long when the external sins of the flesh are getting a good "going over" by the preacher. Certainly the externals can have serious consequences for the believer. However, God's Word is just as scathing in its denunciation of the hidden sins of the spirit. A spirit of bitterness, jealousy, or envy will do just as much damage as a bottle of booze.

Backbiting, slanderous accusation, and gossip are just as bad in the sight of God as adultery.

Pride still goes before destruction, and a haughty spirit before a fall (Proverbs 16:18).

The line of demarkation involves not only a turning away from the sins of the flesh but also a turning away from the sins of the spirit. To whatever degree we are willing to separate from this world and its attitudes, to a corresponding degree we become useful to God.

When have you ever heard of a preacher losing his credentials for a spirit of bitterness? Now there are obvious reasons why we cannot accurately assess a penalty for internal violations of God's standard of holiness. We cannot view a person's heart. But God does.

There is a difference in the lifestyle of the Holy Ghost-filled Christian. That spotless Dove brings a freshness and purity with Him when He moves into a heart. Certainly no Holy Ghost-filled person lays claim to sinless perfection, but we have learned not to sin habitually.

This lifestyle of purity is not a system of rigid restraint that makes a sin out of anything that is pretty or fun. It does not take all the pleasure out of life. Nor does this purity hold us in deadly fear and dread lest we should somehow, unknowingly incur the wrath of God.

Nobody laughs more or gets more true enjoyment out of living than Holy Ghost-filled saints. Even their valleys are high. These folks shout in the sunshine, and they shout in the rain. We have discovered that the presence of God is just as real at midnight as at noonday. We're not afraid that God will hate us if we do something wrong; we just want to see His smile of approval because we have done something right.

There is a difference in the sense of purity for the Holy Ghost saints. We have a hunger for the fullest possible fellowship with the Savior.

CONCLUSION

Pentecostal power is available to every believer today. God longs to make Himself real to His church, but He will never force His attention on anyone. If you do not want the fullness of the Spirit, don't worry, He will never come your way.

But if your heart hungers and thirsts for something more, He will satisfy your longings. You will discover when this swift-winged energy comes into your life, there really is a difference.

The baptism in the Holy Ghost occurs in a time of praise. Following the ascension of our Lord, the disciples "returned to Jerusalem with great joy: and were continually in the temple, praising and blessing God" (Luke 24:52, 53).

You must yield yourself to the Baptizer, Jesus Christ. Surrender every part of your life to Him. Trust yourself to His hands.

When the Holy Ghost comes in, you will discover there *is* a difference.

THE COMPASSION OF JESUS

Doug Beacham

SCRIPTURE: Mark 1:40-42

INTRODUCTION

Most of us can remember our first experience of puppy love as children. It was a time filled with excitement, dreams, and broken hearts. Sadly, for many people, those puppy-love experiences of life become adult nightmares of shattered marriages and expectations that never materialize. Perhaps it is the country music writers of our society who best describe the pain of love. Sometimes the titles have a humorous ring to take the sting out of the universal pain. Johnny Cash sings a little ditty, "I've Been Flushed Down the Bathroom of Your Heart." Syndicated columnist Lewis Grizzard has become wealthy describing the woes of life. In a double entendre reflecting his open heart surgery and failed marriages, Grizzard wrote the book *They Tore Out My Heart and Stomped That Sucker Flat.*

We need to laugh, because we know the seriousness of the pain of life. But deep inside we long for someone to truly care, truly listen to our suffering. In our fast-paced society we pay high fees for counselors to listen to our suffering. Ours is the age of "compassion by the hour."

Into this demoralized, fragmented, and empty world comes the biblical message of compassion. The Old Testament tells us that the Lord is "full of compassion" (Psalm 78:38; 86:15; 111:4; 112:4; 145:8). The Gospels relate compassion as a characteristic of the ministry of Jesus.

In both Testaments compassion is expressed in the dimensions of *feelings* and *actions*. The *feeling* dimension of compassion is expressed in the New Testament word *splanchnizomai*, a verb used of Jesus that expresses an emotional response from the "innards" of a person. The *action* dimension is reflected in the fact that the Lord always has an appropriate response to our need. Our familiar expression "This moves me" reflects both dimensions of compassion. The pain of another strikes us emotionally and moves us to an appropriate response.

The greatest example of the Lord's compassion is the Incarnation. It is in the Word becoming flesh that we discover the depths of God's love for lost humanity and the certainty of His response to our sinful need. In the ministry of Jesus we see the fullness of the Lord's compassion as He ministers to our every need.

COMPASSION FOR THE LOST

Near New Orleans, on Interstate 10, is a billboard advertising Atonement Lutheran Church: "Atonement, This Exit." It is a catchy phrase for the fast-paced scattered sheep of our world. Matthew 9:36 tells us that Jesus saw the multitudes as sheep without a shepherd. He knew their vulnerable position and how defenseless they were. Sheep without a shepherd soon become dead sheep. Out of His loving compassion for the masses of the world, He called for laborers to be sent forth into the harvest.

The evangelistic call of world missions is based on the compassion of Jesus. The Pentecostal churches of the world are arising with various themes of evangelism as we approach the third millennium of the Christian Era. As never before, this is a time for us to truly be moved in heart and appropriate action. It is our opportunity to proclaim to a world headed into despair on the "Interstate Zeros" of life that there is an exit leading to salvation. It is found in the Atonement provided by Jesus Christ, and there is only one exit!

COMPASSION TO TEACH

The feeding of the 5,000 is well-known to most church attenders. We know the story of the little lad who gave bread and fish and got a miracle. But there is a preface to the story that is often neglected. Mark's account tells that Jesus saw the multitude, and out of His compassion He taught them (6:34). What a practical application of an appropriate response! His emotive response of compassion did not paralyze Him with a weeping, overwhelmed sense of pity. Rather, out of His compassion He saw a way to help their condition: He taught them.

Jesus was a teacher. He knew how to communicate the great truths of eternity to simple minds. To the query of the disciples of how we should pray, He gave a simple 30-second prayer that encompasses the totality of Kingdom living. He taught about the kingdom of God—the manifestation of God's rule and kingship on the earth.

In His teaching, Jesus gave purpose and direction to life. He pointed humanity beyond itself to the work and will of the creating Father. God's desire to give meaning to our struggles is vividly expressed in the literary style of Lamentations. This small, five-chapter book gives hope to Judah following her captivity into Babylon. The chaos of sin's destruction, followed by the purging fire of God's punishment, is given order through the Word. In *Five Smooth Stones for Pastoral Work*, Eugene H. Peterson makes a powerful application of material available in most good commentaries. The five poems of Lamentations are acrostic in literary form; that is, they use a certain pattern of the Hebrew alphabet to facilitate memory and convey significance. The Hebrew alphabet had 22 letters from—*aleph* to *taw*. In the first four poems the first verse begins with the first letter of the alphabet, and each verse follows the alphabetic order consecutively to the last letter of the alphabet. The last chapter is a poem of 22 stanzas, conforming to the number of letters in the Hebrew alphabet.

The significance of this is seen when we consider that Jesus Christ is the *Alpha* and *Omega* *(the first and last letters of the Greek alphabet). In other words, in Jesus Christ, His love, His service, His atoning blood, His compassion,* we find both Testaments telling us there are no words that are outside His authority and power to control. That dreaded *C* word, cancer, is within the healing power of the Alpha and Omega! That dreaded *D* word, divorce, is within the reconciling power of the Alpha and Omega! That dreaded *F* word, fear, is within the peace-filled word of the Alpha and Omega! The compassionate teaching of Jesus will set us free!

COMPASSION THAT HEALS

While Mark focused on the *teaching* response of compassion at the feeding of the 5,000 (6:34), Matthew focused on the *healing* response of compassion at the same event (14:14). No doubt a crowd of 5,000 men from Galilee had its share of wounded, hurting people. Jesus' ministry was not simply a how-to manual for eternal life; it was a practicing ministry of release, relief, and re-creation. His teaching of the Kingdom was followed by enabling blinded eyes to see the Messiah and enabling crippled legs to walk in obedience.

Every pastor knows the significance of a caring touch. The medical profession knows that the anxiety-ridden patient can find comfort in the hand-in-hand touch of the physician or nurse. There is a healing power of compassion, commitment, and companionship that flows from the touch of healing.

COMPASSION FOR THE OUTCASTS

Jesus invaded territory long held by Satan: the unclean of society. This was the wasteland of humanity dominated by leprosy and other skin diseases. Its boundaries were established by society, and its call letters had to be announced by the victims: "Unclean, unclean!"

The leper in Mark 1:40-42 fell at Jesus' feet begging the Master to make him clean. No doubt the wretched man had seen others delivered, healed, saved. Faith and hope arose in his heart. The question of the leper was not "Can You heal me?" He had no doubt that the power of this Galilean preacher

61

was sufficient to heal. The question was "Will You heal me?" There was no doubt in Jesus' mind concerning either *can* or *will*. The Master found a man ready to be set free from that which separated him from others. Here was a man ready to accept the responsibilities for entering the fullness of life. Here was a man prepared to leave the security of sickness for the uncertainty of new opportunities found in wholeness. Here was a man ready to live.

CONCLUSION

The Old Testament psalmists discovered in the depths of life that the Lord is full of compassion. Not until centuries later did a blessed generation in Israel have the privilege of seeing, touching, and hearing the fullness of compassion in the flesh. He came as one of us and on the cursed tree became our sin. His twisted body became the avenue of life, reconciliation, peace, and meaning.

Surgeon Richard Selzer, in *Mortal Lessons: Notes on the Art of Surgery*, tells of a young woman who had to have a tumor surgically removed from her face. She and her husband had been warned by Selzer of the possibility that a nerve would be cut in removing all the tumor, leaving her with a twisted lip. Following the operation, Selzer visited the recuperating woman, who asked, "Will my lip always be like this?" He replied, "Yes, it will; it is because the nerve is cut." The woman was silent. Her husband came near to her, smiled, and said, "I like it. It is kind of cute." Selzer then continued, "Unmindful, he bends to kiss her crooked mouth, and I so close I can see how he twists his own lips to accommodate to hers, to show her that their kiss still works."

There He is on the cross, twisted and crooked with my sin and pain, accommodating to me to give the compassionate kiss of life—the kiss that still works.

MANY VOICES, BUT ONLY ONE COUNTS

Danny L. May

SCRIPTURE: Acts 10:9-18

INTRODUCTION

Many voices cry for your attention, but only one counts. Simon Peter was on a rooftop when a voice suddenly began to speak to him. In a trance—a vision—the Lord directed him to go to Cornelius' house (Cornelius was a centurion and a Roman soldier) and preach the gospel. This was quite an awkward undertaking for Simon Peter, a traditional Jew who believed strictly in the Old Testament. The Lord was about to change his thinking and philosophy of ministry.

THE VOICES PETER HEARD

Figuratively, Peter no doubt heard several voices. The *voice of tradition* said, "You are not allowed to eat the things God put in the sheet." So Simon Peter responded something like this: "No, Lord, I'll not rise, kill, and eat these vile things the Old Testament says I should not eat. I'm faithful to tradition. I'm faithful to those things that are a part of my history, and I'm not going to change now. I'm going to hold to my tradition. I can't go to the Gentiles. I can't go to

Cornelius' house. I can't go to those non-Jews who haven't gone through the rituals to become a part of our fellowship."

Simon Peter likely heard the *voice of "We've never done it this way before."* He liked things the way they were and didn't want change. He probably felt he'd better stick with the way things were and not make anyone uncomfortable.

He may have heard the *voice of "What will my friends think?"* I believe Peter was thinking, *If I kill and eat these things, what will all my good Jewish brethren think? What will they think if I suddenly do things differently than I've done them before? What will happen if I change my philosophy of ministry? What will my friends think if I catch a new vision? The other apostles haven't had to deal with this kind of thinking. How will they look at it?*

On the rooftop, Simon Peter probably heard the *voice of "Let's maintain the status quo."* The status quo says, "We don't need a new vision from God. We don't need a fresh start. Everything's in place, so we'll stick with the old vision, the old pattern, the old way of doing things."

Peter probably heard the *voice of "It sounds like a good idea, but what's the hurry?"* One of the greatest ideas the devil puts forth is that while something may be a good idea, we shouldn't get in a hurry to take action. There is no need to get stirred up, to get excited. There's no need for us to be changed or supercharged by the power of God. We should just relax. One day we'll change into what we ought to be; one day we'll be transformed into what God wants us to be, but what's the hurry? Let's think this through, and maybe someday we'll get around to doing what God really wants done.

These voices are still being heard today. But on the rooftop that day only one voice mattered. That voice was God's. He let a sheet down by the four corners and said, "Rise, Peter; kill, and eat. It is My will for you to change your philosophy of ministry. It is My purpose for you to be different than you've ever been before. It is My desire that you be charged with a new vision. It doesn't matter what others think. It doesn't matter what the status quo is. You need to get in a hurry because this opportunity is going to pass, and if you don't do it now, it will never be done."

God's voice said to Peter, "I've got a work for you to do, a job for you to accomplish. I want you to rise, kill, and eat all these foul things a Jew should not eat." Peter explained to the Lord, "But I'm a good traditionalist. I'm a good Jew. I have never eaten those things. Nothing defiled has ever entered my mouth." But God spoke again and said, "What I have cleansed, let no man call common or unclean."

THE VOICE THAT MATTERS

Only one voice matters. It's not my voice or your voice. It's not the voice of the past or even the voice of the future. The voice that matters is the voice of God: "I raised you up to do something, to be something, to accomplish My task, to catch My vision, and to see what I want you to do that I might be glorified and praised."

God's voice called to Simon Peter and calls to us today, "I want you to see things as I see them." To accomplish this we have to have a vision. Richard Gehman, as a non-Christian accompanying Dr. Bob Pierce on overseas missions, wrote about seeing a small child in India with no arms or legs who slithered out of the grass like a snake. When they threw a quarter out of the jeep toward him, the child picked up the quarter with his mouth and wiggled off—without arms, without legs. After following Dr. Pierce for several days, Richard Gehman became a believer.

The title of his book should be our prayer: *Let My Heart Be Broken With the Things That Break the Heart of God.* May our eyes see what the eyes of the Lord see. May we perceive the way He perceives. May we see hurting, broken people and respond to their needs. God wants us to see the harvest field as He sees it. He wants us to see the work load. He wants us to see the need for prayer, the need for fasting. He wants us to be the people He has raised us up to be.

What God was saying to Simon Peter he also says to us "I want you to do what I want you to do—and in My way."

Simon Peter replied, "But this doesn't fit with my religion."

"That's OK," the Lord said, "I want you to go to Cornelius' house and preach to that Roman soldier."

"God, what can You do for a Roman soldier? What can You do for the Gentiles? Surely, they're not going to receive You."

But while Simon Peter was preaching at Cornelius' house, the Spirit of the Lord fell upon him and upon all those who heard the Word. Thank God, we can do things the way the Lord wants them done. We can accomplish much by following the Lord's direction. The work can be done, the vision clearly seen, and the job plainly undertaken in the name of Jesus Christ.

Though many voices are crying, may we hear God's voice, which says, "Do it My way; accomplish it My way. If you do it My way, I'll bless it, honor it, and cause My anointing to fall upon it. I'll cause My glory to surround it and My power to back it up. I'll cause My unction to make it work if you'll only do it the way I want you to do it."

May we also heed His voice as it says, "Go the way I choose for you." Simon Peter could have come down off the roof, enjoyed a meal, and returned to the comfort of the fellowship of the other apostles without revealing that God wanted him to go a different way. He also could have gone out and done great things for the Lord. He could have gone to many other places other than Caesarea Philippi. He could have gone to Bethlehem, where Jesus was born, or he could have gone to Nazareth, where Jesus lived most of His life. And he could have done great and wonderful works. He could have even preached the gospel of the Lord Jesus Christ. He could have declared Jesus' birth, life, ministry, death, burial, resurrection, and ascension.

However, if he had gone his own way, no matter how many good things he did they would have never taken the place of going God's way. We must have a determination to listen to the voice of the Almighty and to go the way which God chooses for us.

Jonah was supposed to go to Nineveh. That was God's way, but he chose to go another direction. He wound up in the belly of a whale, asking God to forgive him.

The prophet Elijah decided to go to the mountains and get in a cave instead of confronting the king and his wife. That was his way; but when he repented and heard the voice of God, he retraced his steps and carried out God's order.

How many times do we lose the freshness of our experience with God by choosing our way instead of His? As a college student I chose my way, but the Lord took me to Isaiah 66 and said to me, "Because you have not chosen My way, I will choose for you something that is not pleasant." It is always best to go the way God chooses for us.

Many voices are speaking to us, but only one counts. The question is, will we hear the voice of God? With the many voices that are crying, will we listen to the voice that really counts?

CONCLUSION

When we think about the many voices we hear and think about all Satan is saying to this generation, we realize his intention to frustrate us. He makes every effort to cause our attention to be diverted to situations other than those the Lord desires us to attend to.

BREAKING OUT OF THE SALTSHAKER

Perry Gillum

SCRIPTURE: Matthew 5:13, 14

INTRODUCTION

"Ye are the salt of the earth: but if the salt have lost his savour, wherewith shall it be salted? it is thenceforth good for nothing, but to be cast out, and to be trodden under foot of men. Ye are the light of the world. A city that is set on an hill cannot be hid" (Matthew 5:13, 14).

When Orville and Wilbur Wright finally succeeded in keeping their homemade airplane in the air, December 17, 1903, they wired a telegram to their sister telling of their great achievement. The telegram read: "First sustained flight today. Fifty-nine seconds. Hope to be home by Christmas."

Upon receiving the news, the sister rushed to the newspaper office and gave the telegram to the editor. The next morning, believe it or not, the newspaper headline said, "Popular Local Bicycle Merchants to Be Home for Holidays."

The scoop of the century was lost because the editor missed the point. We laugh at this account, but many times we have missed the point of some holy scriptures because we have read them too casually, failing to allow their deep significance to reach us and thus set the tone for our life.

The Sermon on the Mount, delivered by our Lord, extols lifestyle virtues that were exactly opposite to those admired and publicly demonstrated by the Greeks and Romans of that day: "Blessed are the poor in spirit . . . the mourners . . . the meek . . . those who hunger and thirst after righteousness . . . the merciful . . . the pure in heart . . . the peacemakers . . . the persecuted" (Matthew 5:3-12). These biblical principles still run counter to the spirit of the age.

CHRIST CHALLENGES DISCIPLES

At no time before in history has the challenge been greater than now for Christ's disciples to break out of the saltshaker and reflect the light of the gospel of our Lord. Jesus Christ did not die to save civilization . . . nor to change the world. He certainly did not die to save only a particular nation. He died to save a people for His name. His sacrifice was sufficient to save every human born from the beginning to the end of time. His death is efficacious only for those who accept His life and His gospel.

Jesus emphatically challenged the big fisherman, Peter, whom He divinely called to be an apostle, when He said, "I will build my church; and the gates of hell shall not prevail against it" (Matthew 16:18).

Obviously the called-out ones (the church) have influence in the world around them as salt and light, as good seed, as a colony of the kingdom of God on earth—provided, of course, they are salty and live a lifestyle illuminated by gospel light. Salt that has lost its saltiness is good-for-nothing. Christ has called for the church to be salt—are we losing our savor? Light that is covered does not shine. Christ is calling the church to be light—is our voltage low?

IN THE WORLD, NOT *OF* THE WORLD

There is an unfortunate tendency among some Christians to withdraw from society. Lurking within some is the inclination to retreat into seclusion, where we are anything but salt and light. Where in the world did this concept come from?

69

Christ at no time directed His disciples to remain aloof and apart from the people of the world. He did not set up secluded societies in which His followers were to be excluded from the stress and strain of human society. Rather, He sent His disciples into the mainstream of the world. He said, "I send you out as sheep among wolves. . . . I send you out to the lost sheep of the house of Israel. . . . As the Father has sent me into the world, so send I you into the world" (see Matthew 10:6, 16; John 20:21). In so doing, He was injecting divine salt and light into society.

Christ's directive was that His character, conduct, and compassion be transmitted through His called-out ones to every part of their world. Daniel was salt for Babylon; Joseph was salt for Egypt; Paul was salt on a ship bound for Rome. In their unique positions these men were not *of* this world, but certainly they were *in* this world. Jesus instructed His disciples in uncomplicated language, Go . . . preach . . . heal the sick, cleanse the lepers, raise the dead, cast out devils: freely ye have received, freely give" (Matthew 10:6-8). He requires no more of His disciples than He performed Himself while He was in the world.

This same Jesus was scorned as a friend of publicans and sinners. He brought good tidings, going from place to place doing good—binding up broken hearts, setting the captives free. He comforted those who mourned and injected strength into those of whom He was a part. Dare we do less?

Is it possible to be His disciple and remain in the saltshaker? The biblical challenge is for each of us to break out of the saltshaker and overturn every bushel that obstructs His liberating gospel light. Christ sends us into situations similar to those in which He ministered and calls us to the same kind of service. He intends that we contribute to the spiritual strength and well-being of the community where we live.

CHARACTERISTICS OF SALT

Salt hinders corruption. As Christians we must be careful to build our character and be sure that the life we live is full testimony that Christ is dwelling with us. Salt also stings! Jesus didn't say that we are to be the honey of the world;

He said we are salt. Our example should influence those about us for good.

Salt penetrates. When used in food, it becomes a part of the food. Here we see the paradox: *in* the world but not *of* the world (John 17:11, 16). There should be penetration but also separation.

Salt must break out of the shaker if it is to penetrate; salt must be applied if it is to permeate; salt must be impregnate if it is to be effective. By divine design, the church is to make an impact on the world with the liberating gospel of Jesus Christ . . . not in word only but also in deed.

Paul turned cities, towns, villages, and nations upside down. Thousands of men, women, boys, and girls surrendered their lives to Christ and became militant disciples, salting and lighting the way for others to follow.

In one of his letters, Paul noted, "And I, brethren, when I came to you, came not with excellency of speech or of wisdom, declaring unto you the testimony of God. For I determined not to know any thing among you, save Jesus Christ, and him crucified. And I was with you in weakness, and in fear, and in much trembling. And my speech and my preaching was not with enticing words of man's wisdom, but in demonstration of the Spirit and of power: that your faith should not stand in the wisdom of men, but in the power of God" (1 Corinthians 2:1-5).

THE CHURCH SHOULD REFLECT CHRIST THROUGH HOLY LIFESTYLE

We must ask ourselves this question: Where is the church's witness? Dogma is not witness; neither is orthodoxy, doctrine, rhetoric, numbers, buildings, programs, success, fame, or public acceptance. If God is not revealed in those who profess faith in Him, where in the world should someone who desires to see God look?

We are to reflect His holiness. His strength, His Spirit, His wisdom, His justice, His love, His faithfulness, His righteousness, His peace, His characteristics and holiness reflected in and through His disciples will turn this world upside down.

Let's start an epidemic of a true lifestyle of holiness among the nations of the world. This can be done only if we are willing to repent of our failure to be salt and light to this generation.

It's never easy to swim upstream, but Christianity calls for an upstream lifestyle. The world in which we live is by biblical definition a system headed by Satan. Following the philosophy of this system leads to eternal separation from God.

CONCLUSION

Biblical discipleship requires both vertical and horizontal relationships. It is possible to have good horizontal relationships with our associates yet be fruitless in our gospel work. Only when our vertical relationship with Christ is in biblical focus can we truly become salt and light.

God is challenging us to lead by example and cleanse the house of God. Failure to be salty and full of light results in loss of divine power. God, in His Holy Word, challenged His disciples to break with mediocrity or face His judgment. God has proclaimed that He will destroy the saltcellars and overturn the bushels that hide His gospel light.

HOLINESS

R. Edward Davenport

SCRIPTURE: Hebrews 12:14

INTRODUCTION

The word *holiness* is found 43 times in Scripture. The Declaration of Faith of the Church of God succinctly states our belief in all this word implies—holiness to be God's standard of living for His people.

The roots of our denomination are firmly planted in the Holiness Movement. In response to our forefathers' seeking God, He later gave the gift of the Holy Spirit, and we became an early herald of the Pentecostal message. We are today a Pentecostal church with a historical foundation in holiness and a commitment to preach and live holy lives. We are a holiness church, and in fact there is no other kind.

Holiness has been mistaken for other things and has been scorned by many. Many Bible-believing people have rejected this biblical doctrine because of misinformation or a total lack of teaching. True doctrinal holiness is not a denomination, not a religious movement, not a social order, not a certain dress code, nor a man-made theology.

Instead, holiness is an attribute of God. He is its only source. All of man's supposed righteousness amounts to filth, but God is holy. Man's claim to holiness is only through God's grace by which He imputes this quality to men (Romans 4:6). Therefore, we become holy by the blood of Christ, the Holy Spirit, and the Word of God.

WHAT HOLINESS IS NOT

To fully understand what holiness is, we must first look at what it is not. It is not the eradication of sin. When a person comes to Jesus Christ and accepts Him as Savior, his sin nature is not totally removed. If this were true, there are at least two things that would immediately happen: there would be no death, and no children would be born with a fallen nature.

The belief that the sin nature is eradicated is contrary to experience. There is not one person who has been washed in the blood of Jesus Christ that has not at some time in his life failed God and committed sin. The only sinless person ever to live was Christ. None of us have ever been able to reach that lofty height.

The Scripture tells us in 1 John 1:8-10, "If we claim to be without sin, we deceive ourselves and the truth is not in us. If we [Christians] confess our sins, He is faithful and just and will forgive us our sins and purify us from all unrighteousness. If we claim we have not sinned, we make him out to be a liar and his word has no place in our lives" (*NIV*). These verses were written to the children of God.

Holiness is not a legalistic code of living. It is not simply keeping a set of rules. We cannot *do* enough to be holy! If it were possible for us to keep the whole law (which it is not) and we were to offend in one point, we are guilty of the whole.

In Romans 7, Paul declared that the law cannot by itself make us holy—not because there is fault with the law but because the flesh is weak. In Romans 8:3, Paul wrote, "For what the law could not do, in that it was weak through the flesh, God sending his own Son in the likeness of sinful flesh, and for sin, condemned sin in the flesh."

Also, holiness is not asceticism or self-denial. It cannot be accomplished by human attempt to subdue the flesh. Asceticism comes from ancient heathenism, and it teaches that all matter is sinful; and since the flesh is matter, it must be subdued by human will.

Paul illustrated this point with Israel: "For I bear them record that they have a zeal of God, but not according to knowledge. For they being ignorant of God's righteousness, and going about to establish their own righteousness, have not submitted themselves unto the righteousness of God" (Romans 10:2, 3). Many people have made shipwreck of their faith simply because of a lack of understanding about true holiness.

WHAT HOLINESS IS

Now let's consider what holiness is. It is first of all *separation*. It is that part of God's nature which makes Him holy and distinct from all else. Holiness speaks of His perfection and glorious majesty. Man experiences this separation through the power of the blood, the Holy Spirit, and the Word. God separates us by His grace from this world and delivers us.

Next, the nature of holiness is *dedication*. It is not only deliverance *from* worldliness, but it is also commitment *to* that which is holy. God's people are holy people, and they are committed to God, His Son, the Holy Spirit, the church, the home, and the community. These people are not wallflowers; they have vision and vitality which they use for the glory of God.

Holiness is also *purification*. Purification is a condition of holiness. It means that we are partakers of the divine nature. "For if the blood of bulls and of goats and the ashes of an heifer sprinkling the unclean, sanctifieth to the purifying of the flesh: how much more shall the blood of Christ, who through the eternal Spirit offered himself without spot to God, purge your conscience from dead works to serve the living God?" (Hebrews 9:13, 14). With the realization that God grants us this purification, it also becomes the responsibility of man to separate himself from the things of the world which are contrary to the holiness of God. (Read 2 Corinthians 6:14—7:1.)

The holiness life also carries with it the meaning of *consecration*. We are to live out the holiness experience day by day. This is what we are called to in 1 Peter 1:15: "But as he which hath called you is holy, so be ye holy in all manner of conversation." We are further taught in Hebrews 12:14 to follow holiness and in 2 Corinthians 7:1 to mature in holiness.

With these holy characteristics in our life (separation, dedication, purification, and consecration), there will also be service. There will be a desire to be involved in the work of our Lord. Because we are the recipients of this grace, we will want to manifest our praise through Christian service. There are at least three ways we may manifest this appreciation. First, we are to offer spiritual sacrifices according to 1 Peter 2:5. Second, we are to offer the sacrifice of praise (Hebrews 13:15). Third, we are to be a living sacrifice (Roman 12:1).

INSTANT OR PROGRESSIVE SANCTIFICATION

There has long been a debate about the time of sanctification. Some have hazarded their personal experience trying to prove a point of view. The great debate has been whether it instant or progressive? The fact is, it is both.

Sanctification is described in Scripture in various ways. It is instantaneous because it becomes a part of our experience at the new birth. It is positional because we obtain a position with and before God "in Christ." It is progressive because it is a lifelong experience. Those people who say they are the same as they were when saved decades ago are to be pitied. This means they have made no progress in the Word of God and the life of holiness. Sanctification is also practical, for we learn daily to perfect or mature in it.

HOW HOLINESS IS OBTAINED

The blood, the Holy Spirit, and the Word of God are three essentials for total sanctification. Through the blood we obtain eternal sanctification. When Jesus poured out His blood at 9Calvary, He obtained this holy status with God for all believers for all eternity. "For by one offering he hath perfected for ever them that are sanctified" (Hebrews 10:14). In 1 John 1:7 we read, "The blood of Jesus Christ His Son cleanseth us from all sin." Also, the blood of Christ has the power to purge our conscience from dead works to serve the living God (Hebrews 9:14).

The Holy Spirit then brings about internal sanctification. In 2 Thessalonians 2:13 we learn, "God hath from the beginning chosen you to salvation through sanctification of the Spirit and belief of the truth." In 1 Peter 1:2 we also discover that we are elect according to the sanctification of the Spirit. The Holy Spirit enters our life at conversion, fills us when we receive the baptism of His Spirit, and works in us all of our life as our sanctifier, equipping us to have an impact upon the world.

Through the Word of God, we then have external sanctification. In John 15:3, Jesus said, "Now ye are clean [holy] through the word which I have spoken unto you." Later Jesus prayed in the Garden and said, "Sanctify them through thy truth: thy word is truth" (John 17:17). As we read and apply the Word of God, it has a daily impact on our life. It is impossible to remain the same person if you study the Word of God every day.

The price for your sanctification has been paid. If you will apply the truth of this message to your life, you can be holy in the sight of God and without blame before men.

WHEN THE LORD MADE ARRANGEMENTS

Bobby Johnson

SCRIPTURE: 1 Kings 17:1-16

INTRODUCTION

This passage of Scripture shows the arrangements the Lord made to sustain Elijah the prophet. These arrangements involved a brook, some ravens, and a widow.

God could have arranged for a river to provide water for Elijah, but instead He used a brook. According to Genesis 1:6-9, water is under God's control! He even measured the waters in the hollow of His hand (Isaiah 40:12). The Bible gives many illustrations of God's controlling water to meet people's needs: the dividing of the Red Sea, bringing water from the rock, causing an iron axhead to swim, and turning water into wine.

The Lord could have used a king to feed Elijah, but instead He made arrangements with a widow. He didn't choose a king with a storehouse of plenty, but He chose a widow whose barrel of meal was almost empty. Now widows are one of God's first concerns. God even uses widows to reveal whether or not we have pure religion: "Pure religion and undefiled before God and the Father is this, To visit the fatherless and widows in their affliction, and to keep himself unspotted from the world" (James 1:27).

The Lord can make arrangements with any phase of His creation. He gave manna from heaven and honey from a carcass. He sent fire from heaven, words through the mouth of a donkey, and conviction by a rooster. He employed hailstones to smite the Canaanites, thunder to discomfit the Philistines, stars to war against Sisera, hornets to fight the Amorites, and the earth to swallow rebellious men such as Nadab and Abihu.

The Lord's arrangements seem foolish to the worldly-minded. "But God hath chosen the foolish things of the world to confound the wise; and God hath chosen the weak things of the world to confound the things which are mighty; and base things of the world, and things which are despised, hath God chosen, yea, and things which are not, to bring to nought things that are: that no flesh should glory in his presence" (1 Corinthians 1:27-29).

THE LORD'S ARRANGEMENTS ARE PERFECTLY TIMED

According to Exodus 17, the Israelites were ready to stone Moses because their thirst for water had become so severe. Moses cried to the Lord, "What am I going to do?" "The Lord said unto Moses, Go on before the people, and take with thee of the elders of Israel; and thy rod, wherewith thou smotest the river, take in thine hand, and go. Behold, I will stand before thee there upon the rock in Horeb; and thou shalt smite the rock, and there shall come water out of it, that the people may drink" (vv. 5, 6).

God was saying, "When you get there, I'll be there. The arrangements will be made."

Verse 6 continues, "And Moses did so in the sight of the elders of Israel." With perfect timing God miraculously brought water out of the rock.

In 2 Kings 19 we read of King Sennacherib's defying the God of Hezekiah. He wrote a letter to Hezekiah, king of Judah, in which he listed the other nations that his army, the Assyrians, had destroyed. He emphatically declared that Judah would be destroyed just as the surrounding nations had been. Sennacherib marched his army toward Judah and camped for the night. But while he marched and camped, Hezekiah prayed: "Lord, bow down thine ear, and hear: open, Lord, thine eyes, and see. . . . I beseech thee, save thou us" (vv. 16, 19).

"And it came to pass that night, that the angel of the Lord went out, and smote in the camp of the Assyrians an hundred fourscore and five thousand [185,000]: and when they arose early in the morning, behold, they were all dead corpses" (v. 35).

In Acts 12 we read about Simon Peter's apprehension, incarceration, and proposed execution. That night, just a few hours before the execution was to take place, God made arrangements for Simon's deliverance.

When Herod would have brought him forth, the same night Peter was sleeping between two soldiers, bound with two chains: and the keepers before the door kept the prison. And, behold, the angel of the Lord came upon him, and a light shined in the prison: and he smote Peter on the side, and raised him up, saying, Arise up quickly. And his chains fell off from his hands. And the angel said unto him, Gird thyself, and bind on thy sandals. And so he did. And he saith unto him, Cast thy garment about thee, and follow me. And he went out, and followed him; and wist not that it was true which was done by the angel; but thought he saw a vision. When they were past the first and the second ward, they came unto the iron gate that leadeth unto the city; which opened to them of his own accord: and they went out, and passed on through one street; and forthwith the angel departed from him (vv. 6-10).

God's timely intervention on Peter's behalf outwitted the purpose of Herod, the expectation of the Jews, and the vigilance of the soldiers. Simon Peter was delivered even as God's people were praying for his deliverance. As the prophet recorded, "And it shall come to pass, that before they call, I will answer; and while they are yet speaking, I will hear" (Isaiah 65:24).

THE ODDS ARE MEANINGLESS WHEN THE LORD MAKES THE ARRANGEMENTS

The Israelites were torn between two opinions. Elijah cried

out, "How long halt ye between two opinions? if the Lord be God, follow him: but if Baal, then follow him" (1 Kings 18:21).

Elijah further stated, "I, even I only, remain a prophet of the Lord; but Baal's prophets are four hundred and fifty men. Let them therefore give us two bullocks; and let them choose one bullock for themselves, and cut it in pieces, and lay it on wood, and put no fire under: and I will dress the other bullock, and lay it on wood, and put no fire under: and call ye on the name of your gods, and I will call on the name of the Lord: and the God that answereth by fire, let him be God" (vv. 22-24).

Note the odds: Elijah was not only outnumbered 450-to-1 by the prophets of Baal, but the prophets of the groves (Asherak) numbered 400, which raised the ratio to 850-to-1. The scene of the challenge was Mount Carmel, the headquarters of idolatry. Images of Baal gleamed on every side. Heathen altars occupied the sacred soil. Smoke arose from the idolatrous sacrifices. The crowd supported the prophets of Baal. They had forsaken God and were drinking in iniquity like water. Among the crowd were King Ahab and Jezebel. One statement from God's Word well describes Ahab: "[He] did more to provoke the Lord . . . to anger than all the kings of Israel that were before him" (1 Kings 16:33). And Jezebel was seemingly the incarnation of iniquity.

The odds were stacked against Elijah, but note his prayer and see the results of God's arrangements: "It came to pass at the time of the offering of the evening sacrifice, that Elijah the prophet came near, and said, Lord God of Abraham, Isaac, and of Israel, let it be known this day that thou art God in Israel, and that I am thy servant, and that I have done all these things at thy word. Hear me, O Lord, hear me, that this people may know that thou art the Lord God, and that thou hast turned their heart back again. Then the fire of the Lord fell and consumed the burnt-sacrifice, and the wood, and the stones, and the dust, and licked up the water that was in the trench. And when all the people saw it, they fell on their faces: and they said, The Lord, he is the God; the Lord, he is the God" (1 Kings 18:36-39).

THERE IS NO REASON TO WORRY WHEN GOD MAKES THE ARRANGEMENTS

Observe the odds against the apostle Paul on his stormy voyage to Rome, as recorded in Acts 27. He was outnumbered 275-to-1. He was outranked by the wisdom of the ship's captain. He was outmatched by the furies of nature. But the Lord sent an angel and informed Paul that arrangements were made for the safety of every man aboard. Paul said to those on board, "And now I exhort you to be of good cheer: for there shall be no loss of any man's life among you, but of the ship. For there stood by me this night the angel of God, whose I am, and whom I serve, saying, Fear not, Paul; thou must be brought before Caesar: and, lo, God hath given thee all them that sail with thee" (vv. 22-24).

Paul placed faith in the Lord's arrangements. He told the crew, "Wherefore, sirs, be of good cheer: for I believe God, that it shall be even as it was told me" (v. 25). Paul's faith outnumbered the faithlessness of the 275 aboard. Paul's faith outmatched the furies of nature. Paul's faith outranked the wisdom of the experienced captain. "And so it came to pass, that they escaped all safe to land" (v. 44).

THINGS HAPPEN WHEN THE LORD MAKES THE ARRANGEMENTS

Lepers are cleansed! "As He [Christ] entered into a certain village, there met him ten men that were lepers, which stood afar off: and they lifted up their voices, and said, Jesus, Master, have mercy on us. And when he saw them, he said unto them, Go shew yourselves unto the priests. And it came to pass, that, as they went, they were cleansed" (Luke 17:12-14).

Sight is given! "I am the light of the world," Jesus declared. "When he had thus spoken, he spat on the ground, and made clay of the spittle, and he anointed the eyes of the blind man with the clay, and said unto him, Go, wash in the pool of Siloam, (which is by interpretation, Sent.) He went his way therefore, and washed, and came seeing" (John 9:5-7).

Believers are empowered! Shortly before His ascension, Jesus said, "And, behold, I send the promise of my Father upon you: but tarry ye in the city of Jerusalem, until ye be endued with power from on high" (Luke 24:49). The disciples returned to Jerusalem, assembled in the Upper Room, and tarried. "And when the day of Pentecost was fully come, they were all with one accord in one place. And suddenly there came a sound from heaven as of a rushing mighty wind, and it filled all the house where they were sitting. And there appeared unto them cloven tongues like as of fire, and it sat upon each of them. And they were all filled with the Holy Ghost, and began to speak with other tongues, as the Spirit gave them utterance" (Acts 2:1-4).

Evangelism continues! Corinth, the meeting place of nations, was recognized as the great emporium of the world and was famed for its wealth, luxury, and vice. Paul entered Corinth as a stranger. He was filled with fear. He didn't have a place to reside or preach, but he did have the spirit of evangelism burning in his soul.

God knew Paul's determination and zeal for evangelism, so He made all the necessary arrangements for him to evangelize Corinth. God sent the angel of Providence into the city before Paul; prepared for him a house (the house of Aquila and Priscilla, exiled Jews); gave him employment (tentmaking, the same trade as Aquila and Priscilla); and opened a door for him to preach the gospel of Christ. When Paul was forced to leave the Jewish synagogue, a house next to the synagogue was opened for the continuance of his ministry. Crispus, the chief ruler of the synagogue, accepted the Lord.

CONCLUSION

The Lord has made all the arrangements we will ever need. He has made the arrangements for today and tomorrow, for time and eternity, for earth and heaven, for life and death.

The Lord has made arrangements for our salvation. Salvation originated with Him. He saw the means; He planned the great achievement; He developed the wondrous scheme. It all was executed through Jesus Christ, the only begotten Son of God.

The Lord has made arrangements for our healing through Christ's sacrifice. "With his stripes we are healed" (Isaiah 53:5); "By whose stripes ye were healed" (1 Peter 2:24).

The Lord has made arrangements for the supplying of our needs. "But my God shall supply all your need according to his riches in glory by Christ Jesus" (Philippians 4:19). "Seek ye first the kingdom of God, and his righteousness; and all these things [food and clothing] shall be added unto you" (Matthew 6:33).

The Lord has made arrangements to be with us in death. "Yea, though I walk through the valley of the shadow of death, I will fear no evil: for thou art with me" (Psalm 23:4).

The Lord has made arrangements for our eternal abode. "Let not your heart be troubled: ye believe in God, believe also in me. In my Father's house are many mansions: if it were not so, I would have told you. I go to prepare a place for you. And if I go and prepare a place for you, I will come again, and receive you unto myself; that where I am, there ye may be also" (John 14:1-3).

GOD'S PERSPECTIVE ON FINANCES

George W. Cline

SCRIPTURE: Jeremiah 10:1-12, 21-23

INTRODUCTION

Learning to see, trust, and inquire of the Lord in all circumstances of life is part of the maturing process of every Christian. In today's culture nothing tests our relationship to Him more than finances. Because most Christians have only learned *about Him*, they discover that their trust erodes when trouble comes. Therefore, it is essential to establish a vital relationship with Father God through Jesus Christ the Lord.

Our life is not to be valued by the resources of our possessions but by the richness of our relationship with the Lord (Luke 12:13-21). The bent nature of fallen man inclines our hearts to see things backward, inverted, and distorted making it difficult to trust and obey the Lord. Therefore worry, selfishness, and bondage characterize our lives. *"Knowing Him as Lord"* brings great freedom in all areas of our lives, even in the area of finances.

To better understand how we can trust a God who is involved in all areas of our lives, we must know His character and His care for all His children. Jeremiah 10 not only gives us insight not only into His character but also instructs us on how to live within the society around us. God seeks a people who are "blameless and pure, children of God without fault in a crooked and depraved generation, in which . . . [they] shine like stars in the universe" (Philippians 2:15, *NIV*).

GOD IS THE GOD OF ALL KNOWLEDGE

He has the answer for every question and insight for every situation. Therefore, we must not "'learn the way of the nations'" (*NASB*), which is to have *what* you want *when* you want it. The result is debt. Debt left unchecked will lead to financial bondage. When our attitudes or priorities are wrong, we will spend our resources on ourselves with little concern for those who have never heard the gospel. Lack of discernment and not counting the cost result in this kind of unscriptural thinking: God will bail me out. Purchasing depreciable items through the use of credit can also lead to financial bondage.

The "way of the nations" is to make you *subject* to someone. The degree of bondage depends on the amount of debt and the relationship of debt to your income. Scripture does not prohibit debt but warns of the risk of bondage to the lender (Proverbs 22:7). The purchase of a house is certainly something that does not depreciate, and most of us cannot own a car unless we go into debt in some way. However, if you make $10,000 a year, don't buy a $50,000 car.

If you are in debt, continue to tithe and to give. Let it be your motivation to allow God to show you His power of freedom in finances. And always make special arrangements with your creditors to continue to pay them. Larry Burkett, a financial expert, said, "This is the most simple economic principle there is: If you don't borrow money, you can't get in debt. The second simple economic principle is: If you don't borrow any more money, you can't get any further in debt."

GOD IS THE GOD OF ALL JUSTICE

"'Do not . . . be terrified by signs in the sky'" (*NIV*), because God will see to it that you get what He has promised. He will not keep things to Himself (see Psalm 145:17-20). Because of His grace you get a different portion than you deserve—you deserve Hell, but you get heaven; and you get all of His righteousness and blessings with it.

An untrusting attitude concerning finances rob us of God's true blessings. Insecurity is the result of building our lives around ourselves and our ability to produce. When we become overly occupied with assets and lust for more, then emotional tension, fear of loss, and ungratefulness plague us. Often our built-in demand for security and protection against poverty causes our financial enslavement.

We can either trust the Lord to provide or we can trust ourself (Jeremiah 17:5-10). Giving is saying, "I trust Him." The tithe is a testimony of God's ownership, and it flows out of recognition of God's gift of victory, resources, and blessings. Tithing indicates our recognition of God's right to all that we have. God alone is the cornerstone of our financial security. If we say, "Jesus is Lord," but have never submitted to giving at least 10 percent away, is He really the Lord of your lives?

Some Christians use their tithe as a financial security blanket by putting it back just in case there is more month than money. Others don't tithe due to ignorance—they don't know what the Bible says. Others don't tithe because they fear that God will not supply. And some walk in plain disobedience—they know that they should tithe but just don't want to. When we neglect the scriptural principle of tithing, that reveals more about our spiritual condition than it does about our financial condition. Somewhere, we have to decide whether or not God is serious when He says something.

God is a God of relationship. That is the whole principle in the Bible about finances. Jesus' response to the Pharisees' giving is interesting (Luke 11:42). Their sin was not in their giving, for they paid tithes; however, they had neglected justice, mercy, and faithfulness. They were failing to deal with their mistreatment of others. God says in 1 Corinthians 13:3 that if we give but don't know how to live with one another in love, our giving profits us nothing.

The majority of our resources for giving comes from working. Work is not part of the curse. Adam worked before he sinned. *Meaningless* work is part of the curse. There are four scriptural reasons why people work: (1) Work is a channel for expressing our creative gifts; (2) work is a great channel for developing character; (3) work shows the excellency of God—we are what God looks like to the people with whom we work; (4) work is a mission field. A lot of people want to change jobs because there are so many non-Christians where they work, but that may be exactly why God has them there.

God uses money (1) to strengthen our trust in Him (if we give all our time to work, we have no time left for Him and His call—Matthew 6:33); (2) to develop our trustworthiness (Luke 16:11); (3) to prove His love (Matthew 7:11); (4) to demonstrate His power over the world (Romans 10:11, 12); (5) to satisfy the needs of others by showing compassion (2 Corinthians 8:1-14).

Christians often wonder how they can give when they barely have enough to meet their own needs. It is only when we believe He owns everything and that He has given us everything that we have that we will trust Him enough to give the firstfruits back to Him. We don't serve God for what we get. If we want God for any other reason than the fact He is God, then we are a materialist. It is as He decides it, not as we desire it. It is our privilege to trust Him.

GOD IS THE GOD OF ALL LOVE

God's care for us is total. We can believe Him for anything and entrust ourselves to His love (Jeremiah 31:3). Many people get into debt because they don't perceive how much that they are loved by God. The society we live in makes it almost impossible for a person without a disciplined lifestyle and a solid relationship with the Lord to understand or to totally embrace the truth that God can and will supply one's every need (Philippians 4:19).

The ease with which credit can be obtained has caused us to look more and more at our own ability to provide our needs and to take our eyes off God. The point is this: The God of all love loves us, and He is intimately concerned about our every need.

It is important to note these principles: (1) In God's economy the first is considered the best. (2) When we give God the first part, which is the best part, He reckons that we would also give Him the rest. That is the Old and New Testament principle. (3) God does not need money. He wants us to give because of what it does within us. Giving is not God's way of getting money; it is His way of maturing His kids.

If we don't know that we are loved, our maturity will be hindered by wrong thinking. We will be consumed by the pressures or anxieties of life. Our mind will be captivated by other things, and we will begin to fear the unknown, the future (Mark 4:12-20).

The pressure or deceitfulness of wealth is to trust in money rather than in the Lord. There is nothing wrong with having money—the Bible never condemns that. However, it does warns against loving or trusting in things other than Him. Riches will not produce the happiness they promise. The pleasures of a materialistic society or the desire, lust, for other things hinders maturity.

GOD IS THE GOD OF ALL WISDOM

God has insight for every situation. Compared to God's wisdom, our wisdom is foolishness. When we don't tithe, we are foolishly saying we don't need anything or anyone else, including the Lord. Tithing is saying that we trust God. Joshua 21:45 says, "Not one of all the Lord's good promises to the house of Israel failed; every one was fulfilled" (NIV). Since He is an unchangeable Lord, everyone of His promises are still true.

Tithing is simply saying, "Jesus, You are Lord of my finances." If we do not make Jesus Lord of our finances, it is because we believe that if we do, we will be deprived in some way or God will require more from us than we want to give. That is the spirit, the mentality, of poverty. That mentality has nothing to do with understanding, believing, or knowing the Father heart of God. God's will and wisdom will release us from the spirit of debt and financial poverty. We get into debt when we fail to trust Him to provide for us.

There is, however, legitimate debt. It is very difficult to own a house without debt, and a car often falls into that category. The criteria we need to use is this: "If I ever have to sell this possession, will it still be worth what I owe on it?" You know you are in wrongful debt when you have to borrow for small things in order to exist. If you are in debt, repent. Turn toward God and turn away from your own desires.

GOD IS THE GOD OF ALL POWER

God can do whatever is necessary to accomplish His purposes. He has the ability to communicate with us about everything. Compared to Him, our power is weak. In Jeremiah 10:21, the Word implies it is not God's inability that causes our lack; it is our failure to seek Him.

The answer to debt is not more income. The answer is submitting to the God of all power and His way. There is nothing wrong with having, but we must have it *His* way. We are in a partnership called "God and Sons." The scriptural guideline for borrowing is clear: When you borrow, it is a promise that you will repay it (Psalm 37:21).

GOD IS THE GOD OF ALL HOLINESS

The God of all holiness desires to come and work His character in us. His heart is to make us like Him so we will respond to situations exactly as He would respond. Somehow we have to live life with an open hand. The only way to do that is to let the God of Holiness work His character, a portion of His life, in us.

The proper goal of giving is never *to get*; it is simply to be an obedient servant. Such giving will liberate us from selfishness.

Jesus warned us to be careful not to be "weighed down with dissipation, drunkenness and the anxieties of life" (Luke 21:34, *NIV*). *Dissipation* is a word that has to do with self-indulgence or wastefulness. That kind of lifestyle will weigh us down and eventually tear us apart.

In giving God control of our finances, we acknowledge that He owns everything that we have. That we believe in God's ownership is proven by our tithing and sacrificial giving. If we give of ourselves—our time, our talent—it will come back in abundance.

But how do we know who to give to? We can go by outward appearances, by hearsay, or by the promptings of the Spirit of God. Learning to be sensitive to the promptings of the Holy Spirit requires that we will be willing to let Him speak about giving anything we have. We have to be willing to try it, even if we are sometimes wrong. Sometimes God has us give to people just because He wants to bless them.

There are four things giving will do for us according to 2 Corinthians 9:6-11: (1) Our giving will determine what we will receive (v. 6)—we receive in proportion to how we have sown; (2) giving reflects our heart attitude (v. 7)—we must check our attitude when we write a check or put money in the offering; (3) giving will make us dependent on God (vv. 8 and 9), which is the whole point; (4) our giving will enable us to give even more (vv. 10, 11).

CONCLUSION

He will work His character in us so we will exhibit Him in everything we do. God's love, grace, and power are measureless, and He never grows tired of you. It does not matter how badly we have messed things up in our life or in the life of our family. Our way is not hidden from Him. He is working on our behalf, even today. He is waiting for us to say, "Daddy, Father, I need You in this area of my life. I submit this to You," and with His measureless grace He comes and overflows that area.

God will be faithful to us because He is righteous and because He is God, not because we are good—it is not based upon our performance. He will always keep His word. He is the God of justice. He will never fail. It has nothing to do with us; it has everything to do with Him. But He did set up principles of obedience for us to follow. The way to love Him is to respond in obedience. The largeness of His creation proves to us His goodness and His grace. He will meet our needs.

CALLED AS PRIESTS

Floyd H. Lawhon

SCRIPTURE: 1 Peter 2:5

INTRODUCTION

It is quite common in our denomination to call our Christian friends "Brother" or "Sister." What would happen if the greeters at the door of the sanctuary each Sunday morning would substitute "Priest" for the common form of address? "Good morning, Priest Brown, Priest James, Priest Mary, or Priest Barbara. Welcome to the temple of the Lord."

Would our attitude change as we entered the sanctuary? Or have we forgotten that according to the Bible, all Christians are priests? Peter, in addressing all the followers of Jesus Christ, who are "begotten . . . again unto a lively hope by the resurrection of Jesus Christ from the dead" (1 Peter 1:3), calls them a "royal priesthood" (2:9). John names all who had been "washed in the Blood of the Lamb" "kings and priests unto God" (Revelation 1:6).

The Bible does not teach that the priest is a certain class in the church called "preachers" or "ministers of the gospel." The division into laity and clergy is a fallacy we have too readily adopted. It is too easy for the average Christian to abrogate his/her responsibility and assign it to the few who sit on the platform of our churches.

WE ARE ALL CALLED

If all are priests, then it is reasonable to consider the attributes of a priest and to determine if we as individuals are prepared to officiate in this capacity.

We learn much from the Old Testament about the role of the priest since the Old Testament is filled with types and symbols which help us to a better understanding of our Christian life. According to the law of Moses, there were two classes of priests—the high priest and the common priest.

The high priest was a type of Christ. He alone was allowed to enter into the Most Holy Place in the tabernacle and the Temple. In his role as High Priest, he sprinkled the mercy seat with the sacrificial blood to atone for the sins of the people. But these High Priests were human. They often failed. They died, and new priests had to be elected to make intercession for the people.

When the blood of bulls and goats was no longer sufficient, our High Priest, Jesus, presented Himself as the sacrifice. He shed His blood on the cross for the remission of our sins, He took the keys of death and hell and entered once and for all into the Holy of Holies, into heaven itself, now to appear in the presence of God for us.

There will never be a change in our High Priest, for Christ forever dwells at the right hand of God. He is a "daysman" (mediator) to stand between us and God and "lay his hand upon [us]" (see Job 9:33). He hears our cries for assistance, knows our needs, sympathizes with us, and is able to save for eternity all those who believe on him.

There is only one High Priest. Heads of denominations are not high priests, the Pope is not a high priest, and high-placed evangelists are not high priests.

The common priest is a type of the Christian. It is not an exact comparison—there are several fundamental differences. According to the law of Moses, a certain tribe among the Jews were called to be priests. They had to be of the tribe of Levi. They had to be willing to offer acceptable service to the Lord. They had to be 30 years of age before they could be priests. They had to be without blemish, free from all physical impurities, infirmities, and imperfections. If one had lost an arm or a hand or a finger, he could not be priest. The halt, the maimed, the diseased, and the blind were all excluded from this honored class.

Under the law of Christ we find no such restrictions as are found under the law of Moses. Just as every descendant of Levi was born into the priesthood, so every Christian can claim the priesthood as his birthright. Jesus has invited the poor and the needy, the halt and the maimed, and the blind to come. It is not necessary to belong to a certain tribe or family or nation in order to be saved. Children, women, slaves —all are welcomed. God has called people from every tribe and nation, from every land and people. God "hath made of one blood all nations of men for to dwell on all the face of the earth," and has given them all power to "seek the Lord . . . and find him" (Acts 17:26, 27). We are all called.

WE ARE CONSECRATED

As priests we have all been consecrated. The Jewish priests were consecrated when they entered upon their work. The law prescribed the ceremonies necessary to their consecration. They were brought to the door of the tabernacle, and their bodies were washed with water. Then the blood of the "ram of consecration" was sprinkled upon their right ear to sanctify their ears for hearing, on the thumb of the right hand to sanctify their hands for serving, and on the great toe of the right foot to sanctify their feet for treading the courts of Jehovah (see Exodus 29; Leviticus 8). This consecration had to be performed just once, and it is a type of the consecration of the Christian.

We can see beauty and reason in these ceremonies when we remember that they are external signs and symbols given to indicate the purity of heart necessary to enjoy God. The inspired writer referred to the consecration of the priests in Hebrews 10:22. He visualized the ceremonies and the priest drawing near to enter upon his duties. He says: "Let us [Christians, priests] draw near [as the priest draws near to the sanctuary] with a true heart, [we must serve the Lord with our hearts, our affections, as well as our minds] in full assurance of faith [we must come in faith, or we cannot

please God], having our hearts sprinkled from an evil conscience [in doing the will of the Lord, we know that we are
accepted and our consciences are clear], and our bodies are
washed with pure water [when we are buried with Christ in
baptism, our bodies are washed with pure water]."

As believer priests we must first of all offer our own body
as a living sacrifice, holy and acceptable to God, which is
our reasonable service (Romans 12:1). We are to glorify God
in our body and our spirit, which are His (1 Corinthians 6:20).

WE ARE CLOTHED

Those who were consecrated to the Jewish priesthood wore
a peculiar dress which distinguished them from all others.
When the high priest passed along, the people saw the seamless
robe with the 72 tassels, made of blue and purple and scarlet,
with its 72 golden bells. They saw on his shoulders the onyx
stones on which were engraved the names of the 12 sons of
Jacob according to their birth. They saw the breastplate and
the plate of gold on which was written "Holiness to the Lord,"
(Exodus 28:36), and they knew he was their high priest.

The common priest also was dressed in white linen with
a girdle around his waist and a bonnet on his head. They
too were differentiated from all others by the dress they wore.

The Christian is to be distinguished by his dress from all
others, but it is not merely the dress of the outward man
that is to mark him as a priest. It is not by a peculiar coat,
dress, or cap that he is to be known and read by all men
but by the adorning of the inner man. The Lord looks not
upon the outward appearance but upon the heart. The Christian is to be "clothed with white robes" (Revelation 7:9), which
is "the righteousness of the saints" (Revelation 19:8).

WE ARE COMMISSIONED

The Jewish priest had duties to perform and blessings and
privileges to enjoy. He entered into the sanctuary. He approached that golden candlestick, which was beaten out of a
talent of pure gold, with its seven branches, all ornamented
with bowls, knobs, and flowers. He trimmed it and fed it
with pure olive oil so it would continually give light to that
room. We see him approach the table of shewbread and place

on it 12 new loaves each Sabbath. He went to the altar of incense, made of acacia wood and overlaid with gold. He places there his offering, which ascended as sweet incense before the throne of God.

The Christian also has duties to perform and privileges and blessings to enjoy. He opens and studies the Word. He looks upon it as the golden candelabrum, the spiritual light to the man of God, the lamp for his feet and the light for his pathway. It presents Christ to him as "the way, the truth, and the life." The table of shewbread is symbolic of the Communion table, at which the one loaf is consumed in grateful remembrance of the death of Christ.

As the Jewish priest came to the altar of incense, so the believer priest comes boldly to the throne of grace to offer up his spiritual sacrifice to God. He has been taught that it is his privilege to come to the throne of grace, in the name of Jesus, and offer his thanksgiving, his adoration, his sweet songs, and his petitions and that God will hear him. He has the privilege of interceding for himself and for others. He is, himself, a priest and need not despair if he cannot find a white-robed priest to intercede for him.

The priest of the Old Testament did not serve only on Sabbath days; there were duties to perform throughout the week. We too as Christian believer priests have obligations to discharge. We are commissioned to preach the gospel of salvation. We are commissioned to minister to the poor, the sick, and the needy. We are commissioned to live exemplary lives that will be a witness to others. We are commissioned to serve as intercessors. We are commissioned to sacrifice of our substance, to do service, to do good for our Lord. We are commissioned to offer praise and worship to God continually —"the fruit of our lips giving thanks to his name" (Hebrews 13:15).

The congregation files into the church on Sunday morning. The pews are filled. Technically the church with 50 in attendance should have 50 priests. Likewise 500 computes to 500 priests. And 5,000— how wonderful! —computes to 5,000 royal priests serving before the Lord. The organ begins to send forth a melody, and the priests on the platform and the priests in the pews, whether a large or small group, in one accord begin to officiate in the temple.

What a high position we are called upon to occupy before the world! We consecrate ourselves to the service of the King of Kings and the Lord of Lords. "Worthy is the Lamb that was slain to receive power, and riches, and wisdom, and strength, and honour, and glory, and blessing. For thou wast slain, and hast redeemed us to God by thy blood out of every kindred, and tongue, and people, and nation; and hast made us unto our God kings and priests" (see Revelation 5:9-12).

In Old Testament times, the glory of the Lord often filled the Temple until the priests were unable to stand. The more priests we have sitting in the pews of our churches, the more of God's glory we will see. Peter made this clear: We are all holy priests, royal priests. We are chosen of God to give Him glory.

All believers are called to be priests!

JESUS WEPT

R.B. Thomas

SCRIPTURE: John 11:35

INTRODUCTION

At least two times in the New Testament we find that Jesus wept. One of those is recorded in John 11:35, from which is drawn the title of this message. The other is found in Luke 19:41, 42, where Jesus beheld the city of Jerusalem and wept. This was a lonely moment in the life of our Lord. "And when he was come near, he beheld the city, and wept over it, saying, If thou hadst known, even thou, at least in this thy day, the things which belong unto thy peace! but now they are hid from thine eyes." Jesus then foretold the judgment and destruction that was coming upon Jerusalem.

MOVED TO TEARS

Greek writers had a choice of two words to express the English equivalent of *weep*. The word used in John 11:35 expresses the simplest form of the English word *weep*, that is, to be moved by emotion to the point of shedding tears.

This is what Jesus did at the graveside of His friend Lazarus. The other Greek word means "to lament," not only by the shedding of tears but also by every outward expression of grief—to bewail or mourn. This is the word used by Luke in writing of Jesus' weeping over Jerusalem.

Jesus was even more emotional at the scene of the city of Jerusalem than at the grave of Lazarus. He had stood in the presence of death and had seen the bitter hurt of Martha and Mary. He saw they were unable to fully comprehend that He is the resurrection and the life, and He was moved to tears. But His tears did not last long, for He knew the purpose of the death of Lazarus and was aware that momentarily he would be restored to life.

Jesus felt much deeper pain as He looked on Jerusalem. He knew Jerusalem was on the brink of a disaster that would destroy the city and being much sorrow into the lives of the people. The death of a soul, the spiritual rejection of a nation, a city, or an individual is always of more concern to Jesus than the passing from this life to the other.

The day was Palm Sunday; it had been a day of triumph. Jesus had ridden on a colt, and the crowds, crying aloud, had proclaimed Him king. No time for tears, you would think. Yet Jesus saw what the multitudes could not see; He felt what they did not feel. To Him it was a time for pain, not praise. As Jesus neared the city—beholding it, knowing what He knew, feeling what He felt—He wept.

What surprising action! What a shock to His friends! Why should Jesus break down like this? Why the tears? Why the sorrow? Why didn't He show pleasure, admiration, joy, and enthusiasm? The city before Him was a panorama of beauty, a majestic sight, the joy of the poet, the rapture of the architect, the rhapsody of the composer. Jerusalem was the City of David, the city of His fathers, and they were ready to make Him king. Why then, with all this adulation, did Jesus weep?

It was a matter of depth—of seeing beyond the surface. The same vision often produces different emotions in different people. In fact, the same vision may evoke different emotions from the same person at different stages of his life. It all depends on how the scene is regarded, what it suggests to the beholder at the time, what it brings forth in associated thought and memories.

An artist looking at Jerusalem might say, "What fine views are here, what an opportunity for pencils and brushes!" A tourist passing the same scene might comment, "What a city to explore, what a place for sight-seeing, what interesting charm awaits in the streets and villages of the city below!" A moralist might say, "What sin, what a wicked city, surely it does not deserve to exist!" But Jesus looked at Jerusalem through the eyes of love and compassion. He saw it through the eyes of a redeemer who shortly must die because of its sin. This melted Him to tears. He knew that salvation was now riding through the streets of the city on a colt and Jerusalem as well as all of Israel did not recognize it. "He came unto his own, and his own received him not." This is why Jesus wept.

WHY HE WEPT

Looking at Jerusalem through the eyes of a redeemer, what did Jesus see that made Him weep? What was the vision which caught His eyes? I am sure that in part it was the immoral, corrupt nature of the city. He saw the corruption of religion with the whited sepulchers of the Pharisees with rotten dead men's bones on the inside. Synagogues were the hideaways of the elite, not the worshiping place of weary souls. He saw the wealthy happily living in luxury while others lived in hunger and rags. He saw the rich man feasting while Lazarus starved at his gate without a crumb. He saw the priest and the rabbi catering to the wealthy and caring not for the sacrifices of sin or the souls of the people. He saw the hungry and the poor, heard their cries for mercy, and perceived that no man cared for their souls. Is it any wonder that Jesus wept?

What was a glittering edifice to Jesus, when the religion of that Temple was in shambles and a sham? What did the loveliness of a city mean to Him when it was a mass of moral filth, poverty, and physical sores? Of what value were wealth and culture if only a few enjoyed them and the rest were ragged and neglected?

With pride one day the disciples of Jesus called His attention to the great white stones of the Temple as though He had never noticed them before. "See these?" they said to Him.

Jesus as though unimpressed said, "Not one stone shall be left upon another" (Mark 13:2). What good were these stones if men's hearts were just as cold and just as hard?

MOVED TO ACTION

Jesus' emotion did not end with emotion, as so often ours does. His emotion and His tears were transmitted into action. He was moved to tears, and His tears moved Him to action. His concern led Him up the Calvary road to the Cross. Surely we can recognize emotions that have taken missionaries all over the world and caused men to dedicate themselves in unselfish Christian service.

The world owes a great debt to its weepers. All of us are indebted to those who turn to the lonely prayer closets and to their crosses that our world might be a better, more Christlike world. But tears for the sake of tears are of little value. Emotion that does not motivate is not worth the time required to express it.

The tragedy of Jerusalem was not her sin, inequality, or poverty. The tragedy was that its inhabitants had a Sin-Bearer and didn't know it. They had a way out but were too blind to see. For all their needs, here on the hill overlooking the city sat the one person who held the answer. The tragedy of Jerusalem was in the rejection of the deliverer God had sent into the world.

The people of Israel thought they needed a king. But if that was what they needed, Jesus could have easily moved in and become king. But they had had kings before now, though they had not had one now for a long time. But they didn't need a king; they needed a Sin-Bearer. They didn't need a political deliverer; they needed a spiritual deliverer.

CONCLUSION

Such is the need of our world. And such is the need of our country. A new king cannot remove the sins of depraved man or of a backslidden nation. Rather, we need a spiritual deliverer.

The tragedy of our time is much like that of Jerusalem in the day of Christ. It is deeper than the fact that we are sinners or even that we are depraved and wicked. The real tragedy is that we have a deliverer but we don't have peace, that we have a Sin-Bearer but we bear our own sins. The tragedy is that we do not recognize Him. Jesus was there, but they didn't know Him. He is here today, and many still don't know Him. The tragedy of Jerusalem and the tragedy of today are much the same.

THE DREAD OF DEBT

Elwood Matthews

SCRIPTURE: Malachi 3:8-11

INTRODUCTION

One of the plights of most nations is their national debt. I can think of no nation of the free world that does not have a staggering deficit. And this country is no exception!

In light of this, it might be proper to say, "As the nation goes, so goes its citizenry." The majority of Americans and citizens of other countries are deeply in debt. They buy things that they don't need and cannot afford to impress people they don't like. There is a craving that drives people to buy, and in far too many cases, on credit. And this creates a dread! A dread of opening the mail to find overdue bills. A dread of meeting a creditor on the street. A dread of going into an establishment where you have a past-due account. A dread of hearing the bill collectors come to the door. A dread of having to tell your companion, "We can't meet our obligations this month."

Yes sir, debt creates a dread!

A CRAVING FOR THINGS

Credit cards, installment payments, and other forms of easy credit have many families "hooked," and their paycheck is already spent before they receive it. This one problem has probably contributed to as much to divorce as any other one cause. Young couples desire to have the same lifestyle as their parents, who have been married for some 40 years, and the inexperienced young husband and wife find themselves deeply in debt for the next 15-25 years with no apparent way out. The constant financial strain brings tension, depression and, in too many cases, divorce. The trouble began with the craving for things. Perhaps that's why John warned, "Love not the world, neither the *things* that are in the world" (1 John 2:15).

This danger is also prevalent in the church, both individually and collectively. How many churches do you know of that have overbuilt their facilities and as a result the congregation has a difficult time fulfilling their financial obligation each month? In fact, there are some lending agencies that will not loan money to churches.

And how many Christians do you know that are heavily obligated to lending agencies? Some have become so far in debt that they don't give to the work of God or pay their tithes. They declare, "I just can't afford to tithe, give offerings, *and* pay debts." But, my frustrated friend, I submit to you that you cannot afford *not* to pay your tithes and give offerings to the work of the Lord. That is the only hope you have of ever getting out of your financial dilemma. Note what the Lord says:

Will a man rob God? Yet ye have robbed me. But ye say, Wherein have we robbed thee? In tithes and offerings. Ye are cursed with a curse: for ye have robbed me, even this whole nation. Bring ye all the tithes into the storehouse, that there may be meat in mine house, and prove me now herewith, saith the Lord of hosts, if I will not open you the windows of heaven, and pour you out a blessing, that there shall not be room enough to receive it. And I will rebuke the devourer for your sakes, and he shall not destroy the fruits of your ground; neither shall your vine cast her fruit before the time in the field, saith the Lord of hosts (Malachi 3:8-11).

104

THE PATH TO RUIN

Time and again, debts have been the downfall of promising ministers. And in too many cases, pastors have left an area for another assignment, leaving behind a number of outstanding debts. This has caused the ministry to lose favor in the community and the church to be reproached. My minister friend, you are a representative of the Lord Jesus Christ. You represent His body here on earth. For His sake, for the church's sake, for the ministry's sake, and for your own sake—pay your debts. And in the event that you should owe a debt and be transferred to another area—don't leave until you have made arrangements with your creditors. Explain to them that you will pay the debt—and be certain that you do. And the same applies to any person who names the name of Christ.

Don't pretend to be a Christian, and especially a minister of the gospel, and refuse to pay a just and honest debt. The Bible is very clear on stealing and fraudulence!

The writer of 2 Kings provides us with an event that should make every preacher beware that he doesn't get himself entangled in debt:

Now there cried a certain woman of the wives of the sons of the prophets unto Elisha, saying, Thy servant my husband is dead; and thou knowest that thy servant did fear the Lord: and the creditor is come to take unto him my two sons to be bondmen. And Elisha said unto her, What shall I do for thee? tell me, what hast thou in the house? And she said, Thine handmaid hath not any thing in the house, save a pot of oil. Then he said, Go, borrow thee vessels abroad of all thy neighbours, even empty vessels; borrow not a few. And when thou art come in, thou shalt shut the door upon thee and upon thy sons, and shalt pour out into all those vessels, and thou shalt set aside that which is full. So she went from him, and shut the door upon her and upon her sons, who brought the vessels to her; and she poured out. And it came to pass, when the vessels were full, that she said unto her son, Bring me yet a vessel. And he said unto her, There is not a vessel more. And the oil stayed. Then she came and told the man of God. And he said, Go, sell the oil, and pay thy debt, and live thou and thy children of the rest (2 Kings 4:1-7).

The death of one of the sons of the prophets—a preacher, in our day—left his widow deeply in debt. How many times have we witnessed that same scene? It appears that we preachers think only of today and of ourselves. We seem to give little consideration for our family's well being should something happen to us. And too often the husband passes away and the wife and children find themselves deeply in debt with no way to pay for the funeral and perhaps an enormous hospital bill, as well as debts incurred by the minister husband/father.

There is another side to the argument that is just as deadly and perhaps even more so. The preacher becomes so interested in providing for the family and leaving them with no worries that his time is spent in making provisions for the flesh to the detriment of the spiritual welfare of his congregation and in many cases his family and himself. It might be said that he became so "earthly minded he is no heavenly good." There must be a balance between the two, and God's Word is the scale.

A DEBT-FREE PLAN

The Mosaic Law gave the creditor the right to claim the debtor and the children of the debtor who could not pay so that they might serve the creditor until the Year of Jubilee, at which time they would be set free. The son of the prophet's creditor laid claim on the two orphaned children.

The bereaved woman was distressed, but she knew where to go for help. She went to Elisha—God's prophet. She poured out her soul to him, reminding him that her husband had feared God. Thank God for that kind of testimony! The preacher might not have been a good manager of his finances, but he feared God—undoubtedly leaving a good testimony.

Elisha gave the woman a plan to pay her husband's debt —though he did not reveal the entire plan. He gave her just enough to test her faith. And it would take faith to go and borrow pots and pans from the neighbors to pour oil into from a small flask or pot.

And God has not changed His method of helping those who sincerely desire to follow His instructions. He gives us just enough revelation to cause us to walk in faith. Even the young man Saul, when he was chosen by the Lord, was only told to go into the city and someone would come and tell him what the Lord wanted him to do (Acts 9:6).

The woman acted in faith. She borrowed vessels, closed the door, and began to pour from the one small pot. And from that vessel the oil flowed until each empty container was filled. As the last one was filled, the oil stopped flowing.

After she acted in faith, Elisha revealed the rest of his plan for her financial security. She was to take the oil and sell it, pay the creditor, and she and her sons were to live on the remaining money. God performed a miracle to help this woman. And I'm convinced that God will help all today who will come to Him in sincerity and desiring to set their house in order financially.

Now mind you, I am not suggesting a prosperity plan —though God gave this woman one. I am suggesting that He will help us get out of a financial strain that is taking away our victory and joy. And He will help churches to get from under an overpowering financial load.

Of course, He expects individuals and churches to have the good sense to stop buying! A person will never get out from under the dread of debt as long as he continues on a buying spree. And, husband, if your wife is addicted to buying, it's time for you to take charge and let her know that the buying stops—until the debts are under control. And, sir, if you are a slave to a SALE—get a grip on yourself and set an example for your wife and family.

Now some may ask, How far do I go with this? How about my home mortgage or my automobile? No doubt there are many other questions.

Romans 13 gives us some excellent advice in this area. The first seven verses deal with our relations to the government. Verses 8-10 apply to a greater relationship:

Owe no man any thing, but to love one another: for he that loveth another hath fulfilled the law. For this, Thou shalt not commit adultery, Thou shalt not kill, Thou shalt not steal, Thou shalt not bear false witness, Thou shalt not covet; and if there be any other commandment, it is briefly comprehended in this saying, namely, Thou shalt love thy neighbour as thyself. Love worketh no ill to his neighbour: therefore love is the fulfilling of the law.

Some are prone to take "Owe no man any thing" a bit far. They conclude that we should never incur financial obligations of any type or that we do not borrow from others in case of need.

Yet a close look at Scripture shows that the Lord does not hold such a strong view. The woman in debt borrowed pots when told to do so by the prophet.

Moses said, "If thou lend money to any of my people that is poor by thee, thou shalt not be to him as an usurer, neither shalt thou lay upon him usury" (Exodus 22:25).

David said of the Lord, "He is ever merciful, and lendeth" (Psalm 37:26). This implies a borrower.

Jesus said, "Give to him that asketh thee, and from him that would borrow of thee turn not thou away" (Matthew 5:42) and "Love ye your enemies, and do good, and lend, hoping for nothing again" (Luke 6:35).

Now I'm aware that these points can be argued, but I have no desire to argue. The Lord condemns the looseness with which we contract debts, particularly the indifference so often displayed in repaying them. Remember what the psalmist said: "The wicked borroweth, and payeth not again" (Psalm 37:21).

CONCLUSION

Common sense is always valuable. I suggest we use it concerning our finances. Do not obligate yourself to more than you can comfortably handle. Do not depend on a raise that may not materialize.

Place God's tithe and your giving to God's work at the top of your financial priority list. Use discretion in buying, and don't become a victim of the credit-card syndrome. Study the Scripture concerning debts. Make your purchases a matter of prayer.

The Lord will help us—but we must also help ourselves to stay from under the cloud of the *dread of debt.*

ABUNDANCE

James M. MacKnight

SCRIPTURE: Ephesians 3:17-19

INTRODUCTION

If you were around during the Great Depression, you could never forget the economic limitations of those days. There was a scarcity of almost everything! Clothing was in short supply; money was limited. In our home, families ate only the bare essentials. Children grew up feeling they would not live long enough to ever discover something of which there was an abundance!

I grew up with such a feeling. But I will never forget the first time I stood on the shores of the Atlantic Ocean—as far as I could see, water stretched out in front of me. A few years later, I stood on Liberian sand in West Africa and realized this was the same body of water but 3,000 miles away. I suddenly became aware of something of which there was plenty.

But the abundance of God's provision in nature is dwarfed when we contemplate the infinite abundance of God's spiritual provision for us in Christ! In John 10:10, Jesus said, "The thief cometh not, but for to steal, and to kill, and to destroy:

I am come that they might have life, and that they might have it more abundantly." This abundance refers both to quantity and quality. God offers to us an abundance of mercy, love, and grace beyond our comprehension.

ABUNDANT MERCY

The apostle Peter spoke of God's abundant mercy which "hath begotten us again unto a lively hope by the resurrection of Jesus Christ from the dead" (1 Peter 1:3). God shows His mercy in goodness and compassion manifested toward those in misery or distress. Mercy is an eternal quality in God, but the exercising of it is not mandatory. God chooses to offer us mercy. Were it a matter of paying a debt, it would no longer be mercy. Mercy is not responding to an obligation but rather showing compassion to the undeserving.

This was graphically illustrated in the story of Esther, who went before King Ahasuerus without being summoned to appear. The law said that if a person were to appear before the king without being summoned, that individual would be put to death unless the king held out his golden scepter. The king was not under any obligation—he could hold out his scepter and show mercy if he so desired. (Of course, Ahasuerus granted mercy to Esther.)

The mercy Peter referred to in 1 Peter 1:3 is the great compassion the Lord showed in providing an atonement for man when he was in misery and despair.

Psalmists and prophets alike praised God for His abundant mercy. The psalmist declared, "I will sing of the mercies of the Lord for ever" (Psalm 89:1). In Jeremiah 33:11, the prophet proclaimed, "Praise the Lord of hosts: for the Lord is good; for his mercy endureth for ever."

God's mercy is of the highest quality and is unlimited in its quantity.

The publican said, "God be merciful to me a sinner" (Luke 18:13). He was saying, "You are not obligated, but please be merciful. Have mercy on me, Oh Lord."

ABUNDANT LOVE

Abundant love is the overriding theme of the writings of the apostle John. In his youth, this man was austere; he was even nicknamed "Son of Thunder." But he was so mellowed by God's love that his writings in later years earned him the title "the apostle of love."

Of all the references to God's love, the most classic verse —the one that shows its abundance best—is recorded in John 3:16: "For God so loved the world, that he gave his only begotten Son, that whosoever believeth in him should not perish, but have everlasting life." The essence of God's love is self-sacrificing for the benefit of the one loved. It manifests itself whether or not the loved one is worthy of love or even capable of returning it. God's love is unequaled love. God's love, therefore, is not based on our response. It is God's nature to love, for He *is* love.

This is in contrast with the heathen gods who hate and are always angry and in contrast with the philosopher who is cold and indifferent. God's love is so abundant and so great He is able to love all people the same.

ABUNDANT GRACE

Paul mentioned "abundant grace" four times in his writings. In the New Testament, *grace* is a word of central importance —the key word, in fact, of Christianity. The New Testament message is the grand announcement that grace has come to mankind, in and through Jesus Christ. "And the Word was made flesh, and dwelt among us . . . full of grace and truth . . . For the law was given by Moses, but grace and truth came by Jesus Christ" (John 1:14, 17).

One of the greatest needs in the world today is to *know* the grace of God. A summons comes from God to receive this grace. "For by grace are ye saved through faith; and that not of yourselves: it is the gift of God: not of works, lest any man should boast" (Ephesians 2:8, 9). God, by the grace manifested through Jesus Christ, bestows the gift of salvation upon us.

Romans 5:17 says, "For if by one man's offence death reigned by one; *much more* they which receive *abundance of grace* and of the gift of righteousness shall reign in life by one, Jesus Christ."

Having experienced the grace of God, Paul and Barnabas

"persuaded them to [the Gentile converts of Antioch] to continue in the grace of God" (Acts 13:43).

To continue in the grace of God is to be built up and to find "an inheritance among all them which are sanctified" (Acts 20:32).

Grace is the sum total of all we experience in the gospel! Again, Paul said it clearly and decisively: "For by grace are ye saved through faith; and that not of yourselves: it is the gift of God."

We receive what we do not deserve, what we could never earn, what we could never become good enough to merit. It is the same experience that Noah enjoyed. The account is recorded in Genesis 6:8: "But Noah found grace in the eyes of the Lord."

A boy was reported missing. As night approached, the whole family, the neighbors, and the fire department were all out searching. They sought for the boy all through the night without success. They decided they would drag the nearby lake for his body in the morning.

Suddenly, the older brother discovered him sitting on the fender of a car. The brother shouted out excitedly, "I've found him—he's all right!" Everyone came running, but Dad outran them all. He grabbed up his boy into his arms, kissed him, and held him very close for a long time. Then the comments started from neighbors! One said the boy ought to be thrashed real hard. A relative said, "Jim, if that were my son, I would punish him severely!"

But the dad, still holding the boy, stepped forward and said, "Friends, I don't want to appear ungrateful for what you have done, and I appreciate your advice—but this is not your boy; he is mine.

"His mother and I have already paid the price of his loss in our hearts and bodies tonight. We had almost given up hope that he would be found alive! *There will be no punishment for my boy tonight.*"

The truth is, we were all spiritually lost—dead in trespasses and sin. We deserved to be punished to the point of eternal death! But God offered us mercy; He showed us love; He dealt with us in grace.

CONCLUSION

We are thankful to the Lord for the abundance of mercy, love, and grace. By drawing upon these freely, we can never diminish their abundance. That is what was demonstrated by the father in the story of the Prodigal Son. When the father saw his son returning home, he had compassion on him. He ran, fell on his neck, and kissed him. The father said, "For this my son was dead, and is alive again; he was lost, and is found" (Luke 15:24).

This is the true story of abundant mercy, love, and grace.

THE ART OF LIVING

Raymond M. Pruitt

SCRIPTURE: Philippians 3:20—4:23

INTRODUCTION

The art of living is the least learned of all arts. Most people have learned the art of coping, of getting along with the demands of life, of making do with half answers; but few know the art of enjoying all of life at its best.

A good many years ago, syndicated columnist Billy Rose reported on a group of American tycoons who met in the 1920s at Chicago's Edgewater Beach Hotel. They represented in personal wealth and financial control more money than there was in the national treasury. Their power and influence was enormous, their "success" fabulous.

Twenty-five years later, Billy Rose wrote another column on those same men. He called the roll and told what had happened to each of them since the Chicago meeting. One, a man who had cornered millions through wheat speculation, had died abroad, insolvent. Another, the president of the nation's largest independent steel company, had died broke. Another, the president of the New York Stock Exchange, had been recently released from prison. A member of the Cabinet

114

in President Harding's administration, after being released from prison for health reasons, had died at home. The greatest exploiter of the bear market on Wall Street had committed suicide. The leader of the world's match monopoly had likewise died by his own hand. Billy Rose summed up his report by saying, "All of these men had learned how to make big money, but not one of them had learned how to live!"

Those men were not alone! To many others, life seems to be only a rat race in which only the rats get the cheese. Even Christians too often fail to get into the stream of abundant living. A lot of professing Christians know nothing of "joy unspeakable" or "peace that passeth understanding." They sing the songs but have never found the reality they sing about.

In the passage in Philippians 3:20—4:23, we are given God's formula for life at its very best. Let us focus on some of the main points.

CITIZENSHIP IN HEAVEN

"Finally, my brethren, rejoice in the Lord. . . . For our conversation [citizenship] is in heaven; from whence also we look for the Saviour, the Lord Jesus Christ: who shall change our vile body, that it may be fashioned like unto his glorious body, according to the working whereby he is able even to subdue all things unto himself. Therefore, my brethren dearly beloved and longed for, my joy and crown, so stand fast in the Lord, my dearly beloved" (Philippians 1:20—4:1).

These verses teach us to understand and to live by the knowledge that we are colonists of heaven. This world is not our home; we're just passing through here. Our treasures and our hopes are there. We live with heaven in view. Our life's decisions are made in the light of heaven, our eternal home. This life and the things of it are temporal, fleeting, changeable. "Here we have no continuing city" (Hebrews 13:14, NKJV), but in heaven there will be no diminishing or fading of the joys and wonders that await the faithful.

Jesus taught the disciples that no accomplishment done here on earth or any honors received are to be compared with the assurance that we are citizens of heaven: "And the seventy returned again with joy, saying, Lord, even the devils are subject unto us through thy name. And he said unto them . . . Notwithstanding in this rejoice not, that the spirits are subject unto you; but rather rejoice, because your names are written in heaven" (Luke 10:17, 18, 20).

The apostle Paul made the same point in Ephesians 2:19 when he reminded his readers: "Now therefore ye are no more strangers and foreigners, but fellowcitizens with the saints, and of the household of God."

The writer of Hebrews also made the same emphasis when writing of the faithful saints of the Old Testament:

These all died in faith, not having received the promises, but having seen them afar off, and were persuaded of them, and embraced them, and confessed that they were strangers and pilgrims on the earth. For they that say such things declare plainly that they seek a country. And truly, if they had been mindful of that country from whence they came out, they might have had opportunity to have returned. But now they desire a better country, that is, an heavenly: wherefore God is not ashamed to be called their God: for he hath prepared for them a city (Hebrews 11:13-16).

It is the normal lifestyle of Christians that they live daily with the consciousness that their true citizenship is in heaven. In the *Letter to Diognetus* (second century), the writer said of the Christians, "They pass their time upon earth, but they have their citizenship in heaven."

We are to be as Jesus when He said, "I am not of this world" (John 8:23). And the apostle John said, "As he is, so are we in this world" (1 John 4:17).

We must recognize that the present generation is dominated by materialistic and humanistic thinking. Most people live in the here and now. For many, this world and the things of this world are all there is. For them, there is nothing more. Consequently, the Christian marches to a different drumbeat We are tuned to a different frequency. Our personal lives, our businesses, our families, and our lifestyles will our worldview. We are different, and it shows!

As we pass through this world, we must leave our mark at every level of society. That's why the Lord leaves us here for a while—to leave our mark, to be His witnesses and His ambassadors. We must succeed as Christians who embrace

Christian values. We must outlive, outthink, outdo, and outdie those who are in the world without Christ.

RIGHT RELATIONSHIPS WITH OTHER PEOPLE

"I beseech Euodias, and beseech Syntyche, that they be of the same mind in the Lord" (Philippians 4:2).

Bad relationships do injury to the individuals involved, as well as bringing disgrace and hindrance to the cause of Christ. Too many churches have a "Sister Odious" and a "Sister Soon-Touchy" who create problems for themselves and for the church.

Admittedly, it is a challenge to always get along in sweet fellowship with everybody all the time, but we are admonished in Scripture to work at it. "Endeavouring to keep the unity of the Spirit in the bond of peace" (Ephesians 4:3). Our goal: Unity in essentials, liberty in nonessentials, love in all things.

The rewards of right relationships are peace and harmony in the church, inner personal peace and boundless love for others, and the blessed approval and favor of the Lord.

RIGHT ATTITUDE TOWARD THE EXPERIENCES OF LIFE

Rejoice in the Lord at all times, in all situations. "Rejoice in the Lord alway: and again I say, Rejoice" (Philippians 4:4).

Paul did not deny that there will be painful situations, bitter tears, and times of anguish. But even in these things, the Christian may rejoice and be exceedingly glad because he knows "the Lord is at hand" (Philippians 4:5). God always has the situation in control, and He will never abandon His children. Before trouble can get to us, it must first go through Him; and when He allows it, He has some purpose in it that will in the end bring glory to Him and blessing to His servants.

We do not always understand the ways of God, nor do we need to. We only know that He is altogether good and works good for those who love and fear Him. Therefore, rejoice! Rejoice through your tears and your pain. The Lord is at hand, and His love for you transcends all understanding.

"Let your moderation [gentleness] be known unto all men" (Philippians 4:5). Since God is always in charge and He never makes a mistake, those who trust in Him never have cause to panic. They can be "cool, calm, and collected" in every circumstance, because "the Lord is at hand."

The Lord is at hand in the sense that He is an ever-present help in the time of need. The Lord is at hand in the sense that His coming is imminent. Therefore, "Do not be anxious about anything, but in everything, by prayer and petition, with thanksgiving, present your requests to God" (Philippians 4:6, *NIV*). D.L. Moody summed up this principle when he said, "Worry about nothing; pray about everything; be thankful for anything."

"Worry is a thin stream of fear trickling through the mind. If encouraged, it cuts a channel into which all our thoughts are drained" (Arthur Somers Roche). A bulletin-board sign read: "Don't let worry kill you off—let the church help."

The peace of God, which is the consequence of unquestionable trust in the faithfulness of God, is the mighty fortress of the Christ-centered life. "And the peace of God, which passeth all understanding, shall keep your hearts and minds through Christ Jesus" (Philippians 4:7).

Let the positive attitude control your thinking. "Finally, brethren, whatsoever things are true, whatsoever things are honest, whatsoever things are just, whatsoever things are pure, whatsoever things are lovely, whatsoever things are of good report; if there be any virtue, and if there be any praise, think on these things" (Philippians 4:8).

Don't allow the Enemy to take control of your mind and drag your thoughts into the gutter of contrariness, complaint, and corruption. By God's grace, we have the capacity to build what Christopher Morley called a beautiful "inscape" in our minds. To a very significant degree, we create our own environment. "Two men looked out prison bars one saw mud; the other, stars."

The Positive Count

Count your blessings instead of your crosses,
Count your gains instead of your losses,
Count your joys instead of your woes,
Count your friends instead of your foes,
Count your courage instead of your fears,
Count your laughs instead of your tears,
Count your full years instead of your lean,

Count your kind deeds instead of your mean,
Count your health instead of your wealth,
Count on God instead of yourself.

—Anonymous

RIGHT ATTITUDE TOWARD POSSESSIONS

Christian commitment and contentment is the key to peace and joy. Possessing these, one can say with the apostle, "I rejoiced in the Lord greatly . . . for I have learned, in whatsoever state I am, therewith to be content. I know both how to be abased, and I know how to abound: every where and in all things I am instructed both to be full and to be hungry, both to abound and to suffer need. I can do all things through Christ which strengtheneth me" (Philippians 4:10-13).

As we live a life of commitment and contentment in Christ, our desires for worldly goods are moderate. Our desires for bettering our material circumstances are tempered by a desire to please the Lord in all things. Whatever our present condition may be, we cheerfully submit to the providence of God in it. We are so comfortable with what He has chosen for us that we do not envy others who may be in more prosperous circumstances. Worldly goods are only of relative value to us. The absolutes in our lives have to do with our relationship with Christ and pleasing Him.

We learn from this passage that contentment depends more upon our attitude than upon our outward condition. Times of material need can become times of learning to trust in the faithfulness of God and to enjoy Him. (It is noteworthy that Paul was in prison for preaching the gospel when he wrote this joyful Epistle to the Philippians.)

Life here can be beautiful even when the going gets rough. It all depends on where we have chosen to fix our foundations —in the here and now or in the Lord Jesus Christ.

Great Christians have demonstrated that life can be beautiful even in the midst of severe trouble. Following the Chicago fire of 1871, Horatio G. Spafford arranged for his family to take a trip to Europe. Mrs. Spafford and the four daughters were to go ahead, and Mr. Spafford would join them a few days later.

119

The ship on which the happy mother and her four daughters sailed, the *Ville du Havre*, never got further than halfway across the Atlantic. In the dead of a November night, it was rammed by a sailing vessel and cut in two. In the appalling confusion and disaster that followed, Mrs. Spafford saw all four of her daughters swept away to their deaths in the cold Atlantic waters. A falling mast knocked Mrs. Spafford unconscious, and a wave freakishly deposited her on a piece of wreckage where she later regained consciousness.

When she and a few other survivors reached Cardiff, Wales, Mrs. Spafford cabled two words to her husband: "Saved alone." Taking the earliest ship he could get, he hastened to be with his grieving wife. It was when his ship reached the approximate spot where the *Ville du Havre* had met its doom that God gave Mr. Spafford the inspiration, insight, and courage to write that beautiful hymn:

When peace, like a river, attendeth my way,
When sorrows like sea billows roll;
Whatever my lot, Thou hast taught me to say,
It is well, it is well with my soul.

—*Hymns of the Spirit,* p. 131

CONCLUSION

It is God's desire for His children to enjoy life to the full. In Christ, this is possible, even though we have pain and trouble. The Lord is always at hand. When we appreciate our citizenship in heaven, have a right relationship with other people, a right attitude toward life, and a right attitude toward earthly possessions, nothing can destroy our peace or spoil our joy in the Lord.

NO MAN IS AN ISLAND

Bennie Triplett

SCRIPTURE: Romans 12:4, 5

INTRODUCTION

The great English poet John Donne wrote, "No man is an island, entire of itself; every man is a piece of the continent, a part of the main." *The Living Bible* paraphrases verse 5 of our text, "We belong to each other, and each needs all the others." Goodspeed states, "We are individually parts of one another." *The New Testament in Basic English* says, "We are dependent on one another."

WHAT IS AN ISLAND?

An island is a tract of land, smaller than a continent, which is surrounded by water. It can also be regarded as anything that resembles an island, such as a position of isolation, like a traffic island or a safety zone.

Independence. Let us ask ourselves, Is an island really an island? If we could see things as God sees them, we would realize that most things in life are connected, related, intertwined.

I remember the first time I went to Lake Lanier, a beautiful lake outside Atlanta, Georgia. I was in the boat with my good friend, Homer Sims, who remarked, "The water has been kind of low lately, and I don't know what we're going to find today. Right now there are a lot of islands out here."

His boat had a depth finder on it. As we were riding along, he said, "There is something under here 50 feet deep, 40 feet, 30 feet, 20 feet, 10 feet." Then he started turning away, as if he were dodging something under the water. It wasn't long until the motor was bumping and we had to make some adjustments in our rig. From a distance it looked as if nothing was there, but as we got closer, land came up fast underneath the boat. If I had looked around under the water, I would have seen how each individual island was connected underneath the surface.

Interdependence. Archaeologists, historians, and scientists believe the land masses which are now divided and surrounded by water were once connected. Many scholars believe there was a time when men could travel from one continent to another without crossing a body of water. Many things in our world are connected and related, though they do not seem to be. They are interdependent upon one another. No man is an island! No man stands alone!

NO PART OF NATURE STANDS ALONE

Nature is interconnected and balanced. I marveled when my biology professor said to me, "You breathe in oxygen and breathe out carbon dioxide."

"Where do we get this oxygen?" I asked.

He responded, "The trees breathe in carbon dioxide and breathe out oxygen."

We examined a leaf under a microscope to see how it was designed to breathe. Through a process called photosynthesis, the trees help to purify and produce the oxygen we breathe. God—as Creator, supreme architect, and designer—has so correlated all of nature that there is an unbelievable balance, interrelatedness and interdependence. No part of nature stands alone.

NO PART OF THE UNIVERSE STANDS ALONE

The pull of the sun, the gyrations of the planets, the variations of gravity, and the fixations of the constellations are very concise and coordinated. Even though the earth is spinning like a top, we all manage to stand up straight, keep our balance, and stay on board. The days, months, and length of the seasons; the ebb and flow of the tides of the oceans, seas, gulfs, and major waterways—all are connected to the sun, moon, and stars. The sun has never failed, and the tides can certainly be counted on. The seasons, daytime, and nighttime are irrefutable witnesses that all the elements of the universe are inextricably tied together, unified and mutually dependent one upon the other.

NO NATION OR CULTURE COMPLETELY STANDS ALONE

Most nations and cultures used to exist autonomously. Even in our own nation our past pride caused us to think, "We don't need anything; we have it all!" Ask the nations of the Middle East if there is anything we need. As the family of man depletes many of its natural resources, national and cultural autonomy will become less and less. Rapid transportation and mass communication have brought us closer together and taught us to be more interdependent upon one another.

NO MAN STANDS ALONE

Man is interrelated. In 1 Corinthians 12:12 Paul described how man is so related. It is man's nature to think he is autonomous and in need of nothing. He prefers to believe that no part of his being is mutually dependent upon the other, but it is. God has miraculously and marvelously made man and put him together.

Man is organically related. Scripture reflects this: "If the foot shall say, Because I am not the hand, I am not of the body; is it therefore not of the body? And if the ear shall say, Because I am not the eye, I am not of the body; is it therefore not of the body? If the whole body were an eye, where were the hearing? If the whole were hearing, where were the smelling? But now hath God set the members every one of them in the body, as it hath pleased him. And if they were all one member, where were the body? But now are

123

they many members, yet but one body" (1 Corinthians 12:15-20).

The members of the body are cooperatively related. Man's total being is cooperatively related, one part working with the other. All its members are synchronized and attuned to function together.

And the eye cannot say unto the hand, I have no need of thee: nor again the head to the feet, I have no need of you. Nay, much more those members of the body, which seem to be more feeble, are necessary: And those members of the body, which we think to be less honourable, upon these we bestow more abundant honour; and our uncomely parts have more abundant comeliness (1 Corinthians 12:21-23).

The members of the body are sympathetically related. In 1 Corinthians 12:24-26 Paul commented, "For our comely parts have no need: but God hath tempered the body together, having given more abundant honour to that part which lacked: that there should be no schism in the body; but that the members should have the same care one for another. And whether one member suffer, all the members suffer with it; or one member be honoured, all the members rejoice with it."

Man's being is sympathetically connected and harmoniously interrelated. If the tip of your little finger touches the wrong part of the coffee pot, your brain sends emergency signals throughout a network of nerve endings, muscles, tissues, and sinews. It does not have to call a committee meeting or ask the chairman of the board. Your whole body automatically goes into action when your little finger is burned. Your heart pumps faster, the blood flows more rapidly, and all the healing agencies of your body react to heal and correct that burned finger.

Because the body is interconnected, I cannot be happy or sad without everything about me becoming happy or sad. Have you ever taken time to notice that when you get happy, all of you gets happy? You cannot isolate happiness. I don't ever remember laughing when my face and my voice or mind laughed separately. In the body of Christ—the family of God —when one weeps, we all weep. When one rejoices, we all rejoice. No man is an island. No man stands alone. As individuals we are interconnected organically, cooperatively, and sympathetically.

How are we related otherwise? Do we need one another?

SHARING OUR BURDENS

The Bible says, "Confess your faults one to another, and pray one for another" (James 5:16).

In Galatians 6:2 we read, "Bear ye one another's burdens, and so fulfil the law of Christ."

Hebrews 3:13 says, "But exhort one another daily, while it is called To day; lest any of you be hardened through the deceitfulness of sin."

SHARING OUR LOVE

In John 13:35 Christ said, "By this shall all men know that ye are my disciples, if ye have love one to another." He seemed to be saying to His followers, "You have been ambitious, envious, and at odds with each other for supremacy, but this cannot be. You must learn to love as I love, for by this love shall all men know you are Christians."

Disciples of other teachers and leaders were known by their habits or some particular creed or ritual. But the followers of Jesus Christ were known by the love they had for one another. "Beloved, let us love one another: for love is of God; and every one that loveth is born of God, and knoweth God. He that loveth not knoweth not God; for God is love" (1 John 4:7, 8).

We should never stop loving like Jesus loves, for "by this shall all men *know* that . . . [we] are . . . His disciples."

SHARING OUR FORGIVENESS

Colossians 3:13 instructs us regarding our relationship with others: "Forbearing one another, and forgiving one another . . . even as Christ forgave you."

We are admonished in Ephesians 4:32, "Be ye kind one to another, tenderhearted, forgiving one another, even as God for Christ's sake hath forgiven you."

Romans 14:7, 8 reminds us, "For none of us liveth to himself, and no man dieth to himself. For whether we live,

125

we live unto the Lord; and whether we die, we die unto the Lord: whether we live therefore, or die, we are the Lord's."

CONCLUSION

If you think you are an island unto yourself and have no need of others, you should read Revelation 3:14-22:

And unto the angel of the church of the Laodiceans write; These things saith the Amen, the faithful and true witness, the beginning of the creation of God; I know thy works, that thou art neither cold nor hot: I would thou wert cold or hot. So then because thou art lukewarm, and neither cold or hot, I will spue thee out of my mouth. Because thou sayest, I am rich, and increased with goods, and have need of nothing; and knowest not that thou art wretched, and miserable, and poor, and blind, and naked: I counsel thee to buy of me gold tried in the fire, that thou mayest be rich; and white raiment, that thou mayest be clothed, and that the shame of thy nakedness do not appear; and anoint thine eyes with eyesalve, that thou mayest see. As many as I love, I rebuke and chasten: be zealous therefore, and repent. Behold, I stand at the door, and knock: if any man hear my voice, and open the door, I will come in to him, and will sup with him, and he with me. To him that overcometh will I grant to sit with me in my throne, even as I also overcame, and am set down with my Father in his throne. He that hath an ear, let him hear what the Spirit saith unto the churches.

Do you still think you have no need of anyone and that no one needs you? Just as the universe, the human body, and all of existence are interwoven and interdependent, so is the family of man. Each of us has need of the other. No man is an island. No one stands alone.

We must take one more step in our journey through reality, and that is toward our relationship with God. Without the reality of God, there would be no consciousness, no existence, no meaningful relationships. The first words in the sacred Scriptures exclaim, "In the beginning God . . . " (Genesis 1:1). In a world of gadgets, rockets, computers, material, and magical marvels, the best and most important things we have are God and each other.

GENEROSITY

C.M. Ward

SCRIPTURE: Proverbs 11:25; Luke 6:38; 2 Corinthians 9:6; James 1:5

INTRODUCTION

The law of giving is, If you are generous, generosity will in turn flow to you. "Give, and it shall be given unto you" (Luke 6:38).

Paul made the application of this law a part of his ministry. "He which soweth sparingly shall reap also sparingly; and he which soweth bountifully shall reap also bountifully" (2 Corinthians 9:6).

A Scrooge-like person cuts himself off from help.

"The liberal soul shall be made fat: and he that watereth shall be watered also himself" (Proverbs 11:25). There is a law of return, but it doesn't always mean a return in kind.

INVESTMENT

The late entrepreneur Fred Waring taught me more about giving than anyone else. He reduced the concept of giving to one word: *investment*. He did not consider that giving was a loss, a goodbye to personal wealth, or a tip-of-the-hat charity. To him it was an opportunity for investment.

God is not only a good God, He is a *giver*—"God, that giveth to all men liberally" (James 1:5).

In sickness you are hardly in a position to ask for healing—*a gift*—if your daily practice has been to withhold. All you dare ask—after repentance—is mercy.

GREED

Greed shrivels. You can almost see the pain when the offering plate is passed. You can almost hear the groan of agony when an appeal is made. The nongiver becomes withdrawn and fearful in spirit. When the spirit is diseased, the body is affected. You cannot violate God's laws without suffering. You need help, but how can you expect to be helped when you haven't helped?

It is risky business to set yourself against the odds. Reaping follows sowing. The nongiver has built no credit. The nongiver bankrupts his own energy sources, attempting to hoard and promoting selfishness.

Your body is your scoreboard, reflecting your thoughts and your conduct.

How often personal damage could be avoided by giving even a little! The obstinate and the rude say, "I'm going to have it my way or else," causing real harm. Internal organs are under stress, veins in the neck bulge, and the heart beats too rapidly—all because of an unwillingness to give a little.

Many physicians have said to a patient, "You must adjust your lifestyle. Whether you continue to live depends upon it." The adamant ones choose a life of imprisonment to self-centeredness. An unwillingness to give up one's own selfish will cancels the very forces of nature which would contribute to healing and health.

Happiness is an asset to health. The determination to have your own way at any cost will never produce good cheer. Autocratic people are lonely people, and loneliness is devastating. The person who says, "I won't join in congregational singing because I object to the choice of the song" is out of the flow. Lack of participation blocks circulation. A miserable state of mind can contribute to abnormal blood pressure.

Perhaps the rich man at whose gate Lazarus was laid died sooner than he otherwise would have if he had been more generous. He certainly was not as happy as he would have been with a more charitable attitude. His "good things" were not enough. His smallness showed through. He shrank every day. He became mean, withdrawn, a man of extreme poverty in the midst of his vast wealth. In the end, his wealth could not buy him even a cup of water to help relieve his misery. "There is that withholdeth more than is meet, but it tendeth to poverty" (Proverbs 11:24).

GENEROSITY VS. RECKLESSNESS

Generosity is not *recklessness*. The law of giving does not include the spendthrift. Prudence is a virtue.

To dwell in suspicion is deteriorating. To have not one good word for anyone upsets the stomach, causes sleeplessness, and clouds the mind with dark thoughts. To have a sunny disposition is much better. The jolly man in town who has a good word for everybody is well-liked by all.

Jesus knew another man who would rather build barns than share. His attitude made it impossible to save him. His affluence choked the life out of him. "To him that asketh . . . turn not thou away!" (Matthew 5:42).

Too many queue into healing lines to find a cheap remedy. They wouldn't dare treat a doctor the way they treat the gospel. They give no thought to returning thanks by performing a service. Their selfish intent is to recover immediately without a thought of recompense.

God's blessing is withheld until you learn to give. Skinflints sign their own death certificate. God withholds His benefits from such. Jairus was a liberal man; his daughter was healed. Mary was a liberal woman, and Jesus commended her for pouring ointment on His feet.

"Cast thy bread upon the waters: for thou shalt find it after many days" (Ecclesiastes 11:1). You never know on what occasion the need for previous investment may arise. A blood transfusion, the loan of a summer cottage, or a vapor steam system may be an immediate dividend. How often in Western drama we hear, "I owe you one!"

Samson was a generous man, though at times he misdirected his generosity. But he had banked it. God was pleased to return to him his gift of strength even though Samson had erred.

Jesus warned against being a selfish, clamlike, tightfisted person. But in the parable of the talents, He showed how the investor was rewarded. The master took the talent from the introspective pessimist who had allowed it to lie idle and gave it to the one who believed in putting his resources into circulation. There's no sense in hoarding your possessions. As has been said, "You can never take it with you; there's no pocket in a shroud."

A time will come when you will need more than material gifts. You will need what hospital, bank, and church cannot supply. For this reason, you should bank in heaven toward that day. "Lay not up for yourselves treasures upon earth . . . but lay up for yourselves treasures in heaven" (Matthew 6:19, 20). When you ask for strength or an extension of life, will heaven check your balance and reply, "Overdrawn—no funds"?

Circulation is the key to spiritual as well as physical health.

I grew up in a family of pioneers. At Mother's table were always extra chairs. The lonely were invited. Those marred at birth were seated with us and served the same amount. Mother found room for the homeless and the deserted. We learned to respect the unfortunate. And God supplied. He poured in as my parents poured out. My father would say, "God's hand will always be bigger than mine." I am glad I grew up in a home of givers.

FREEDOM

Jesus said, "Freely ye have received, freely give" (Matthew 10:8). *Freedom* in giving is the catalyst of well-being. When you stop giving, you cut off the source of blessing; you become restricted, narrow, reclusive; and spiritual death sets in.

Jesus reached out toward children and nature. He drew strength from His Father's handiwork. *He gave.* Power went out from Him to meet human need. We do not have an anemic Christ.

I have discovered that giving people are the contented, healthy, working members of church congregations. I have also learned that complainers, murmurers, and those who argue are the ones in the congregation who are robbing God and who resist church spending. It was the same stymieing attitude that twisted Judas' thinking. He felt Jesus was unworthy of expenditure.

CONCLUSION

Keep an open heart of compassion. You are a steward—a *manager*. Testify by your open hand that there are more blessings where those came from.

"Give, and it *shall* be given unto you." It is not open to debate—it will happen. You become a candidate for God's largess.

Do you need a "good gift" today? Healing and health are beyond price. Change your lifestyle, and allow the law of giving to work in your life.

FOLLOW THE CLOUD

B.E. Underwood

SCRIPTURE: Exodus 13:20-22

INTRODUCTION

God never leaves His people without clear guidance for their journey. This is revealed in the history of Israel. His method for leading Israel was by the cloud.

The history of the cloud is one of the dominant themes of the Old Testament. The first reference to the cloud found in Exodus 13:20-22:

And they took their journey from Succoth, and encamped in Etham, in the edge of the wilderness. And the Lord went before them by day in a pillar of a cloud, to lead them the way; and by night in a pillar of fire, to give them light; to go by day and night: He took not away the pillar of the cloud by day, nor the pillar of fire by night, from before the people.

This happened prior to their leaving Egypt. God provided the cloud while the Israelites were yet in Egypt. It was to be a sign of Jehovah's presence and guidance for His people.

During their exit from Egypt the cloud served them well. In Exodus 14:19-20, we read:

And the angel of God, which went before the camp of Israel, removed and went behind them; and the pillar of the cloud went from before their face, and stood behind them: And it came between the camp of the Egyptians and the camp of Israel; and it was a cloud and darkness to them, but it gave light by night to these: so that the one came not near the other all the night.

In verse 24 we learn that God operated from that cloud. "And it came to pass, that in the morning watch the Lord looked unto the host of the Egyptians through the pillar of fire and of the cloud, and troubled the host of the Egyptians."

Following their passage through the Red Sea, Israel continued to follow the cloud. In Exodus 16:10 we find that "the glory of the Lord appeared in the cloud." God then spoke to His people.

Moses met Jehovah on Mt. Sinai, and Jehovah proclaimed, "Lo, I come unto thee in a thick cloud, that the people may hear when I speak with thee, and believe thee for ever" (Exodus 19:9).

Later Moses was called again to meet with God on the mountain, and again the cloud appeared:

And Moses went up into the mount, and a cloud covered the mount. And the glory of the Lord abode upon mount Sinai, and the cloud covered it six days: and the seventh day he called unto Moses out of the midst of the cloud. And the sight of the glory of the Lord was like devouring fire on the top of the mount in the eyes of the children of Israel. And Moses went into the midst of the cloud, and gat him up into the mount: and Moses was in the mount forty days and forty nights (Exodus 24:15-18).

The completion of the tent of the testimony provided another opportunity for the cloud. In Exodus 33:9 we read: "And it came to pass, as Moses entered into the tabernacle, the cloudy pillar descended, and stood at the door of the tabernacle, and the Lord talked with Moses."

When Moses carried the two tables of stone to the mount for God to write again the ten commandments, the cloud was also present:

The Lord descended in the cloud, and stood with him there, and proclaimed the name of the Lord. And the Lord passed by before him, and proclaimed, The Lord, The Lord God, merciful and gracious, longsuffering, and abundant in goodness and truth, keeping mercy for thousands, forgiving iniquity and transgression and sin, and that will by no means clear the guilty; visiting the iniquity of the fathers upon the children, and upon the children's children, unto the third and to the fourth generation (Exodus 34:5-7).

The cloud rested upon the tabernacle and gave guidance to the camp of Israel:

Then a cloud covered the tent of the congregation, and the glory of the Lord filled the tabernacle. And Moses was not able to enter into the tent of the congregation, because the cloud abode thereon, and the glory of the Lord filled the tabernacle. And when the cloud was taken up from over the tabernacle, the children of Israel went onward in their journeys: But if the cloud were not taken up, then they journeyed not till the day that it was taken up. For the cloud of the Lord was upon the tabernacle by day, and fire was on it by night, in the sight of all the house of Israel, throughout all their journeys (Exodus 40:34-38).

This glory cloud is called the "Shekinah." The word *Shekinah* means "dwelling place of God" and speaks of the fact that the glory (or presence) of Jehovah resided in the cloud. This residing presence of God was the guiding light that led Israel from place to place and from camp to camp.

THE EARLY CHURCH FOLLOWED THE CLOUD

Believers today are still led by the residing presence of Jehovah. He does not reside in a cloud above the church building but in the lives of His people. This indwelling Holy Spirit is the "cloud" for the church in this dispensation.

Paul tells us in Romans 8:14 that the sons of God are led by the Spirit of God. This Holy Spirit's ministry brought into existence the modern Pentecostal Movement.

When the latter-rain outpouring of the Spirit began just after the turn of the 20th century, a mighty cloud moved across the earth. The major decision for many believers was whether or not to follow the cloud. Some struck camp and began to follow the moving of the cloud. Others refused to follow and insisted on staying in the camp, where they had previously seen the manifestation of God's power.

It is significant that this great Pentecostal phenomenon of the 20th century has been called a movement. It is a mighty movement of God's people toward His ultimate and eternal purpose.

Certain characteristics of the cloud may help us understand God's guidance. The cloud was both fire and cloud—revelation and covering. It was both disclosure and concealment. God's glory was manifested, but there was also a covering for the manifested presence. This has ever been the characteristic of God's revelation of Himself. No man can ever stand in the presence of God's full glory.

The absolute uncertainty of the cloud's movement kept the children of Israel alert. They never knew when it would move. It might move by day or by night. They had to stay vigilant always to know when they should move. They never knew how long they were to remain in camp. They must be prepared to stay for only one day, but they must also be ready for a one-year camp.

The most important factor in their camping was to stay in touch with the cloud. Anyone who failed to move with the cloud would be left behind. No matter how comfortable and well-placed the camp site, it never determined the length of the stay. Only the cloud made the decision to move or to stay.

This poses an important question for those committed to following the Lord. Shall we follow the cloud or maintain the camp?

SHALL WE FOLLOW THE CLOUD?

It is easy to begin feeling at home in the camp. The surroundings become familiar and pleasant. The memories in the ashes of former camp fires can be attractive. In fact, one can become preoccupied with rekindling the flames. Many campers have lost sight of the cloud while bent over yesterday's ash heap. This temptation can blind one to the fact that God's people are pilgrims and must never settle down until they reach their destination. (And we are not there yet!)

It is always appealing to settle down in places where God's glory has been manifested. Simon Peter thought it a good idea to build three tabernacles on the Mount of Transfiguration. He could not see that the cloud was moving down into the valley. He would build monuments to the manifestation of the glory.

Many others have made similar proposals that have fallen upon receptive ears. Countless tabernacles have been built upon the ashes of former camp fires. And those who are committed to their rekindling think that those who have moved on have betrayed the fire. But the fire still resides in the moving cloud—not in the ashes of the camp.

But if we are to be led by the Spirit of God just as Israel was led by the cloud and the fire, how can we discern the leadership of the spirit?

This question need not concern those who make little of the leadership and ministry of the Spirit. But those of us who are part of the great Pentecostal Movement are committed to the ministry of the Spirit. We affirm the dynamic leadership He gives to the church. This is the primary reason for the tremendous growth of this movement.

THOSE WHO FOLLOW THE CLOUD

Those who follow the cloud must have the ability to recognize what the Spirit is saying to the church. They must be able to discern what God is doing *now*, not just what He did yesterday. This ability to recognize what God is doing is vital to the continued usefulness of the Pentecostal revival.

They must be able to discern the difference between the Spirit of God and other spirits that would pose as glory clouds above the camp. The gift of the discerning of spirits is the Spirit's provision for this need. It is axiomatic that if God is leading by His Spirit, Satan will try to imitate this leadership in order to deceive the people of God. We must be equipped to deal with this deception.

Satan will use both demon spirits and human beings to imitate the glory cloud. Both doctrines of demons and miracles of demons will be used to deceive. And just as often the doctrines of men (traditions of men) will be used to replace the Spirit of God. We must be equipped continually with the gift of the discerning of spirits in order to identify the source of both doctrines and deeds.

Satan's modus operandi is revealed in Matthew 16:21-23. Simon Peter had just made that majestic confession that Jesus was "the Christ, the Son of the living God" (Matthew 16:16). He had been receptive to the revelation of God and was commended by Jesus for his perception. Simon seemed to be out in front of the others in his spiritual understanding. But when Jesus continued His revelation of the purpose of God, "Peter took him aside and began to rebuke him. 'Never, Lord!' he said, 'This shall never happen to you!'" (Matthew 16:22, NIV). Jesus discerned the spirits involved in this resistance to the will of God. "Jesus turned and said to Peter, 'Get behind me, Satan! You are a stumbling block to me; you do not have in mind the things of God, but the things of men'" (Matthew 16:23, NIV).

Three spirits were at work in this situation. The Spirit of God moving in Jesus was at work preparing the disciples for God's next great move in man's redemption. Satan was present to thwart God's work. This is evident by the way Jesus addressed Simon Peter. He knew who was behind this effort to reject the truth.

Peter was not demon possessed. Many Pentecostal saints make the mistake of supposing every situation to be a manifestation of either demon possession or Holy Spirit possession.

It's true that Satan is ever at work to whatever degree he is permitted to influence a situation. And on this occasion he was using the spirit of human nature apart from God to pervert the revelation of God. Jesus identified Peter's attitude as coming from his minding "the things of men." Satan is addressed as the culprit in this mind-set, but he was working through the spirit of the culture in which Peter lived and thought.

Some of the so-called revelations being proclaimed within the Pentecostal/Charismatic community today are much like the position of Simon Peter. They are motivated by minds that are more occupied with the things of men than with the things of God.

For example, the prosperity doctrine suits the materialism of our Western culture. No politician could think of a more appealing doctrine to win votes than to proclaim that God wills for all His children to prosper materially and live their lives in luxury. Few scriptures have ever been as misused and distorted as 3 John 2: "Beloved, I wish above all things that thou mayest prosper and be in health, even as thy soul prospereth." This common salutation from the ancient world has been taken to mean that God has revealed a basic theology of prosperity. This doctrine has led many believers to reject the plain teaching of Jesus concerning self-denial. Instead of self-denial they adopt an attitude of self-indulgence. The gift of the discerning of spirits will quickly identify the source of this error.

The same is true of the divine health doctrine being proclaimed by some proponents of revelation knowledge. Who would reject a guarantee that sickness would never touch him? This doctrine is often proclaimed in the midst of glaring contradictions to its claim.

Why are Pentecostal people the most susceptible to this deception? Could it be that Satan has chosen to attack the movement at this point for the purpose of discrediting the mighty miracles of healing that have attended the movement from its inception?

Some are troubled by the fact that Pentecostal people seem to be so gullible. But it may be natural that Satan would invade the ranks of those who are most obedient to the Lord's command and promise with regard to signs and wonders in order to work his devilish havoc.

CONCLUSION

The people of God are to be a discerning people. Thus they will surely see the scriptural source of such devious doctrines. This is our God-given protection against deception.

But in the midst of this discerning, we must be alert to the primary purpose of this gift. It is to recognize the voice of God. We must listen to what the Spirit is saying to the church.

We must follow the cloud!

AN UNYIELDING RESOLVE

Cullen L. Hicks

SCRIPTURE: Joshua 24:14, 15

INTRODUCTION

Advancement and progress toward any worthy goal, especially if it is of a spiritual nature, will meet with opposition. Unless we possess true determination, with a willingness to be persistent, the adversary of our soul will stop us short of the goal.

Joshua was a man of true determination and resolution of heart. Because of his courage and resolution, he has won the admiration of God-fearing people of every generation. The words he spoke to Israel, recorded in our Scripture text, are words which have challenged thousands—even millions —through the centuries to resolve to serve God as Joshua did.

THE MAN WHO ISSUED THE CHALLENGE

Joshua was the commander in chief of the armies of Israel, the people of God. As governor of Israel, Joshua was the most influential man in all the nation. On this occasion he had gathered all Israel together in Shechem with their judges, officers, and elders. He was not reluctant nor ashamed to boldly declare to them, "As for me and my house, we will serve the Lord."

Joshua knew that godliness does no harm to one's dignity. On the contrary, godliness enhances and ennobles any individual, regardless of his title.

However, many seem to feel that only the foolish and the weak-minded acknowledge and serve God; some think salvation is good only for little children and the elderly. They think that the mature, the cultured, and the brilliant-minded can get along without God.

However, God is worshiped and served by people of all ranks and stations in life. There is much truth in the statement "Nowhere does religion shine to more advantage than in and among those of position and power." Those in elevated positions have more opportunities for doing good for others. They are able, by virtue of their position, to exert a more far-reaching influence.

THE INFLUENCE OF THOSE IN ELEVATED POSITIONS

The example and influence of those in authority can and does have much to do with the morals and manners of a nation, a state, or a community. It can be proven from the Bible, as well as from world history, that morals, manners, and fashions filter downward from leadership to the populace. If those of high office are true worshipers of God and who practice and teach His ways, they will surely draw others after them. On the other hand, if they are infidels—giving no consideration to God nor His values—they are like poisonous and evil fountainheads, transmitting corruption into the lives of all who drink from the fountain of their influence. That is why Solomon said, "When the righteous are in authority, the people rejoice: but when the wicked beareth rule, the people mourn" (Proverbs 29:2).

Manasseh is an example of a wicked leader. The Bible says, "Manasseh seduced them to do more evil than did the nations whom the Lord destroyed before the children of Israel" (2 Kings 21:9). It is also said that Manasseh "made Judah also to sin with his idols" (v. 11).

Asa, a righteous king of Judah, exerted great influence for good during his reign. "He took away the sodomites out of the land, and removed all the idols that his fathers had made. And also Maachah his mother, even her he removed from being queen, because she had made an idol in a grove" (1 Kings 15:12, 13).

In both instances, a nation went the way of its leader. That is generally the way things work in a nation, a church, or a family. May the Lord raise up leaders who will set a godly example—in our nation, our churches, and our homes.

THE WILLINGNESS TO STAND ALONE

Joshua was not indifferent to the welfare of others—he wanted others to serve the God he served. But he had resolved not to allow himself to be governed or influenced by what others did. If others would not follow God, then he would walk alone. In effect, he said to Israel, "If no one else in the nation of Israel chooses to serve the Lord, my household and I will still serve the Lord."

Oh, how we need people today who possess such a made-up mind! It seems that very few are willing to stand alone. Many are manipulated and governed by the opinions and actions of others. They would rather bow than to be cast into the furnace, where the presence of the fourth Man is manifested.

Be assured that if you are determined to obey God, you will find yourself alone time and time again. Your willingness to stand alone will often be put to the test. Can you say with Joshua, "As for me . . . I will serve the Lord"?

The people of Israel had chronically failed to take such a stand. They were often up and down, off and on—really undecided about who they wanted to serve. They were fence-straddlers, halfway wanting to serve the true God and halfway wanting to hold onto other gods. So Joshua issued the challenge: "Make up your mind. Stop playing religion. Make your choice. Choose this day whom you will serve."

Then Joshua mentioned the gods from which they could choose. First, he mentioned the gods which their fathers served "on the other side of the flood [the Euphrates]"—that is, the gods of their ancestors or the gods of tradition. Joshua knew that then, even as now, many people are hung up on following the religion of their fathers, even if that religion is vain.

Next he mentioned the gods of the Amorites, in whose land they were dwelling, that is, the gods of their neighbors. In effect, he was saying, "If you desire the affections and fellowship of this idolatrous people, then serve their gods and you shall have it. Indulge in their excesses and pleasures if you want them for friends. Bow with them before their idol gods and they will receive you. But as for me and my house, we will serve the Lord."

The church today needs thunderous voices to cry forth the same challenge to an undecided, vacillating religious world. The condition of the church world demands such a voice. Oh, that our leaders would take such a stand!

THE MEANING OF JOSHUA'S STATEMENT

What did Joshua mean when he said, "As for me and my house, we will serve the Lord"? Did he mean he could force religion on his family and dictate the way they served God? Of course not. He knew that true worship had to be voluntary. He also knew that in the end, everyone would answer for himself. I think he was saying, "As for those living under my roof over whom I have authority and influence, I will require them to give attendance to the things of God, and I will lead them by example."

Having grown up on a farm, the son of a sharecropper, I have often heard my father talk to his farmer friends about his plans regarding his crops. He would say something like this: "I am going to plant 20 acres of cotton and 25 acres of corn this year." Now Dad and Mother had five sons and two daughters, so this meant the children were involved in the planting, raising, and harvesting of the crop. When Dad said, "I am going to plant . . . ," he was referring to his family or household. When planting time or harvesttime came, Dad would tell us it was time to go to the fields. Even though we were sometimes reluctant and even unwilling to do so, we would obey him by following his example and instructions.

Joshua recognized the heavy responsibility that was his as head of a household. If our world had more fathers who would firmly resolve to take their stand and lead their families in serving God, the family life and the spiritual life of our nation and other nations would improve dramatically.

All fathers have a great responsibility to their family. Should a father not strive to provide for his children's physical needs, he would not be considered humane. Yet there are many fathers (and mothers) who commit a more injurious crime by disregarding their children's spiritual and eternal welfare.

Paul's words in 1 Timothy 5:8 read, "If any provide not for his own, and specially for those of his own house, he hath denied the faith, and is worse than an infidel." While this scripture is probably speaking of material provisions, it could also apply to spiritual provisions as well.

THE NECESSITY OF DETERMINATION AND RESOLVE

Without determination and resolve, we will not go far on our way to heaven. The Enemy will dispute every step of progress on the upward way, so unless our heart is fixed like flint, we will surely not remain steadfast.

Paul was so determined to "win Christ" that he, knowing that bonds and afflictions awaited him, said, "But none of these things move me, neither count I my life dear unto myself, so that I might finish my course with joy, and the ministry, which I have received of the Lord Jesus" (Acts 20:24).

Outward circumstances could not turn Paul aside or draw him off course. He had put his hand to the plow and would not look back. Even if his very sanity be questioned, he steadfastly affirmed, "I know whom I have believed, and am persuaded that he is able to keep that which I have committed unto him against that day" (2 Timothy 1:12). All the forces of evil and darkness came against him, yet he could say, "Nay, in all these things we are more than conquerors through him that loved us" (Romans 8:37).

Paul knew that he was not the only one whom the Enemy would endeavor to discourage and turn back from following the Lord, for he said to Timothy, "Yea, and all that will live godly in Christ Jesus shall suffer persecution" (2 Timothy 3:12).

The writer to the Hebrew Christians exhorted them to "call to remembrance the former days, in which, after ye were illuminated, ye endured a great fight of afflictions." Then he admonished them, "Cast not away therefore your confidence.

. . . For ye have need of patience, that, after ye have done the will of God, ye might receive the promise" (Hebrews 10:32, 35, 36).

CONCLUSION

Jesus met with the greatest of opposition on His way to the Cross. But He had come into the world for that hour when He would cry, "It is finished." Although He could have called 10,000 angels to His rescue, He was determined to go all the way to Calvary. "For the joy that was set before him [in bringing many sons and daughters to glory, He] endured the cross, despising the shame" (Hebrews 12:2). He was determined to finish the work the Father gave Him to do. What about you? Are you resolved to follow Jesus though all of hell assail you? Can you say with resolve and determination of heart, "As for me and my house, we will serve the Lord"?

THE MAKING OF AN ELDER

Ronald D. Williams

SCRIPTURE: 1 Peter 5:1-11

INTRODUCTION

Of all biblical personalities, we identify most closely with Simon Peter. Of all the apostles, his career is the most vivid; his character, the most human and real. We recall his early life as a fisherman, then his leaving all to follow Jesus and becoming one of the most intimate of the Lord's disciples.

We admire his attempt to walk on water, frown upon his idea of three tents at the Transfiguration, criticize his denial of the Lord, and admire his courage on the Day of Pentecost. We are astounded at his miracles of healing, warned by his treatment of Ananias and Sapphira, and touched by the warmth of his letters in his old age.

Simon Peter—brave, impulsive, confident, unstable, yet so affectionate . . . so much like ourselves today. And it is with this empathy that we hear the apostle near the closing of his life, share in his experience, and receive exhortation and instruction.

It was also about this time in Peter's life, A.D. 60, that he dictated, or at least contributed background material, to his understudy, John Mark. In Peter's letter, there are words, phrases, and pictures which are direct flashbacks of memory from Peter's days with the Master. We thus turn back history's pages to 30 years in the life of Peter to derive benefit and understanding for today.

THE SOURCE OF OUR ELDERSHIP (1 Peter 5:1)

Peter expressed his oneness with the churches of Asia Minor as an elder. To be an elder in those days was no easy position. It did not carry the honored title or professional prestige which leadership in today's church seems to provide. On the contrary, it spoke of the first to be persecuted, imprisoned, or blamed for acts committed in the name of the church. One never dared to aspire to the position for personal gain; thus the words of Paul are significant when he wrote that to aspire to be an elder was an ambition of double honor.

From where did Peter's eldership come? Peter takes us back to the Easter Sunday morning in Mark 16:1-8, bright with sunlight and the light of the Resurrection. The words of the angel had been relayed through Mary Magdalene and James' mother instructing the disciples to go into Galilee where they would be reunited with the risen Lord. This account carefully adds the words "And Peter" (v. 7).

Much had happened to Jesus since in the judgment hall He had caught a glimpse of Peter, full of fearful denial. He had conquered sin by sacrifice, bowed His head in death, confronted the devil and forces of darkness, snatching away the keys of hell and of death. He had entered the grave and proclaimed His finished work to the captives. He had risen from the grave in triumphant splendor. Yet through all of it, the Master's love was *stronger than death* . . . especially for Peter. He now seems to be reversing Peter's previous words, "Though all men shall be offended because of thee, yet will I never be offended" (Matthew 26:33).

Jesus' love was *stronger than failure*. Peter had failed so miserably. He had misunderstood the divine plan, even endangering the Lord in the garden. He had betrayed his vows and denied Jesus three times. Still, Jesus called for him.

In our roles as elders, we must above all realize the source of our calling. It is not of man's choice or due to our merits.

God has called us in spite of our weaknesses and given us a share in His work. We too must echo the words of St. Francis of Assisi. When asked why God had chosen him to play such an important part in the church, he answered, "He chose me because He could find none more worthless, and He wished to confound the nobility and grandeur, the strength, the beauty and the learning of this world."

Peter said that eldership is a privilege, and we, like him, are elders, witnesses, and partakers of God's glory. We have no other claim.

THE DEMANDS OF OUR ELDERSHIP (1 Peter 5:2-4)

Peter instructs us to "feed the flock." Where have we heard these words before? It was on another beautiful morning, recorded in John 21.

Jesus had already showed Himself alive to Peter. Peter had been restored into fellowship. Now, restless as he always was, Peter and the disciples went fishing on the Sea of Tiberias (Sea of Galilee). The entire night turned out to be a failure.

At sunrise Jesus came, and the disciples did not recognize Him. He instructed them to cast on the opposite side of the boat. Their catch was greater than they could bear. John, always full of spiritual sensitivity and insight, told Peter it was the Lord. Peter swam to Jesus and found breakfast already prepared.

Full with a hearty breakfast, Peter then heard Jesus' very famous question: "Peter, do you love Me more than all these —your vocation, friends, honor?" Jesus called Peter to a *passionate devotion to Him*. And today Christ demands the same of us, for leadership is not self-centeredness but a relationship to the Master himself.

Twice, Jesus asked Peter if his love was from above but finally had to use the word depicting human origin. Peter, with *unfeigned humility*, confessed the weakness of his love. His lack of love was fully compensated for by the strength of his humble confession, and Jesus turned his lack into fullness. We, too, need to learn the strength and power derived from the consistent confession, in unfeigned humility, of our frail humanity.

Jesus then instructed Peter to feed the lambs and prophesied so accurately of the suffering that was to be in the apostle's future. What *immovable courage* was demanded of Peter! It is one thing to wear the crown of glory, but another to wear the crown of thorns.

Peter, in this passage, alludes to these qualities in us when he beseeches us to take on the work willingly, not of force; to be interested not in personal gain but in service; to be not dictatorial but an example; and to be accountable and courageous.

Yes, Peter, we hear you.

THE PRUNING OF OUR ELDERSHIP (1 Peter 5:5-7)

Reading further, our eyes fall on another phrase, "clothed with humility." The phrase literally means "to tie up the garment of a slave and gird oneself for service." And immediately, our minds accompany Peter back to that night in the Upper Room, recorded in John 13.

Having eaten the Passover lamb, the Lamb of God himself rose, tied up His garment, and proceeded to gird Himself to wash the feet of His beloved disciples. Coming to Peter, He found the disciple stubborn, shouting, "You will never wash my feet! It's below Your dignity as the Son of God to act as a slave!"

It could be said that Jesus' action was an embarrassment to Peter and definitely not in Peter's concept of how things should be. Through the gentle rebuke of the Master, Peter learned to *submit to authority*, whether or not it fit his thinking.

By washing the feet of the disciples, Jesus taught them that true leadership *submit to serving others*. Jesus had said He came not to be served but to serve. Now His followers were to be living examples of it. True leadership is achieved not by reducing others to service but in the giving of oneself in selfless service to others.

Jesus then prayed, "Father, the hour is come" (John 17:1). This referred to the Cross, both for the disciples and for the Lord. In the same manner that Jesus had to *submit to God's plan*, so did the Twelve. Not only do we need to submit to those in authority and to the service of others, but we must, through painful and precious experience, learn to allow God's plan to be revealed in His way, not our own.

Peter said to be subject to the elders, be clothed with humility, cast your care on Him, feed the flock.

THE BALANCE OF OUR ELDERSHIP (1 Peter 5:8, 9)

Peter fully recognized the need to "be sober" and to "be vigilant," because "the devil, as a roaring lion, walketh about, seeking whom he may devour."

Mark 1:21-39 records Peter's first trip with Jesus. They entered the city of Capernaum, and on the Sabbath, Jesus began to teach in the synagogue. He spoke with such authority that all were astonished.

A man possessed of an unclean spirit cried out against the Lord. Jesus was equal to the task and deliver this man from the power of Satan. Immediately, Peter realized that *association with Christ would inevitably involve them in spiritual warfare.*

Peter returned home, with Jesus accompanying him. They found Peter's mother-in-law ill with a fever. Jesus kindly lifted her up, healed her, and she served them. Peter learned the second lesson of the day: *There is a need for gentleness in serving.*

How different from his own personality! Yet strength is never perfected until it is tender. In Acts 3 we learn how Peter did the same for the lame man at the Gate Beautiful and later, in Acts 9, for Dorcas.

That evening the folk of the city brought all the diseased, sick, and demon-possessed, and Jesus ministered to them. Imprinted on Peter's heart and mind was the *anguish of the world.* Jesus never let His work cause Him to lose sight of the real purpose of His coming. Neither did Peter.

Finally, at the height of demands upon Him, Jesus departed to a lonely place to pray. Peter came searching for the Lord and learned the *source of His power.* Jesus totally relied on the power of prayer for His success.

To assume the responsibility of leadership in the body of Christ immediately exposes you to spiritual warfare and conflict. Satan will not allow you to rest. But as you are faithful, you, too, will be equal to the task. In fulfilling that task, there are three necessities that must always be kept in perspective and balance: a gentle manner, a vision of the world's need, and the source of your power—prayer.

CONCLUSION (1 Peter 5:10, 11)

Peter concluded by writing, "But the God of all grace, who hath called us unto his eternal glory by Christ Jesus, after that ye have suffered a while, make you perfect, stablish, strengthen, settle you. To him be glory and dominion for ever and ever. Amen."

Perfect, to be forgiven and qualified by Him; *established*, to be prepared by Him; *strengthened*, to be pruned by Him; and *settled*, to have His perceptions—these are the spiritual graces which are ours for true eldership in the church.

A few months ago I was asked to represent my own denomination at a conference in Canada, performing the task of an elder to that wonderful group of churches. My enjoyment of flying over the majestic Canadian Rockies was interrupted by a gnawing thought: *How do I do the work of an elder while I'm here?*

The Holy Spirit immediately checked me. He reminded me that I *am* an elder; I do not *do* "elder" things. Eldership is wrapped around my relationship, my character, my calling to servanthood, rather than a relegated position, a performance, or a sovereign authority over a body of believers or churches. Once again I remembered that the term *elder* simply means "an older brother," called by God, matured by experience, and a model to the younger part of God's family.

We can be *all* of these, because God is the God of *all* grace.

EPENETUS—FIRSTFRUITS OF ASIA

James A. Cross

SCRIPTURE: Romans 16:5

INTRODUCTION

Do you recall the name of your first convert in one of your pastorates? Do you recall the name of your first convert in the beginning of your ministry? Very likely it would be hard to recall the name of that person. Paul paid an everlasting tribute to his first convert in Asia. Little is known about this person, but Paul remembered him, and his name is recorded for our benefit and consideration.

PAUL'S FIRST CONVERT IN EPHESUS

On his third missionary journey Paul was allowed to preach the gospel in Asia. His original plan was changed by the Holy Spirit, so that his entry into Asia was delayed for a few years. Being directed by the Holy Spirit, Paul now entered Asia and into Ephesus particularly.

The city of Ephesus was the largest, richest, and perhaps the most influential city where Paul founded a church. Perhaps here his success in preaching and beginning churches found its highest achievement.

Though Ephesus was a beautiful city with finely paved streets and large public buildings, it was a wicked city. A temple erected to honor the goddess Diana was a very prominent place in Paul's day. When he arrived in the city, the temple was about five centuries old. It had been dedicated to the worship of the Greek goddess Artemis, afterward identified with the Roman Diana. The size of the building was 350 feet in length and 150 feet wide, with columns towering 60 feet above the floor.

In this city Paul had the opportunity to begin one of the seven churches mentioned by John in Revelation 2, 3. Paul stayed in this city longer than at any other place. Acts 20:31 states that he labored among them "three years."

Ephesus was the center for spreading the Word of the Lord throughout all the provinces of Asia. It is here that he immortalized the name of his first soul won to Jesus by mentioning him in Romans 16:5, "Salute Epaenetus my well-beloved who is the firstfruits of Asia unto Christ" (ASV). "Greet my beloved Epaenetus, who was the first convert in Asia for Christ" (RSV).

The Scripture does not tell us where Paul encountered Epenetus. It may have been on the streets of the city or in the synagogue where Paul taught for three months. Perhaps his conversion happened on a one-to-one basis, or he may have been one of the first converts to publicly declare his belief in Jesus. You may be assured that Paul gave Epenetus a thorough grounding in the Scriptures as he "reasoned with . . . [him] out of the scriptures" (Acts 17:2).

The first convert did not come easily. Paul recounted some of the seed-sowing and labors in planting the Word:

You know how I lived the whole time I was with you, from the first day I came into the province of Asia. I served the Lord with great humility and with tears. . . . You know that I have not hesitated to preach anything that would be helpful to you but have taught you publicly and from house to house. I have declared to both Jews and Greeks that they must turn to God in repentance and have faith in our Lord Jesus. Remember that for three years I never stopped warning each of you night and day with tears. (Acts 20:18-21, 31 NIV).

Paul's labor, prayers, fastings, and persecutions resulted in a harvest of souls for God and His church. But, oh, the joy of that first convert, Epenetus. "He that goeth forth and weepeth, bearing precious seed, shall doubtless come again with rejoicing, bringing his sheaves with him" (Psalm 126:6). "For what is our hope, or joy, or crown of rejoicing? Are not even ye in the presence of our Lord Jesus Christ at his coming? For ye are our glory and joy" (1 Thessalonians 2:19, 20).

EPENETUS LIVED HIS CHRISTIAN EXPERIENCE

Epenetus, by being the first convert, had a tremendous responsibility thrust upon him. Everyone's eyes were upon him. How would this Gentile react? Could this newfound experience bear him up and keep him in times of trials and tests? Would he continue in this new way after his pastor left Ephesus?

As a first convert he stood alone. Only Paul could identify with him in this newfound way. No doubt at his work he suffered ridicule from his fellow workers. I am sure that Satan was present to assault him with doubts and fears, and with many different temptations. I am confident Paul had instructed him in leaning on the Word of the Lord and he defeated the devil with "Thus saith the Lord." With every temptation overcome, Epenetus felt renewed strength and overcoming victory. The reality of "God with us" (Matthew 1:23) and Jesus' assurance, "I am with you always" (28:20) gave reason for thanksgiving for Christ's abiding presence.

Epenetus influenced others by his steadfast trust in the Lord Jesus. The daily life he lived made a lasting impression on those who observed him in times of trials and temptations. Others began to realize that the newfound way was a reality in Epenetus' life every day of the week.

Epenetus won others to the Lord Jesus Christ. He did so by being a living testimony in work, worship, and commitment to Jesus. He dedicated his all to the service of Jesus, and his dedication made a difference in others. Epenetus must have remembered Paul's teaching about Jesus and His method of building the Kingdom. No doubt Paul told him about Andrew's finding his brother Simon and his bringing him to

Jesus, saying, "We have found the Messiah." I rather expect that Epenetus led his kinsfolk and neighbors to the service where they were converted.

Epenetus supported the church with his tithes and offerings. No doubt Paul taught from the prophets and from Malachi about tithing. We know what Paul believed about tithing and giving from his writings in 1 Corinthians 9:3-14, especially verse 14: "Even so hath the Lord ordained that they which preach the gospel should live of the gospel." He also wrote in 1 Corinthians 16:2, "Upon the first day of the week let every one of you lay by him in store, as God hath prospered him, that there be no gatherings when I come." The action and life of Epenetus was so faithful that Paul was justified in labeling him "the firstfruits of Asia." And the proof lies in calling him "my beloved Epaenetus."

EPENETUS LIVED VICTORIOUSLY FOR JESUS CHRIST

Epenetus lived so faithfully for Christ that Paul regarded him worthy of mention. Had Epenetus failed the Lord, he doubtless would have been forgotten. The careful teaching that was bestowed upon Epenetus was not lost. The sown seed was carefully cultivated, and lavish care was bestowed upon its growth. "Here was doubtless a renewed and holy person, adorning the Christian profession, and by ripeness and beauty and service ableness of character fitted to be regarded as the firstfruits of a province. Now, the firstfruits may be as good in quality as the harvest that follows" (*Pulpit Commentary*, Volume 18, p. 460).

The field the Apostle Paul planted yielded a great harvest. Although the goddess Diana had been worshiped there for many years, Paul preached Christ and made inroads in the lives of many. The influence of Diana decreased. A flourishing church was established, and pilgrims who came to worship Diana came to know God. It is recorded that the apostle John became one of its early leaders. In A.D. 262 the temple was destroyed and never rebuilt. Diana was dead. Ephesus became a Christian city.

Yes, Epenetus lived victoriously. The fruit that followed after him was of the same substance as the firstfruits. It is said that Epenetus later moved to Rome, and I am sure he exercised the same influence there that he had in Ephesus. He was a beloved brother and one who remained faithful.

CONCLUSION

The influence of Epenetus lived after him. The firstfruits grew into a harvest. Six other churches were established to form a great Christian circle. Who can measure the reach of a single life?

Henry Ward Beecher said, "The humblest individual exerts some influence, either for good or evil, upon others." Carlyle said, "The work that an unknown man has done is like a vein of water flowing hidden underground, secretly making the ground green."

Will you be another Epenetus?

CONFESSION, A BIBLE WORD

Roy H. Hicks

SCRIPTURE: Romans 10:9, 10

INTRODUCTION

The word *confession* is not only a Bible word, it is a *good* Bible word. However, some ministers of the gospel have set aside some good Bible words, such as this one, and have ignored them because they have suffered the abuse of misinterpretation. Some other Bible-based words that have suffered abuse are *submission, rapture, tongues,* and *prosperity.*

If the abuse of a word leads to its being set aside, then it necessarily follows that we also set aside its doctrine! So it takes fortitude, in the face of the criticism that stems from these abuses, to continue to preach the truth. *Confession,* as a good Bible word, needs to be emphasized, not set aside.

WHAT DO WE CONFESS?

First, we confess our sins (1 John 1:9). John the Beloved was writing to Christians; he was not writing to sinners. *The Amplified Bible* defines *confession* close to its root meaning as "freely admit."

156

On the subject of confession, Christians are taught everything from automatic forgiveness of every spiritual failure to the other extreme of feeling utterly condemned over every failure. Here John wrote about sins. They must be confessed, or there is no forgiveness. If an individual is truly walking in the light of the Lord, he will be aware of his sins that need to be confessed.

We also confess Jesus Christ as our Lord (Romans 10:9). It is possible that one can believe (intellectually) that Jesus is the Christ and still not be saved. Even Satan and his fallen angels believe in this way, but they are not saved, because they do not confess Jesus to be their Lord. Jesus must become our Lord in order for us to be saved. This means not only confessing Him to be the Son of God but accepting Him as our personal Savior and Lord. Believe, yes! But we must also confess what we believe.

We confess God's promises. God's promises are His Word. According to Hebrews 11:13-16, there are established principles for confessing His promises:

1. They had faith in His promises.

2. They were persuaded of His promises.

3. They embraced His promises.

But this group did not live to see or experience the fulfillment of God's promises. In this, we are taught not to confess just to get a reward. We confess God's Word because it is His Word. Even when all else seems to fail and we do not receive the promise, we still confess the Word.

Some have endeavored to bypass godly principles by making confession a formula. This twisting of the Scripture results in unfortunate experiences. One young man was said to have been confessing a Mercedes, . . . with a Volkswagen faith!

The difference between the principles of faith and a mere formula is this. If we are using a mere formula and we fail in our confession, we lay the formula aside. But faith principles cannot be laid aside, even when they seem to fail. The believers described in Hebrews 11 all died confessing that God had prepared for them a country. They died without seeing it, but they never stopped confessing His promise, because it was more than just a formula; it was a principle. Right now, at this moment, they are in that eternal city they confessed.

WHEN DO WE CONFESS?

Romans 10:9 implies that confession which leads to salvation is done continually. Greek scholars all agree that confession (Greek: *homologia*) is a continuous-action word. It is not sufficient to have confessed Jesus as Lord last year or yesterday. We must continually confess His lordship over our lives. The church will never experience backsliding if we will learn to confess Jesus as Lord every day.

We should maintain a positive confession of God's Word even in negative situations. Jesus taught that by our words we shall be justified and by our words we shall be condemned. Born-again Christians can let their light shine in a dark world only by being positive. In fact, as Christians, we are the only ones who have eternal hope, and we can share our hope by a positive lifestyle.

I met a pastor who was complaining about how difficult things were in his city. He complained of the shallowness of his church members and of all the problems of his church. He finally said, "It's so bad I don't know what I'm going to do." I asked him if he believed God could do all things. He answered in the affirmative. "But," I said, "you did not say that! You said you didn't know what you were going to do. A Christian would trust God!"

We confess, admit to, and acknowledge God's Word *before* the trial or test comes. Speaking God's promises well ahead of any kind of trial will prepare us to go through that situation. If the doctor says you have cancer, that is devastating news. And if you have not already been confessing constantly that Jesus is your healer, it is going to be more difficult to confess Him now. Paul the apostle said, "We walk by faith, not by sight" (2 Corinthians 5:7). The five senses will fail us where spiritual truths are concerned. *We must learn to go beyond the senses by speaking God's promises into our spirit before we need them.* If we will confess God's Word before we need it, the Holy Spirit will bring it out of our spirit when we do.

HOW DO WE CONFESS?

We confess with praise, with thanksgiving, and with worship. In both Hebrew and Greek, confession has a dual meaning. The Hebrew word *yadah* means "to confess with worship." It means coming to God with an open hand as opposed to a closed one. The word *Judah* means "a confessor, one who acknowledges God and confesses that all good comes from His hand, giving Him praise that is due His grace and mercy." (*Adam Clarke Commentary*).

The Greek word *homologeo* is best translated, "the fruit of our lips giving thanks to his name" (Hebrews 13:15). Offering the sacrifice of praise is here described by one Greek word—*homologeo*, that is "to confess."

CONCLUSION

Many much-publicized failures seem to plague faith-teaching ministries. If we who believe in the message of faith's confession of the Word will stay true to God's Word and confess, always with praise and thanksgiving, there will be more positive results and fewer failures.

We cannot confess for a better job while complaining about the one we have. We must thank God every day that we have a job! We must stop trying to pray in a better car while constantly complaining about the bucket of bolts we are driving! Let us thank God for the one we have! And we cannot confess for better health while being constant complainers.

Remember, confession is not only a great Bible word, but the salvation of our souls is impossible without it. Jesus taught that if you confess Him before men, He will confess you before the Father and the angels (see Matthew 10:32; Luke 12:8).

GOD AT HIS BEST

Robert P. Frazier

SCRIPTURE: Matthew 11:6

INTRODUCTION

Picture John the Baptist imprisoned and succumbing to doubt and discouragement. John 10:41 observes that "John did no miracle."

Although Jesus was John's cousin, the prison environment shaded his faith, and John sent two disciples to verify the person and work of Christ. In the face of John's wavering faith, Jesus not only verified His personal ministry (which He refused to do on occasion with the Pharisees), but after John's disciples left, Jesus verified John's ministry before His own disciples and made the amazing statement that "there hath not risen a greater than John the Baptist" (Matthew 11:11).

Such a positive statement of affirmation represents Jesus at His best.

God is never better than at a man's worst moment. Consider the following three examples.

ADAM IN DISGRACE

Since the troubles of this and all previous generations can be traced to Adam's fall, he also bears the terrible blame for the contagion of sin passed along to the human family. As the *New England Primer* succinctly stated, "In Adam's fall, we sinned all."

But instead of facing God and admitting his guilt, Adam cowardly hid with his wife. Upon discovery, he attempted to blame Eve for the problem. This *has* to be the absolute lowest point of Adam's life.

John Newton could identify with Adam's sin. He had fallen into such disgrace that his father ostracized him and fellow sailors reviled him. He was held in such low regard that on one occasion when he fell overboard in a drunken stupor, his shipmates rescued him by throwing a harpoon in his leg. He held a reputation as a cruel shipmaster while hauling loads of slaves.

It was during a terrible storm at sea that Christ found John Newton, and he later wrote "Amazing Grace":

> *Amazing grace! how sweet the sound,*
> *That saved a wretch like me!*
> *I once was lost, but now am found,*
> *Was blind, but now I see.*
>
> *Thro' many dangers, toils, and snares,*
> *I have already come;*
> *'Tis grace hath bro't me safe thus far,*
> *And grace will lead me home.*

Amidst the blackness of Adam's despair, God was at His best! To live eternally in a world cursed by sin would certainly be unbearable. To exist forever in a body suffering the debilitating effects of sin is unthinkable. Thus, when God pronounced death upon the family of man, one might say it was a supreme act of mercy. Henceforth, man would suffer but a brief span of time and would have opportunity for redemption and eventual reception back into paradise. Because every man must face the reality of death as a result of the curse, every man must also prepare himself by experiencing a relationship with the second Adam, Jesus.

God was at His best when He said, "Die."

JOB IN DESPAIR

The tragic day of Job 3:1-13 dawned upon a pitiful man who had lost family, wealth, and friends. His suicidal frame of mind had him cursing the day he was born and praying for God to kill him.

R.A. Torrey understood Job's feelings of despair. Torrey was raised by a godly and prayerful mother who never ceased believing her son would be saved. He went away from that influence and sought to build a reputation for himself in the eyes of the world.

The young skeptic's life did not go as planned. Tragedy slipped up on him. One night in a hotel he arose from his bed and reached for a nearby revolver, determined to end it all. Like a bolt of lightning, there flashed upon his memory the last words of his mother: "Son, in your darkest hour, remember your mother's words."

As a result of his encounter with God, Torrey went on to be one of the most influential preachers in America.

God's response to Job's shocking prayer was an earsplitting silence. He would not be lured into a debate concerning His actions, but He would give a full accounting soon. By refusing death to Job at his low point of despair, God was at His best!

God was at His best when He said no.

MANKIND IN DEFIANCE

Jesus Christ, incarnate God, lived as a man and went about doing good. His goal was not personal enjoyment but human redemption. He was the one truly altruistic person ever to walk this earth.

Imagine then the scene of Calvary, with Christ poised to achieve the victory of the ages. Humanity perched on the stark branches of unbelief and screamed out its defiance: "You saved others, save Yourself." "If you are king of the Jews, save Yourself."

Coupled with the screamed insults were the swooping attacks upon His person. He was spit upon, slugged, whipped, and beaten.

Amidst this demonic defiance, Jesus prayed, "Father, forgive them. They know not what they do."

Mankind deserved annihilation for its defiance but instead received forgiveness.

God was at His best when man was at his worst. We don't audibly hear the Father's answer to the prayer of His Son, but we know it was yes.

When God said yes, sin was vaporized and blown away on the fresh breeze of forgiveness.

When God said yes, His Word became a sharpened sword to slice away the veil of obstruction that we might have full and free access to the eternal Word.

When God said yes, that Word of liberty echoed throughout the chambers of hell and set the chains and bars rattling in their sockets in preparation for the coming of the conquering Christ.

When God said yes, the Holy Spirit shot like an arrow to lodge in the hearts of men, convicting them of sin.

When God said yes, armies of angels sprang into action to minister to those who would become the heirs of salvation.

When God said yes, the earth gave a shudder of anticipation that a redeemed race might plant their blessed feet on the four corners of the globe.

When God said yes, the shocked sun forgot to shine.

When God said yes, His Word immediately flashed to the ends of the universe and back again and set the heavens vibrating to the tune "Redeemed":

> *Redeemed, redeemed, redeemed by the blood of the Lamb, Redeemed, redeemed, His child and forever I am!*

BY MY SPIRIT, SAITH THE LORD

Daniel Greenlee

SCRIPTURE: Zechariah 4:6-9

INTRODUCTION

The people of God had been warned centuries before that if they should forget the Lord and that it was by His provision they entered the Promised Land, they would forfeit God's blessings.

And so it was.

For 70 years they found themselves enslaved to their adversaries in a strange land and culture. Yet in the midst of captivity, they repented and found forgiveness and blessing.

As Jeremiah had prophesied, the king allowed them to return to their own land to rebuild their Temple and city. Yet because they had become so pleased with the climate and relative comfort of this land, only a small remnant returned. They had almost forgotten their own identity and language.

It is upon this small remnant of believers that we focus our attention in this sermon.

HISTORICAL BACKGROUND OF THE TIMES

When the people of God returned to their city, they found the ruination and destruction of war that brought them into 9captivity. There was very little to start with beyond their own vision and determination to see the promise of God realized again for their people.

From the very beginning they were plagued with opposition from their critics in an attempt to abort the vision of their hearts. There were accusations and threats planned against them in order to frustrate their efforts.

When we determine to believe God for His provision and promise, we discover continual spiritual harassment from our critics and the archenemy himself in an attempt to discourage us and cause us to give up before we complete the task.

Eventually the opposition resulted in a sense of pessimism and lethargy among the people. After years of working on the Temple, their attention turned to their own comfort, and they built houses for themselves. In fact, there were some in that day who suggested that the Temple be built later, in another generation.

Our lesson finds that 16 years had lapsed, and the Temple was still not completed. They had found convenient excuses for their neglect and loss of vision. There was an erosion of their spiritual priorities.

God's remedy was to send two prophets to speak His word to get them back on course. Haggai would come with five fiery sermons, rebuking them for their lethargy. The younger Zechariah would come with a message of encouragement that God would provide His grace and strength for them to finish the Temple.

HAGGAI, THE FIERY PREACHER (Haggai 1:1-9)

Haggai immediately attacked the misplaced priorities of the people. They had become intoxicated with materialism and the comforts of life. In the long run they had lost the vision for the things of God. They had succumbed to "give-up-itis." They simply had quit the business of God. Because of adversity and fear, they had given up.

Haggai's sermons cried for them to consider their ways and see that God was still very much involved in what was happening in their lives. They had focused their attention upon their own convenience and comforts, only to become frustrated. They were now involved in making money and increasing their goods and yet were no better off than before. The more they made, the less they were able to keep for themselves. It is as if they were being asked, "Can you not see that God has blown upon these things and that your lack of prosperity is His dealing?"

There is a temptation to change our theology whenever we experience momentary setbacks. It was easier for them to change their theology about the Temple than to persist through the challenges of the times.

From the beginning the Serpent has asked, "Did God really say that?" Throughout the ages that same question in revised form attempts to undermine the integrity of our faith. It's easier just to give in and say, "Maybe God really didn't say that."

But God had indeed spoken to them about rebuilding the Temple and the city of God. Haggai challenged them to realign their priorities and complete the building of the Temple.

We must continue to "seek first the Kingdom" before "these things" are added unto us. The people repented and rallied behind their leader in a new singleness of mind and purpose to complete the task. Sometimes a rebuke, spoken at the right time, is just what we need to give us the correct perspective. So it was with Israel. Haggai's rebuke brought a sense of repentance and revival to the people of God.

ZECHARIAH, THE ENCOURAGER (Zechariah 4:6-9)

Ever notice how diverse are the ministries and personalities God uses to accomplish His purpose? While God raised up Haggai to motivate the people through a warning rebuke, He raised up the younger Zechariah to encourage and comfort the leadership and the people. Some of us respond best when we are firmly rebuked. Others respond better when someone comes along beside us with encouragement. "Pick up your burden; you can make it; God will help you."

Zechariah specifically had a message of encouragement for Zerubbabel, their leader. In the midst of their discouragement, they needed a fresh assurance from the Lord to inspire their faith. They needed to see that they were involved in much more than a building program to complete the Temple; they were involved in building a future for generations to come. There was a promise that the Temple would be filled with the glory of the Lord. Though that promise might not be fulfilled in their day, it would be fulfilled.

We are people of hope and vision. It is this hope that sustains us. We continue to believe for the fullness of the kingdom of God. Even though it may not come completely in our day, we build with the assurance that it will come to pass! God's message is that future blessings are contingent upon present obedience to His call and will. We aren't called to build our own comfort. We are called to something much higher—to build for the future, for eternity.

The elements of Zechariah's prophecy included an assurance that the task would be accomplished by the Spirit of God, the obstacles would be removed, the people would succeed in its completion, and they would realize it would be done by the grace of God.

David prayed, "From the end of the earth will I cry unto thee, when my heart is overwhelmed: lead me to the rock that is higher than I" (Psalm 61:2). Overwhelmed is just how Zechariah felt—overwhelmed by the fulfilled awesomeness of the task.

It's easy to be overwhelmed when we equate our abilities with the challenge set before us. We always come up short—not enough time, talent, strength, ability, or resources. God's answer to Zechariah's discouragement was to remind Him that he was never expected to fulfill the task without divine enabling. "Zechariah, this won't be done by your strength or ability. It'll be done by My Spirit."

Thus it has been throughout the ages. It was the Holy Spirit that brought into reality the Creation in the very beginning, and it has always been the Holy Spirit that has been working upon the earth to bring about the sovereign will and purposes of the Father. It is still the Holy Spirit, working through us, to will and to perform the Father's will.

Don't worry about the obstacles, they'll be removed. God who rules over all the earth will deal with the obstacles in His time and in His way. Jesus challenged His disciples to simply believe God's word. By believing, they would be able to speak to mountains and they would be cast into the midst of the sea. When we see our sufficiency in the Spirit of God, we are able to surmount difficulties and succeed in the task.

Zerubbabel had laid the foundations, and the prophet assured him that he would set the capstone completing the task. It is a picture of God's persistent grace. Although Zerubbabel wavered, God remained faithful. It would take longer than anticipated, but if he continued to rely upon God's provision and not give up, he would not be defeated.

In reality we are never really defeated until we completely give up. Don't give up. The God who has been working in you will continue working in you until the task is completed. He is faithful.

And yet a word of balance—it will be done by God's grace. No one would understand that better than Zerubbabel. They wouldn't finish the task because of their strength or faithfulness. It wasn't because they were some great people. It would be because of God's greatness and faithfulness. They would cry, "Grace, grace unto it" (Zechariah 4:7). When we stand in the presence of our Lord and experience His love and affirmation, we too shall cry, "Grace, grace, grace!"

Faith comes by hearing a word from the Lord. Because Zechariah brought them a fresh word from God, there was the release of a new faith to arise and complete the rebuilding of the Temple. Revival came, and they fulfilled the destiny that God had called them to.

APPLICATIONS

Like the people of Israel we can become overwhelmed by the magnitude of the challenge before us. In fact we usually are overwhelmed when we focus upon our own abilities. We need to be reminded of the words of Jesus that we are His church, that it is He who is building His church, and that the church will be triumphant even over the gates of hell. It is a picture of His sufficiency, His ability, His victory!

Paul understood that concept well when he encouraged the Philippians through a difficult passage of growth when he could not come personally to their assistance. "He which hath begun a good work in you will perform it [complete it, fulfill it] until the day of Jesus Christ" (Philippians 1:6). It would have been easy for Paul to have been overwhelmed by his concern for the church. Yet he saw a higher principle; God was working here! And because this was the work of God, it would continue and would be completed.

CONCLUSION

As we stand in the place of Zerubbabel, we must hear the words of God's prophet. God's Spirit, His grace, will continue to persist in our lives to enable us to fulfill His will. He doesn't expect us to accomplish these things within our own ability. He has provided His ability for our insufficiency. We started by grace, we continue by grace, and grace will lead us on to the fulfillment of the will of God for each of our lives. God will complete the task in us and through us.

TIME: THE FAMILY TREASURE

Paul L. Walker

SCRIPTURE: Ecclesiastes 3:1-14*

INTRODUCTION

There is an old saying: "Time waits for no one." As old as it is and as many times as it has been used, this saying still conveys a relevant message—that time management and happiness go hand in hand. Or to put it another way, the way we use our time is a barometer for the level of our joy. We are what we do, and doing obviously involves the utilization of time.

The writer of Ecclesiastes—the teacher—said, "To everything there is a season, a time every purpose under heaven" (Ecclesiastes 3:1). This passage reminds us of the importance of treasuring our time, because the joy of life is directly correlated to the investment of our time.

In this regard I recently ran a check on several married couples I had counseled during the past two years. These couples were chosen at random, and to my surprise, scheduling and the use of time were very prominent in causing conflict in the majority of the cases. It suddenly became apparent —"Time is a family treasure."

Thus, when we talk about treasuring our time, we are not simply mouthing theoretical nonsense. Time is a precious gift from God, and its use is a determining factor in whether we live a life of productivity or succumb to the hectic struggle.

THE CONCERN

Because time is a precious gift, the biblical message is concerned with the brevity of time. Psalm 90:12 petitions God by saying, "So teach us to number our days, that we may gain a heart of wisdom." Ecclesiastes 12:1 gives the admonition to "remember now your Creator in the days of your youth, before the difficult days come, and the years draw near when you say, 'I have no pleasure in them.'" "The time is short," warns 1 Corinthians 7:29, and "the form of this world is passing away" (v. 31).

The apostle Paul was concerned about the utilization of time in the most productive ways, and he cautioned the Ephesians to be careful how they live, "not as fools but as wise, redeeming the time, because the days are evil" (Ephesians 5:15, 16). He expressed the same urgency to the Colossians and told them to be wise in the way they act toward outsiders, "redeeming the time" (Colossians 4:5).

If we want balance, meaning, order, tranquillity, congruence, peace, and joy in our lives, it is important for us to share this biblical concern so that we, too, as families redeem the time. We need to make the most of every opportunity.

THE CONTROL

The secret for treasuring our time is control, not only in setting our schedules but in disciplining ourselves to keep our commitments. We can't manufacture, market or store time, but we can learn the meaning of control. In fact, this is what the teacher had in mind when he said that God "has made everything beautiful in its time" (Ecclesiastes 3:11).

He then went on to explain the meaning of this statement by saying, "Also He has put eternity in their hearts, except that no one find out the work that God does from beginning to end" (Ecclesiastes 3:11).

Having established the importance of time, the teacher moved ahead with a personal note and shared, "I know that there is nothing better for them than to rejoice, and to do good in their lives, and also that every man should eat and drink and enjoy the good of all his labor—it is the gift of God" (Ecclesiastes 3:12, 13).

Here is our challenge: We are to use time in such a way that we can rejoice and do good, because we all want to eat, drink and find enjoyment in our life's work.

The consideration, however, is for us to recognize what the teacher told us in verse 14, "I know that whatever God does, it shall be forever. Nothing can be added to it, and nothing taken from it. God does it, that men should fear before Him." The control of our time has at its base the reverence of God and respect for the gift of life.

THE CONTEXT

With this scriptural basis for treasuring our time before us, it is necessary to live our lives in the context of God's will for the use of our time. Like the writer of Ecclesiastes, we sense the ambivalence of life and share his concern that materialism leads to a mind-set that cries out, "Vanity of vanities . . . all is vanity" (Ecclesiastes 12:8).

We recognize that we have a duty to God and are responsible for the use of the resources He gives us. Thus, we agree with the teacher, "Let us hear the conclusion of the whole matter: Fear God and keep His commandments, for this is the whole duty of man" (Ecclesiastes 12:13).

The point is that each family needs a biblical philosophy of time that delivers it from the tyranny of the world's rat race. This means that the family strives to arrange priorities with God first, others second, and the self last. Without a biblical philosophy of time, we find ourselves saying: "I really want to increase my prayer life, but I just don't have time." "I would really like to improve the relationship with my spouse and family, but I just don't have time." "I honestly want to become more involved in the work of the church and its ministries, but I just don't have time." "I wish I could do more personal things and really grow as a person and a

Christian, but I just don't have time." "I really need to exercise, but I just don't have time."

So, what is a biblical philosophy of time?

EVERY GOOD GIFT COMES FROM GOD

In our modern era we have learned to do many things. We have split the atom, harnessed computers, and ushered in the space age, but the genius behind it all is a gift from God. As the teacher said, "He has put eternity in their hearts" (Ecclesiastes 3:11). In other words, we are to live our lives in such a way that we see every good gift as a blessing from God.

Moses had to constantly remind Israel of this, and in Deuteronomy 8:18 we hear him say, "'And you shall remember the Lord your God, for it is He who gives you power to get wealth, that He may establish His covenant which He swore to your fathers, as it is this day.'"

Time and time again the prophets reminded Israel of the same theme, and Haggai echoed the words of the Lord, "'The silver is Mine, and the gold is Mine,' says the Lord of hosts" (Haggai 2:8).

In the New Testament, James unequivocally stated, "Every good gift and every perfect gift is from above, and comes down from the Father of lights, with whom there is no variation or shadow of turning" (James 1:17).

Our problem is we get caught in the Nebuchadnezzar syndrome. We forget the source of our blessings.

In Daniel 4 Nebuchadnezzar, the king of Babylon, walked on his balcony and overlooked the greatest city in the world during that era. There he was, the man who had conquered all the known nations. Nebuchadnezzar had everything at his fingertips and everything under his control.

He looked at the great wall that was over 350 feet high and 87 feet thick. He viewed the 250 watchtowers on the wall and admired the hanging gardens—a wonder of the world —overshadowing the city some 300 feet in the air. He surveyed the 53 temples and the 180 altars dedicated to the heathen god, Ishtar, and then said, "'Is not this great Babylon, that I have built for a royal dwelling by my mighty power and for the honor of my majesty?'" (Daniel 4:30).

At that point God withdrew His blessings. Nebuchadnezzar forgot that every good gift comes from God. The result was a severe case of madness. "He was driven from men and ate grass like oxen; his body was wet with the dew of heaven till his hair had grown like eagles' feathers and his nails like birds' claws" (Daniel 4:33).

Although the consequences may not be so drastic in our own lives, we are suffering from the same kind of selfishness as Nebuchadnezzar. And our selfishness has brought us everything from high blood pressure and urban decay to the absence of community and integrity in relationships.

In a practical sense, we experience the results of selfishness in the erosion of quality in almost every area of life, work, and service. As a result of the me-first worldview, for instance, drastic measures are now needed to deal with automobiles and appliances in constant need of repair. Many items seem to break down as soon as their warranties expire. We cope with fluctuations of supply and demand that intermittently attack the dollar, creating a bizarre kind of inflation. Prices seem to keep rising even though consumer demand often slumps. Unemployment plagues us as we move from an industrial society to a service society. Billions of dollars are doled out to people on welfare, and the influx of foreign-made clothing and goods often forces American enterprises to go bankrupt or to close shop. Families fall apart, and the divorce rate soars.

Somewhere along the line we have forgotten that we did not build this country solely with our hands. Whatever we have accomplished in establishing our high level of affluence, we have accomplished because we were founded on the knowledge that every good gift comes from God and is to be used to its most productive end.

We keep our joy when we use God's gifts to the best advantage for His glory, the ministry to others, and our own highest good.

APPROPRIATE USE OF GOD'S GIFTS YIELDS SPIRITUAL BENEFITS

In Ecclesiastes 3:12, 13 the teacher made it clear that the gifts of God properly appropriated result in happiness, goodness, prosperity, and satisfaction.

174

Once we establish a time philosophy on the premise that every good gift comes from God and then utilize our time to appropriate these gifts according to God's Word, the results are astounding.

This is what the psalmist was talking about when he said, "Delight yourself also in the Lord, and He shall give you the desires of your heart" (Psalm 37:4).

This is the formula propounded by Proverbs 3:9, 10, "Honor the Lord with your possessions, and with the firstfruits of all your increase; so your barns will be filled with plenty, and your vats will overflow with new wine."

This is Christ's message to His disciples in Luke 6:38, "'Give, and it will be given to you: good measure, pressed down, shaken together, and running over will be put into your bosom. For with the same measure that you use, it will be measured back to you.'"

The process is not only to view time as a gift of God but to schedule the appropriate sharing and utilization of all our resources as a sacrifice of praise (see Hebrews 13:15, 16).

In this regard the Bible talks about four levels of giving:

1. *Proportionate Giving*: Deuteronomy 16:17 tells us to give as we are able, which means we are to give in keeping with our respective fiscal capabilities. As the Scripture says, "Every man shall give as he is able, according to the blessing of the Lord your God which He has given you."

2. *Systematic Giving*: In 1 Corinthians 16:2 we are reminded to give each Lord's Day in a regular fashion. As Paul stated, "On the first day of the week let each one of you lay something aside, storing up as he may prosper, that there be no collections when I come." This level of giving involves planning and budgeting for the Lord's work in the same way that we plan and budget to meet our own needs.

3. *Sacrificial Giving*: We are encouraged in 2 Corinthians 9:7 to give as we purpose in our hearts with a cheerful attitude, and in Matthew 10:8 we are told the importance of freely giving as we freely receive. In these two instances our giving is to be over and above what is required in mere tithing. The joy of giving is the result of sharing abundantly in a way that helps others that are less fortunate.

4. *Expectant Giving*: Malachi 3:10 assures us that we can expect a blessing we cannot contain, and Christ promised that our investment in the Kingdom will bring us a return 100 times as much in this present age "and in the age to come, eternal life" (Mark 10:30).

In this regard, tithing is the norm in that it is the way God has chosen to establish His kingdom through the agency of the church. However, it is not giving for the sake of giving. Rather, it is through the consecration of ourselves in the experience of giving that the relationship with the Father will produce reciprocal blessings from His boundless resources. In this way we prosper in order to share that prosperity for the teaching, preaching, and practice of the gospel throughout the world. This is the mission of the church financed by believers who tithe relying on the faithfulness of the Father. This is the family plan for prosperity.

Using God's resources is directly connected to our scheduling, and the way we schedule determines the level of our joy. When we fail to use God's gifts appropriately, we run the risk of losing our sense of peace and contentment.

ASSUME ACCOUNTABILITY

A biblical philosophy of time demands a sense of accountability. This is what the teacher meant when he explained that everything God has done for us is so that we will revere Him (see Ecclesiastes 3:14). Ecclesiastes 3:1-8 gives us insight into the importance of this accountability, for there is

A time to be born, and a time to die;
A time to plant, and a time to pluck what is planted;
A time to kill, and a time to heal;
A time to break down, and a time to build up;
A time to weep, and a time to laugh;
A time to mourn, and a time to dance;
A time to cast away stones, and a time to gather stones;
A time to embrace, and a time to refrain from embracing;
A time to gain, and a time to lose;
A time to keep, and a time to throw away;
A time to tear, and a time to sew;
A time to keep silence, and a time to speak;

A time to love, and a time to hate;
A time for war, and a time of peace.

This is what Paul was driving at when he stated emphatically, "Let a man so consider us, as servants of Christ and stewards of the mysteries of God. Moreover it is required in stewards that one be found faithful" (1 Corinthians 4:1, 2). We are accountable to God to use our resources as persons who have been trusted with "the mysteries of God."

Paul brought the matter into sharp focus when he told the Corinthians, "He who sows sparingly will also reap sparingly, and he who sows bountifully will also reap bountifully" (2 Corinthians 9:6).

The end result is that "You are enriched in everything for all liberality, which cause thanksgiving through us to God" (2 Corinthians 9:11).

THE BOTTOM LINE

The bottom line is we must use our time in such a way that will make the biblical philosophy work.

I remember the Bullock family sitting as a group in my office. The husband and wife were on the verge of divorce.

He was a design consultant who had done extremely well, but he worked long hours and was away from home a lot. His absence put an extra burden on his wife, who had the full responsibility for rearing a teenage girl, a grammar-school son, and a 2-year-old baby. In the wife's words, "I have had it. I can no longer cope with the problems of three children and cover for an absentee father. He is just never around when I need him."

His side of the story was, "We have to eat. I have spent a lifetime building this business. It is just now paying off. I'm not about to neglect it, regardless of what she says."

The daughter made her pitch by saying, "Dad is never around to see my softball games or do anything with me. He comes in late and leaves early. On the weekends he plays golf or has to go to the office. It's like we don't even have a father."

It took a while, but we started by charting the biblical

philosophy of time and then working on a schedule that could relieve the situation and provide more togetherness.

In the process, a methodology emerged to treasure time and make the moments count.

First, they analyzed their regular use of time. They explored such questions as (1) Just exactly how is each family member engaged? (2) What time is the family at home, and how is that time used? (3) Is it really necessary for the husband to spend all that time at the office? (4) Does the daughter really have to be on the go that much? (5) Can the wife rearrange some things and meet her husband in town for lunch and, on occasion, travel with him?

It soon became apparent that while the schedules were tight, more time was available than they thought.

Second, they made scheduling a family affair. Every weekend a family council was held, and the schedules for the coming week were synchronized. During this time the father was able to arrange his week to accommodate the daughter's game schedules more often than he had thought possible. Also, by planning far enough in advance for such things as family outings, dinners out together, husband-wife dates, and goofing-off time with his son, family priorities were put on par with many of the business demands.

Third, the day was started with a family devotion. This was tough because it meant beginning breakfast 30 minutes earlier so the family could eat with the father, who left early to miss the morning traffic jams.

It took some doing, but after a while each person adjusted. The agenda called for eating breakfast and then sharing 10 to 15 minutes of an appropriate Bible reading, short personal observations, testimonies, requests for prayer, and a final prayer together for God's blessings during the day.

Fourth, spiritual vitamins were given consistent priority. Sometimes we call them the grooves of grace, but if we are to grow as Christians, it is important that these seven basic spiritual vitamins be considered:

(1) Study of the Word, formally and informally; (2) prayer, corporate and personal; (3) giving, financially and benevolently; (4) witnessing, in word and in deed; (5) fellowship with others in spiritual interaction; (6) service, in the church and for the

needs of others; and (7) growth, through Christian education, in-depth spiritual experiences, and regular attendance at public worship.

The family members learned to treasure their time, and in the words of the husband, "It's like we have a brand-new lease on life. Sometimes the whole system breaks down and we have to regroup, but we have found a method that works for us."

So, here it is. We treasure our time when we

1. Analyze: Check out our committed time and our wasted time, and then decide how much time we really have to use—to treasure for its highest good.

2. Synchronize: Share the family priorities and then decide what events are necessary, determine when these events can be attended, and make scheduling in advance an important priority.

3. Spiritualize: Make devotional time a regular part of daily activities.

4. Programize: Take the seven spiritual vitamins consistently to live in the grooves of grace in the church and the home.

5. Personalize: Set aside individual time for private relaxation and activity.

This is the bottom line. If we want to keep our joy, we must treasure our time with a biblical philosophy that recognizes that every gift comes from God, that the appropriate use of God's gifts yields spiritual benefits, and that we are accountable for the way these gifts are used in our lives.

*All scriptures in this sermon are from the *New King James Version*.

ELIJAH PRAYED

R.L. Brandt

SCRIPTURE: James 5:16-18

INTRODUCTION

I can think of no subject of more consequence to a nation, to a church, or to an individual than prayer.

Herbert Lockyer wrote, "All God's people are praying people. As soon will you find a living man without breath, as a living Christian without prayer." Jesus himself said, "Men ought always to pray, and not to faint" (Luke 18:1). The implication is clear: If you do not pray, you will faint. If you do pray, you will not faint.

Once when preparing a message on prayer, I made a random listing of 15 prayers that were made by godly individuals or groups in Bible times. I was fascinated to discover that in six of the 15 examples I had chosen, angelic intervention was involved in the answers to their petitions. Suddenly Hebrews 1:14 took on new dimensions of meaning: "Are they not all ministering spirits, sent forth to minister for them who shall be heirs of salvation?"

For example, a Gentile military officer named Cornelius prayed, and God dispatched an angel to direct him (see Acts

10:3-6). The early church prayed while Peter was hopelessly bound in the inner prison, and an angel appeared to effect a profound deliverance (see Acts 12:7-10). After Paul had fasted and prayed in the face of almost certain death for himself and his shipmates, he announced with joy and certainty, "And now I exhort you to be of good cheer: for there shall be no loss of any man's life among you, but of the ship. For there stood by me this night the angel of God, whose I am, and whom I serve" (Acts 27:22, 23).

The point is this: Prayer brings divine intervention by whatever means God chooses, including the blessed ministry of angels.

It is time that our nation, our churches, and we as individual Christians relearn the holy art of prayer. We can learn some valuable lessons from Elijah, one of the most effective prayers in all of Scripture.

HE PRAYED EFFECTUALLY AND FERVENTLY

The word *effectual* in James 5:16 comes from the Greek word *energeo*, no doubt related to our English word *energy*. The essential meaning is "active, efficient." Elijah prayed with such energy, action, and efficiency as to obtain undeniable and miraculous results.

Need we be reminded that as God's Spirit-filled children we have access to an energy far beyond our own? For "the Spirit also helpeth our infirmities [that is, our feebleness]: for we know not what we should pray for as we ought: but the Spirit itself maketh intercession for us with groanings which cannot be uttered" (Romans 8:26). The *dunamis* of the Spirit —that is, the supernatural power and energy of the Spirit —equips us to pray effectually.

Jesus left us an enviable example of effectual praying. Our Lord "offered up prayers and supplications with strong crying and tears . . . and was heard" (Hebrews 5:7).

Elsewhere in the New Testament the word translated "fervent" springs from the Greek word *zelos* for example, 2 Corinthians 7:7, a word akin to our English *zeal*. The root word conveys the idea of "hot" or "heat," and the implication is "white hot," "hot until it glows," "ardor, zeal." When blind Bartimaeus prayed, "he began to cry out, and say, Jesus, thou son of David, have mercy on me" (Mark 10:47). There was a fervency in his praying, bespeaking his faith, which gained for him the desired end, enabling him to go his way with his sight fully restored.

HE PRAYED EARNESTLY AND PERSISTENTLY

The Greek word *proseuchomai* is translated into our English "prayed earnestly" (James 5:17). The meaning is "to pray with worship, to pray to God, to supplicate."

Worship and due recognition of the One to whom prayer is made are important ingredients in successful praying. Our Lord taught us to pray, "Our Father which art in heaven, Hallowed be thy name" (Luke 11:2).

In projecting Elijah's earnest praying, James made a simple yet profound statement: "Elias [Elijah] was a man subject to like passions as we are, and he prayed earnestly" (James 5:17). It is rather easy to think that Elijah was superhuman. Yet under divine inspiration, and for our encouragement, James asserted Elijah was a man—he was like we are. He bore the burden of his own humanity. Yet he prayed earnestly and obtained a response from God.

What a strange prayer—"that it might not rain." What a negative request! The country languished, the crops failed, and the people went hungry—all because the prophet had prayed that it wouldn't rain. What sense does that make?

It can be shown that there was no element of selfishness or vengeful ambition in Elijah's prayer. In fact, he suffered fiercely as a result of his own praying. He was compelled to sit by the brook Cherith to quench his thirst, but the brook eventually dried up. He had to endure the loathsome experience of having his food delivered by a bird that was repulsive to any Jew—the raven. Later he had to suffer the embarrassment of being sustained by a widow. And he had to flee from Ahab and his pursuers to preserve his life. Then why did he pray as he did?

Elijah prayed persistently—that is, with continuing insistence. Today, however, some teach that to pray more than once for something is to admit to lack of faith. However, the Scriptures do not support such a view. Jesus himself prayed three times over the same matter in Gethsemane (see Matthew

26:39-44); Daniel prayed 21 days before he got his answer (see Daniel 10:12-14); Paul fasted and prayed many days aboard ship before an angel visited him with an answer (Acts 27:21-24); and Elijah prayed for rain seven times before he obtained his request.

Elijah's prayer posture on Mount Carmel is noteworthy. "He cast himself down upon the earth, and put his face between his knees" (1 Kings 18:42). It has been observed that this was the posture of an Israeli woman in travail. How fitting then that God's servant, concerned with the spiritual rebirth of his own nation, should engage in a type of travail to accomplish his mission.

But why should Elijah have to pray as he did? Did he not have a promise from God, "Go, shew thyself unto Ahab; and I will send rain upon the earth" (1 Kings 18:1)? We may well ponder the reason and glean a great lesson. It appears certain that God has somehow limited His intervention in human affairs to the active involvement of His servants. He depends on our faith and prayers to release His benefits. It can be rightly concluded that He needs our prayers.

While serving as district superintendent in one of our northern districts, I became aware of the development of a political underground which threatened to divide the district and adversely affect my own ministry. I said little about it but made it a matter of constant prayer.

As has been my habit through the years, I prayed earnestly on the basis of Philippians 4:6, 7: "Be careful for nothing; but in every thing by prayer and supplication with thanksgiving let your requests be made known unto God. And the peace of God, which passeth all understanding, shall keep your hearts and minds through Christ Jesus." Even so, the condition did not improve but rather worsened. Nevertheless, I prayed on, sometimes quoting that passage several times in a single day.

Months passed with no sign of an answer. Then one day the passage I had quoted so often became like a living thing laying hold on my heart. As Martin Luther said, "The words of Paul are living things; they have hands and they have feet." That day, though there were no outward evidences to support my conviction, I knew God was going to resolve the problem.

Six months passed with no evident change of circumstances. Yet my spirit rested in complete assurance and confidence. And then one day the problem melted away like a Montana snow before a chinook and never again raised its head during the many years I served that district. Persistence in prayer paid off.

HE PRAYED IN THE WILL OF GOD

"And this is the confidence that we have in him, that, if we ask any thing according to his will, he heareth us: And if we know that he hear us, whatsoever we ask, we know that we have the petitions that we desired of him" (1 John 5:14, 15).

Howbeit, there is another side to this coin. James said, "Ye ask, and receive not, because ye ask amiss, that ye may consume it upon your lusts" (James 4:3). The key word is *amiss*. It is translated from the Greek *kakos*, which means "badly" (that is, "outside of God's will"). *Lusts* is translated from the Greek *hedones* ("pleasures"), referring to sensual delights. The idea is that when we ask to please ourselves or for our sensual delight, we do not ask in God's will.

Elijah's praying had no selfish element in it. His own testimony was, "I have done all these things at thy word" (1 Kings 18:36). When he prayed that it would not rain, he prayed in the will of God. When he prayed down the fire upon the altar, he prayed in the will of God. And when he prayed that it would rain again, he prayed in the will of God.

The question rises, How can I pray in the will of God? There are several answers:

Pray in the Spirit.

"Likewise the Spirit also helpeth our infirmities: for we know not what we should pray for as we ought: but the Spirit itself maketh intercession for us with groanings which cannot be uttered. And he that searcheth the hearts knoweth what is the mind of the Spirit, because he maketh intercession for the saints according to the will of God" (Romans 8:26, 27).

Pray with Paul.

The Books of Ephesians, Philippians, and Colossians record five exemplary prayers offered by Paul. They are there by divine inspiration. In them is revealed God's will for His children and His church. Thus when Paul's prayers become our prayers, we can know we are praying according to God's will. Furthermore, to pray with Paul is to enter vast new dimensions of praying—dimensions we tend to neglect because of our earthly-mindednesses.

Pray for what God has already revealed as His will.

"For this is the will of God, even your sanctification, that ye should abstain from fornication: that every one of you should know how to possess his vessel in sanctification and honour" (1 Thessalonians 4:3, 4).

"In every thing give thanks: for this is the will of God in Christ Jesus concerning you" (1 Thessalonians 5:18).

"For so is the will of God, that with well doing ye may put to silence the ignorance of foolish men" (1 Peter 2:15).

"The Lord is . . . not willing that any should perish, but that all should come to repentance" (2 Peter 3:9). Thus to pray for lost mankind is to pray according to God's will.

"Pray ye therefore the Lord of the harvest, that he will send forth labourers into his harvest" (Matthew 9:38).

These are but a few examples of praying according to God's revealed will.

CONCLUSION

The challenge before us is to pray as Elijah prayed—effectually and fervently, earnestly and persistently, and according to God's will. The bottom line is to pray according to the will of God so that you can say with Elijah, "I have done all these things at thy word."

MOIST EYES AND A MELTED HEART

Roy D. King

SCRIPTURE: Genesis 43:30, 31

INTRODUCTION

The scene is from the Old Testament. Joseph stood before his brothers. The compassion and concern he felt for them was masked by his brusqueness. The years of separation made him a stranger to his own household. They did not know him. The one before them in regal robes was the aloof prime minister of the reigning empire of that era, to them a powerful political figure and not their dreamer.

They wailed before him as beggars because of the crushing famine at home. Their domestic plight compelled them to be polite, but they were frantic in the presence of the man who could label them spies and imprison them. They were strangers to this land. Who really cared for this nondescript band of Israelite brothers? Jacob, their father, had given them a crash course in foreign diplomacy for fear they would foul the family's only hope for survival. Now they were in danger of never returning to Canaan with food for their families.

A HEART MELTED BY LOVE

Joseph wiped his eyes because his heart melted. The bondage of his brothers' blindness was keen. It could have been otherwise. They had plotted his murder. They had mercilessly sold their brother to slavery. They had deceived their father for decades. They had not understood him then; would they understand him now?

He wept not because of their hunger. He had bread to give, more than enough. It was not sympathy but love that moved him emotionally.

Material needs he could easily meet. Reconciliation and reunion without guilt or remorse would have to be the work of a greater force.

He restrained himself. They must of themselves awake to his true identity. His heart melted. He submitted to the sovereign promptings. He was determined that his brethren should enjoy deliverance and learn a divine lesson. They would learn without guilt or regret that while they meant evil in their deception of the father and the sale of a brother as a slave, God meant it for good to the salvation of many people (Genesis 50:20).

Like the sons of Jacob the human family stands on the brink of apparent disaster. A quagmire of social dilemmas plays havoc with the future. Famine-stricken and destitute people of many nations have jettisoned pride and now beg from whomsoever. There is a universal struggle for survival amid a concert of insurrection, injustice, and intrigue.

Our sins have gotten us into deep trouble. Our behavioral patterns have evil tendencies. Whether by jealousy, blind prejudice, or plain stupidity, ours is a complex problem.

We are hurting; we need help. Well did the prophet cry, "My people are destroyed for lack of knowledge" (Hosea 4:6).

Is there help? Is there hope? Definitely! In the midst of the chaotic conditions across the face of man's world, stands Jesus Christ, a Greater than Joseph. He has received the promise of the Father and is pouring out His Spirit as foretold by the prophet Joel, "And it shall come to pass afterward, that I will pour out my spirit upon all flesh. . . . And it shall come to pass, that whosoever shall call on the name of the Lord shall be delivered" (Joel 2:28, 32).

The prophecy is certain. God is doing even as He has promised. However, if we are going to be a part of the solution and not a part of the problem that stalks the land, there is a price to pay.

Joseph stood before his brothers with bread. He could alleviate their hunger pains. He had the resources to provide for their families and flocks. His ability to do so was the reward of his integrity, a reward that offered help and hope to a people in need.

The need of our world is great, but grain or dollars, as vital as they are, will not save precious souls. We stand, as Joseph did, with the ability to feed. To be mere dispensers of grain is insufficient to meet a deeper need. Hearts filled with a Christlike compassion will move us to disseminate the gospel of Christ—the only means of reconciliation with God.

A HEART BURDENED FOR RIGHTEOUSNESS

The anger and deceit of his brethren, the attempted seduction and false accusation of Potiphar's wife, and the forgetfulness of a companion in prison never robbed Joseph of his sensitivity to the sovereign actions of a compassionate God. Joseph's concern for honesty in Potiphar's house was not solely because of his loyalty to his master. In the hour of testing he cried out, "How then can I do this great wickedness, and sin against God?" (Genesis 39:9). It was not his fear of detection and punishment that deterred this young Hebrew from compromise; it was his fear of the God of Abraham, Isaac, and Jacob.

The grace that sustained him in his sufferings gave great strength to his acts of kindness, mercy, and love. It was with great grace and power that Joseph stood before his brethren and all of Egypt.

God's laws have not changed. "The integrity of the upright shall guide them: but the perverseness of transgressors shall destroy them. Riches profit not in the day of wrath: but righteousness delivereth from death. The righteousness of the perfect shall direct his way: but the wicked shall fall by his own wickedness" (Proverbs 11:3-5).

God himself has not changed. The perverseness and the crookedness of faithless transgressors cannot frustrate His divine purpose. "He abideth faithful" (2 Timothy 2:13).

As heralds of the liberating message of the gospel, we are called to constantly examine our service to Christ. The Bible, our guidebook, is concerned about the kind of people we are. What we are determines what we do and how we act and react in the various situations and circumstances of life.

God has not brought us through persecution and into phenomenal growth to be forgetful or unmindful of a people in need. Moist eyes and melted hearts are the need of this hour.

The mandate of the church has not changed. We face our greatest opportunities; these are the most challenging moments in the history of the church. There has never been such a global move of the Holy Spirit. There has never been a time of such intense hunger.

Can we refute the fact that we have never had it better? God has given us the means, the men, and the methods to respond to the hunger, the hurt, and the self-inflicted harassment brought about by ignorance, lust, and greed. These ever leave in their wake a carnage of innocent victims.

We are called to respond to the world's needs with integrity. Corruption in the proclaimer taints the proclamation. We are called upon to demonstrate that our relationship with God is unimpaired. "There is therefore now no condemnation to them which are in Christ Jesus, who walk not after the flesh, but after the Spirit" (Romans 8:1).

Our code of morals is to be guided by righteous principles, and as a body we are to be complete and undivided.

A HEART PREPARED TO RESPOND

There is no argument—the need is great for a fresh baptism of trustworthiness, incorruptibility, and dependability. We need a demonstration of manhood that has risen above being false to a trust, a responsibility, or a pledge.

It is not necessary to outline the ills that plague us as a people. The media, without any inhibition, gives a daily commentary on the vice and violence, the sin and sensuality, the crime and carnage, the war and worry, the hate and hurt, the disease and disaster, the famine and fatigue that blanket society. The hidden subtlety of this social morass is a religion without a Savior, a church without the Holy Ghost, and a baptism without the anointing.

The foundations of our preparations are the timeless bulwarks of the Christian church. They include education, but greater knowledge is not the supreme goal. The needs of humanity are not wrapped up in greater political influence, although we must speak with candor and clarity to governments and power structures. Our deepest need as a people of God is a return to the fathomless potential of fervent intercession and the earnest study of the Scriptures, our sufficient source for faith and practice. Spiritual disciplines are the prerequisites for distinctive service to our generation.

The church of the Lord Jesus Christ must respond.

We know there is victory, for there is a man called Jesus and He has all power. His compassion stirs and motivates us. His commission compels us to open our eyes and our hearts to a truth-starved world.

There is hope! Jesus Christ is the answer!

CONCLUSION

We are living witnesses of abundant grace. Clouds of witnesses attest to God's faithfulness to all generations. Let us earnestly plead for a genuine affirmation of a living faith in a living Christ and, by God's grace, for a pledge of allegiance to biblical principles that will bring honor and glory to His name.

It is not the hour to be judgmental. A sick society needs a physician. Our Lord did not come to call the righteous but sinners to repentance (Matthew 9:13). "For God sent not his Son into the world to condemn the world; but that the world through him might be saved" (John 3:17).

The hungry and the thirsty, the bruised and the hurt will respond to a church that reaches out in sincerity and love. Weary travelers with real needs stand near us expectantly. Their lives may be shrouded with sin and shackled with guilt. Will we turn away to celebrate our grandeur or reach out in grace?

"I WILL BUILD MY CHURCH"

G. Earl Beatty

SCRIPTURE: Matthew 16:13-20

INTRODUCTION

A motley mob of men, indeed, stood around the Galilean and heard His declaration. Who can know what connotation the men applied when the word *church* was verbalized? "I will build my church," He had said. They may have identified with the elaborate Temple that had been built by Solomon. They may have remembered the story of its destruction. They could have well remembered the sad replica built by Zerubbabel, finished in 515 B.C. They might have immediately visualized their present-day Temple, which had taken 46 years to build and was called Herod's Temple. Obviously it was an elaborate building because the disciples called attention to the magnificent stones and architecture, when Jesus said, "'Not one stone will be left on another'" (Luke 21:6, *NIV*).

But the church has a wider influence than that building, or any building for that matter. The church is an extension of Christ himself and, as such, is inherently holy, unified, and singular in its purpose. *If it is divided, it is not the church; if it is the church, it is not divided.*

The Corinthian writer tackled the thankless task of pulling a fragmented church together. Some were partial to Paul, some were partial to Cephas, some were partial to Apollos, and some of the most pious of all (I use that word in its hypocritical definition) were those who said, "We are of Christ" (see 1 Corinthians 1:12). They most likely had made themselves leaders of their own group, and possibly Christ had no more to do with them than He did with the other factions. Paul said these were carnal and fleshly attitudes.

I am therefore devoting this message to identifying the church and its Lord. Three primary purposes become apparent in the process.

THE ACCLAMATION OF HIS GLORY

The Word of God declares that God will be glorified (Leviticus 10:3; Haggai 1:8). Not one generation has gone by without the name of God ringing from the lips of created beings—first, the angels, then the human race, all of whom were created to give glory to His name.

Things looked dark in the fleeting days of Eden when Adam and Eve hid from God and no more walked with Him in the cool of the day. Outside the Garden, the blood of innocent animals and worship brought glory to a just God. God raised up Noah who found favor in His eyes. Abraham was called from Mesopotamia with a promise: "By you all the families of the earth will bless themselves" (Genesis 12:3, RSV). Literally He was saying that in magnifying the Lord, there would be an inherent blessing for that people.

Each succeeding generation had the choice of listening to godly men who pointed them to the Lord of Glory, or they chose to go their own ways. More and more, the cycle of Israel's disobedience, captivity, repentance, and restoration pointed toward a redemption. In the obscurity of a Judean night, as shepherds quietly watched over their charges, messengers from the glory world initiated an entirely new song of praise, "Glory to God in the highest, and on earth peace, good will toward men" (Luke 2:14).

How long will it take the human race to realize that redemption involves even more than rescuing from eternal death? It is also an act of preserving a people who will glorify His name. Paul said most appropriately, "Ye are bought with a price" (1 Corinthians 7:23).

Praise is contagious. The angels praised Him. The shepherds praised Him. Their audience praised Him. The wise men worshiped Him, and wise men still worship Him.

All through the centuries, since that first one, Jesus has had a church. His solemn promise there in Caesarea Philippi in response to Peter's acclamation was simply, "I will build my church" (Matthew 16:18).

With appreciation and a deep sense of gratitude, I acknowledge that there is a great move of the Evangelical church today to disciple new believers, that there are literally thousands of missionaries around the world, and that by means of radio, television, printed media, and word of mouth the gospel is being preached on every continent of the globe. But we must never forget that the underlying promise is, "*I* will build my church."

Five hundred faithful men and women stood at the feet of the crucified Lord and heard Him say, "All power is given unto me in heaven and in earth" (Matthew 28:18). They received His charge that they were to go into all the world and make disciples. As the Lord of the harvest left them that day, two men in white raiment underscored His commission. "Why," they inquired, "are you standing here gazing up into heaven? This same Jesus . . . will come again" (see Acts 1:11). (And he might have added, "I will require an accounting.")

A new vision entered the church in those early days. A horizontal dimension had been added to the heavenly one. Men would glorify God, but they would take most seriously the task of discipling the world's population. The Holy Spirit, who was the promise of the Father, was poured out on those who tarried at Jerusalem, with the result that by the end of the first century, more than 200,000 converts were scattered throughout the Middle East and Europe. The promise had been fulfilled, "'He dwells with you and will be in you'" (John 14:17, *NKJV*). The Holy Spirit had empowered them to do the work, and they had glorified God in the midst of the most powerful and pagan empire on earth. In fact, by the time Constantine was converted in the beginning of the fourth century, it is estimated that a 10th of the Roman Empire was Christian.

Discipling is the work of the Kingdom, and it is the work which assures the presence of the risen Lord with the church. The church still is claiming the universe for Him. While Muslims, Hindus, Buddhists, atheists, agnostics, and humanists idolize their various gods, the church is still declaring His glory over the earth, a confirmation of Isaiah 11:9.

THE AFFIRMATION OF HIS LORDSHIP

If the primary purpose of the church is to declare and acclaim the glory of Christ, then that church must affirm His lordship. It is one thing to say, "Jesus is Lord," and quite another to make him Lord of one's life. Jesus said, "Why call ye me, Lord, Lord, and do not the things which I say?" (Luke 6:46).

Lordship Calls for Obedience

Obedience is the basic test of lordship. If we recognize that Jesus is Lord, then we are doing the work of the Kingdom. Our capitalist republic is one of the most effective governments in the world. We have a high standard of living; we have freedom of expression; we worship whatever god we choose. Some worship gods made of brick and mortar; some worship gods with wheels; some worship gods who live in stadiums; some worship gods of wealth. The god we choose is the one that calls the shots in our lives, and we obey. That is why Jesus made the observation that whatever god we serve is the one we obey. That isn't too difficult to understand. There are simply people who don't think of their gods as gods. They obviously don't recognize the God of the universe.

The Lordship of Christ Calls for Holiness

It is amazing to me that we talk about holiness as though it were something you take off at night and put back on in the morning, so that when you meet your world, people will say, "There goes a holy person; he looks holy, his actions and words are holy, therefore, he is holy."

Jesus identified holiness as the response of the heart. One who is holy of heart will be holy in action. However, one who is holy in action, *may* be a sinner. Remember, Jesus said that Satan can transform himself into an angel of light; and without some concept of holiness in the heart, there is no way we can tell holy people from unholy people. We simply observe that they seem to be good people.

Holiness has to do with character. What happens when someone crosses us? How do we act when someone has a differing opinion? How do we react when well-made plans are disrupted? This can be a real test of holiness of heart.

The Lordship of Christ Calls for Accountability

So much emphasis is placed on position and status in our world that many people seek it at all costs. This often results in leadership without accountability. One who has not learned to be accountable to God will likely be accountable to no one. We are cultivating a generation of people who are highly incensed when their hand is called for some wrongdoing. I have a brother-in-law who began a career in law enforcement as a state trooper. When someone was stopped for breaking the speed limit, the usual response was, "Obviously my speedometer was wrong" or "Obviously your speedometer was wrong" or "Everyone else was passing me: why didn't you stop them?"

We somehow feel wrongdoing is relative. Why should I be punished when everyone else gets away with it? There is a big difference between true repentance, a godly sorrow for sin and a turning away from it, and the self-initiated sorrow that stems from getting caught.

When man is accountable to God, then his attitudes and actions are directed by the lordship of Christ. Mere chance does not determine whether we are right or wrong. A toss of the dice to see which action seems appropriate is not a sufficient gauge. Praying until we have the mind of Christ is the only acceptable way.

The affirmation of the lordship of Christ in the church is the standard by which that church moves forward to accomplish the work of evangelism. We may get lost individually in the shuffle, but if Jesus is not Lord, then the church is simply another man-made, man-governed organization that will serve its immediate purpose and then die.

195

THE APPLICATION OF HIS AUTHORITY

The third purpose of the church, the application of His authority, is related to the second. This authority was much more apparent in the early church than it is in the 20th century. An obedient, holy, accountable people will have no problem allowing Jesus to be Lord of the church.

Elijah on Mount Carmel stood not on a concept of his own self-sufficiency but on the sovereign authority of Almighty God. His cry to Israel was, "Let God be God." There was no evidence of the frenzy of the prophets of Baal in Elijah's demeanor. This was no uncertain prophet making excuses for an impotent god. With confidence he simply said, "Let the God who answers be God."

Our plans for the future need to be just as sure as those of Elijah. He built the altar, completed all the man-made preparations that were necessary, and then prayed. He was being a channel through which God could convince a backslidden nation that there is only one God. God's authority may be applied the same way now. We do what is within our power, pray, and let God be God. We need not make excuses for Him. We need not explain why God heals in one situation and doesn't in another. We don't need to make excuses for why some people fail and others remain faithful. We must be responsible for our own souls and our own lives and then be channels for His love and grace to this generation.

It is considered appropriate to seek recognition and to be applauded, but that belongs to this world's kingdom. Those leaders in the Book of Acts were not applauded. They were beaten, stoned, jailed, mocked, and threatened. That, however, is not the end of the story. Let's transfer this group of men and all the church triumphant to the next world. The record is in Revelation 19:

I heard what seemed to be the voice of a great multitude, like the sound of many waters and like the sound of mighty thunder, peals, crying, "Hallelujah! For the Lord our God the Almighty reigns. Let us rejoice and exult and give him the glory, for the marriage of the Lamb has come, and his Bride has made herself ready; it was granted her to be clothed with fine linen, bright and pure"—for the fine linen is the righteous deeds of the saints. And the angel said to me, "Write this: Blessed are those who are invited to the marriage supper of the Lamb." (vv. 6-9, RSV).

CONCLUSION

If the church is the church, then it will be united; it will acclaim God's glory; it will affirm His lordship by obedience, by holiness, and by accountability to Him; and it will be a channel through which He applies His authority. The ultimate statement and promise is "I will build my church."

WHAT IS YOUR TREASURE?

D. Chris Thompson

SCRIPTURE: Luke 12:34 (Supplemental reading—Luke 12:15-21; Matthew 6:19-24)

INTRODUCTION

Years ago Dad shared a community legend with an acquaintance of mine. The legend involved the burial of several sacks of $20 gold pieces in a local swamp. The money had never been recovered. The acquaintance just happened to own an expensive metal detector. For the next several days he stayed in the swamp looking for the buried treasure. In fact, his lengthy search contributed to his losing his job and being forced to move from the community.

If man can identify his treasure, he will find the focus of his heart. He may ask himself several questions: What do I think about most? What do I talk about most? What do I spend most of my time doing? What would I rather be doing?

A person's treasure may be his family, his work, his property, his quest for power, his reputation, his hobbies, his leisure time, his bank accounts, or it may be his relationship with Jesus Christ. Whatever the treasure, the text remains true: "Where your treasure is, there will your heart be also" (Luke 12:34).

THE MEANING OF THE TEXT

The text is more than a prediction. It is stating of a universal principle. Whatever man's station in life, whether he is a saint or sinner, his heart is where his treasure is, and his treasure will be put where his heart is. Thus if a man loves God, he will deposit his treasures in heaven by using both his talents and his possessions for the glory of God. Then as he lays up more and more treasure on the other side, his interest in heaven and heavenly things will increase, and his heart will be more firmly anchored in the heavenly world.

Luke 12:34 thus becomes a measuring rod by which one can determine the depth of his devotion. It can also serve as a warning. Whenever one sees himself becoming more interested in earthly possessions than in heavenly treasures, it is time for a serious soul examination; it is time for a transfer of deposits from the earthly to the heavenly bank.

The Lord also reminded His disciples that they could not serve two masters. This is a universal principle of life—one cannot serve God and mammon. It can readily be said one cannot serve God and treasure, unless his treasure is God, without doing any damage to Scripture.

Things do not produce a rich and full life, neither do they bring happiness. In studying about those who have lived rich and useful lives, one learns just how remarkably unimportant things were to them. The abundance of things produces anxieties and discontent more often than it produces happiness. Often those who have the most of this world's goods have never once known the thrill of lasting accomplishment. What really counts in life is God! Such spiritual treasures as love, contentment, peace, a clear conscience, a feeling of accomplishment, a sense of mission, and a hope of heaven follow close behind.

The parable of the rich fool illustrates the principle stated in verse 15. The rich man made the mistake of thinking that life consisted in the abundance of the things he possessed. As a result he not only lost his soul but became, for all time to come, the very personification of the fool and one of the world's best illustrations of how not to live.

THE TREASURE OF JESUS

Not only is Jesus the Son of God and the redeemer of mankind, but He is a perfect example to all believers of true Christianity. His life, His words, and His actions present a vivid portrait of total commitment to His heavenly Father. His treasure was in the right place.

What is the secret of His life? Is it His deity—His being the Son of God? Is it key His being baptized with the Holy Ghost?

There is no simple answer to these questions. Perhaps if we could examine His heart, we could begin to understand His perfect humanity better. Is it possible to understand the focus of His heart? The answer is a most emphatic *yes!* It can be done by discovering His treasure.

What was the treasure of Jesus? There is a clue in His surrender in the Garden of Gethsemane: "Not my will, but thine, be done" (Luke 22:42). It is further uncovered in His statement in John 4:34: "Jesus saith unto them, My meat is to do the will of him that sent me, and to finish his work." His treasure was to do the will of His heavenly Father. That was the focus of His life. He talked about it. It was constantly on His mind. He lived it out. It was the most important thing in His earthly existence.

Paul declared the treasure of the Lord in Philippians 2:5-8. He "thought it not robbery to be equal with God." It seems reasonable to assume that Christ, being the revelation of God, might have claimed His right to be recognized as equal with God. But contrary to the accusation of His enemies (John 5:17, 18), this is precisely what He refused to do—insist upon His own rights or usurp the place of God. He refused to seek self-enrichment or self-gratification.

He "made himself of no reputation" (v. 7)—literally, "emptied Himself." Here is the well-known *kenosis* passage. There are many interpretations here. The simplest interpretation is the best. It seems unnecessary to ask, as many have done, Of what did Christ empty Himself? His deity? His divine nature? His divine prerogatives? His equality with God? Paul simply said that Christ emptied Himself. The Greek verb *kenoun* means "to pour out," with Christ himself as the object. Thus

Christ emptied Himself of Himself. At no time did He allow selfish considerations to dominate His spotless life.

His treasure was to do the will of Him who had sent Him. The road was rocky, but the final destination was glorious.

As Christ's treasure was doing His Father's will, so the Christian's treasure can be his relationship with Jesus Christ. I have always been amazed at the depth of the relationship and trust of my wife's relationship with Christ. She has many treasures in her life—her family, her pleasant personality, her antiques, her crafts—but *the* treasure in her life is Jesus. I remember an incident in her life that proves the depth of her trust and faith. Before we were married, she was on a journey to sing at a friend's wedding. She arrived late at night at a bus station in Richmond. She had to change buses, but the change was with another bus line several blocks away. No cab or any other means of transportation was available. By faith she took her suitcase in hand and started walking the necessary blocks through a very difficult section of town. A strong-looking young man approached her and asked to carry her suitcase. She hesitated, but something whispered to her that it would be all right. After guiding her safely to her destination, the young man left as quickly as he had come. To this day I believe he was a messenger sent by the Lord—perhaps even an angel. Who knows? When one's treasure is Jesus, there are numberless benefits available.

THE APOSTLE PAUL'S TREASURE

Most would admit that Saul of Tarsus, later called Paul, was one of the greatest Christians who has ever lived. At least 13 books of the New Testament, more probably 14, were written by him. What was his treasure? It is easily discovered from his writings.

In 2 Corinthians 4:7 he wrote, "But we have this treasure in earthen vessels, that the excellency of the power may be of God, and not of us." The key to understanding his statement is found in the context. In verse 1 he wrote, "Therefore seeing we have this ministry, as we have received mercy, we faint not." Paul's treasure was the ministry of Christ given to him by the Lord, beginning with his Damascus-road experience. His focus of life was to know Him and to make Him known.

This was what he lived for. For to him, to live was Christ and to die was gain (Philippians 1:21).

The totality of his existence was centered around Christ. A careful study of Colossians 1 reveals just how much his entire being focused on the Lord. He saw Jesus as the source of grace and peace (v. 2), the object of faith and the source of love (v. 4), man's hope (v. 5), man's deliverer and King (v. 13), the redeemer of mankind (v. 14), the image of God (v. 15), the Creator (v. 17), the head of the church (v. 18), and man's reconciler (v. 20).

Jesus was his treasure. His heart had been won by the Lord, and Christ continued to reign on the throne of Paul's heart.

CONCLUSION

Self-evaluation is beneficial for a man. It is even crucial for an organization. Every man would do well to seek to objectively view his life and to discover what is the focus of his life. What does he think about most? What does he most readily speak of? In simple terms, what is his treasure?

If he discovers that Christ is not the substance of his treasure, then he can be assured that his heart does not completely belong to the Lord. Remember, as a man "thinketh in his heart, so is he" (Proverbs 23:7).

Jesus so readily desires to enter every heart and reign there. With Him on the throne, a man reaches his fullest potential and finds self-satisfaction and his reason for being. Remember, the Treasure of the Ages said, "Come to Me, all who are weary and heavy-laden, and I will give you rest" (Matthew 11:28, *NASB*).

Yet the irony is that with the immediate availability of Christ's love and blessings, men still choose other treasures —treasures that moth and rust will corrupt and thieves break through and steal (Matthew 6:19). Yet, praise the Lord, it doesn't have to be that way.

Jesus *can* and *should* be our treasure!

FATHER, MOTHER, AND CHILDREN

B.L. Kelley

SCRIPTURE: Ephesians 5:18—6:4

INTRODUCTION

The traditional family has long been the symbol of a strong, stable, and progressive society. It is my desire that we have and keep a godly appreciation for the family.

Some leaders suggest that we are seeing the death of marriage as we know it. The unrighteous acts of adultery, fornication, homosexuality, abortion, juvenile delinquency, crime, and sexual rebellion are like cords strangling the family. But I believe God has a standard that can make marriage and the family what it ought to be.

A few years ago the *Saturday Evening Post* published "The Seven Ages of the Married." It went as follows:

Year 1. "Sugar Dumpling, I'm really worried about my baby girl. You've got a bad sniffle, and there is no telling about these things with all this strep going around. I'm putting you in the hospital this afternoon for a general checkup and a good rest."

Year 2. "Listen, Darling, I don't like the sound of that

cough. I've called Dr. Miller and asked him to rush over here. Now you go to bed like a good girl."

Year 3. "Maybe you'd better lie down, Honey. Nothing like a little rest when you feel lousy. I'll bring you something. Have you got any canned soup?"

Year 4. "Now look, Dear, be sensible. After you've fed the kids, washed the dishes, and finished the floors, you'd better lie down."

Year 5. "Why don't you take a couple of aspirin?"

Year 6. "I wish you would just gargle or something instead of sitting around all evening barking like a seal."

Year 7. "For Pete's sake, stop sneezing! Are you trying to give me pneumonia?"

One of the basic problems in the family is self-love, self-centeredness, self-satisfaction. We fall more and more in love with ourselves, and too much ego will wreck the family unit. Paul recognized the problem: "Men shall be lovers of their own selves" (2 Timothy 3:2).

THE BIBLE HAS THE ANSWER (5:18-21)

The Spirit-controlled life is God's answer for harmony in the family.

"And be not drunk with wine, wherein is excess" (Ephesians 5:18). In the Greco-Roman world of Paul's day, they drank wine to induce worship. They believed that wine brought about the necessary state of ecstasy that lifted the worshiper to a level of communion with the gods that was otherwise impossible.

We are not called on to lose control through wine and find a false communion. Rather, we are to be controlled by the Spirit and find true communion. The result of being filled with the Spirit is summed up for us in the form of an admonition in verses 19-21. What joy we find in our relationship to God through His Holy Spirit, "speaking to . . . [ourselves] in psalms and hymns and spiritual songs, singing and making melody in . . . [our] heart to the Lord" (v. 19).

The first thing a Spirit-controlled life should have is a sense of inner peace, inner contentment, inner joy. These feelings result naturally in songs of praise and worship.

"Giving thanks always for all things unto God and the Father in the name of the Lord Jesus Christ" (v. 20). A Spirit-controlled person not only has a song in his heart but openly gives thanks to God as well. Our thanks is always unto God.

"Submitting yourselves one to another in the fear of God" (v. 21). God's purpose is unity, and that is accomplished through submission. This is God's plan and purpose in the family as well as the church.

THE BIBLE SPEAKS TO THE WIFE (5:22-24)

"Wives, submit to your own husbands, as to the Lord" (Ephesians 5:22, NKJV). Notice the word here and in Colossians 3:18 is submit, not obey. Obey is reserved for children and servants. The idea conveyed is a spirit of submission. The word own emphasizes the intimate personal relationship. This is your own husband, not someone detached from you. He is your own—you possess him, and he possesses you. Submission does not mean you are inferior—not at all! Jesus submitted to God but was equal with God. Submission is based on love. It is a relationship. He is your own husband as God's gift to you, your own possession "as to the Lord." This is very important.

THE BIBLE SPEAKS TO THE HUSBAND (5:25-33)

Sacrificial love—"Husbands, love your wives, just as Christ also loved the church and gave Himself for it" (Ephesians 5:25, NKJV).

In this verse we find the words "gave Himself for it." Jesus loved us enough to leave heaven, come to earth, take on human form, suffer, and die. He loved the church. The world says, "Be the macho man, the big shot. Don't let anyone step on your territory; fight back; grab for all you can get, because you deserve it."

Purifying love—"That He might sanctify and cleanse it with the washing of water by the word, that He might present it to Himself a glorious church, not having spot or wrinkle or any such thing, but that it should be holy and without blemish" (vv. 26, 27, NKJV). The love a man has for his wife is also to be a purifying love. No one wants to defile someone he loves. Young people especially need to be instructed by the admonitions of Paul. The husband who really loves his wife will not ask her to do anything that violates her conscience.

Caring love—"So husbands ought to love their own wives as their own bodies; he who loves his wife loves himself. For no one ever hated his own flesh, but nourishes and cherishes it, just as the Lord does the church" (vv. 28, 29, *NKJV*). We spend a lot of time on ourselves—exercising, eating the right foods, wearing nice clothes. The man is to love his wife as he loves his own body. The wife is to submit to her own husband. There is nothing humiliating, nothing degrading, nothing inconsistent with intellectual, moral, or spiritual submission. It is simply necessary for domestic order and to fulfill God's plan.

THE BIBLE SPEAKS TO CHILDREN (6:1-4)

The word *children* means "offspring." If you still stick your feet under Dad's table, then this is for you.

Teenagers are having a difficult time today. However, it is not my sympathy they need. They need my prayers and an understanding ear.

"Children, obey your parents." These are the last days, and children still need to be obedient to parents. Some of the spiritual problems among our children may be caused by parents' neglect of their children.

Verse 4 says, "Fathers, do not provoke your children to wrath" (*NKJV*). This refers to the emotional irritation that comes to parents and children. How can parents irritate or provoke their children?

1. *By being over protective*—Fixing the boundaries too narrow, placing no trust in your children, and making your discipline all rules with no liberty will make your children feel boxed in, and resentment and bitterness will result.

2. *By showing favoritism*—Always comparing one child with the others—"Why can't you be like your brother? He always does his homework"—makes the child feel like a lemon on the assembly line.

3. *By depreciating their worth*—If when company comes your children are always told to eat in the kitchen, always

told to be quiet and go to the den or to their room, what do you think this will do to their feeling of self-worth and individual importance?

4. *By offering only discouragement*—Never rewarding them for anything, making them feel that no matter how much they succeed, it is never enough can sabotage your children's self-esteem. Often parents who treat their children like this are trying to get their children to be what they never were. (A girl committed suicide because she could not measure up to her parents' demands.)

5. *By never demonstrating affection*—Children who are never hugged or kissed have a difficult time expressing affection toward others.

6. *By having a lack of standards*—Children need to see principles demonstrated in their parents' lives. Earn their trust. Set guidelines.

7. *By constantly voicing criticism*—Criticism does not lead to responsibility. Children who hear only criticism learn to condemn themselves, find fault with others, doubt their own judgment, and distrust everybody.

8. *By neglecting them or showing indifference*—Children who are too often ignored and whose parents show little or no interest in their activities or welfare grow up feeling unloved and uncherished. Play with your children. Spend time with each one individually.

9. *By overdisciplining them*—If you make your children feel that everything they do is wrong, if you hit them in anger, if you frequently yell or scream at them, if when they spill the milk you are thoroughly exasperated, you need to work on your own self-control. Sit down together and talk. Your children need guidance and affection, not harsh words and physical blows.

CONCLUSION

The rearing of a family in a sin-sick world is no easy undertaking. But God's Word gives guidelines that assure harmony in the family and in turn sets an example for other families to follow.

CHURCH AFLAME

John E. Hedgepeth

SCRIPTURE: Isaiah 4:4, 5

INTRODUCTION

Make no mistake about it, the church is under attack. It's open season for attacks on pastors and the church as well. This world system seems to be driving the church into a corner, challenging, "Produce your credentials. Let us see what you really are. Are you really alive as you claim to be, or are you dead? Do you have the goods to back up your doctrine and your widespread claims, or is the church just another institution that preaches one thing and practices another?"

In a world that is marked by the coldness of a Laodicean age, the church can be alive and on fire, but only as the Holy Spirit runs deeply into our souls and blasts and melts away our carelessness, unconcern, compromise, and deadness. Isaiah declared:

After the Lord has washed away the moral filth of the daughters of Zion [pride, vanity, haughtiness], and shall have purged the blood stains of Jerusalem from the midst of it by the spirit and blast of judgment and by the spirit and blast of burning and sifting. And the Lord will create

*over the whole site . . . a cloud and smoke by day, and
the shining of a flaming fire by night; for over all the glory
shall be a canopy—a defense [of divine love and protection]"*
(Isaiah 4:4, 5, *Amp.*).

John the Baptist declared, "He that cometh after me is
mightier than I . . . he shall baptize you with the Holy
Ghost, and with fire" (Matthew 3:11).

Luke stated, "And there appeared unto them cloven tongues
like as of fire and it sat upon each of them" (Acts 2:3). This
verse pictures the Holy Spirit as a blast of power and as
forked tongues of fire sitting upon the believers.

God speaks again and says, "Our God is a consuming fire"
(Hebrews 12:29).

THE CHURCH AFLAME RECOGNIZES PEOPLE

The church is not buildings, bureaucracies, denominations,
creeds, and programs. The church is people—the everyday,
down-to-earth people who are the "called-out ones." They have
been called out of the world to perform a ministry to the
people of the world, and only the burning blast of the Holy
Spirit will enable them to do it.

Edwin Hatch penned this prayer for his day:

*Breathe on me, Breath of God, till I am wholly Thine,
Till all this earthly part of me, glows with Thy fire divine.*

Charles Wesley wanted God to blast him and burn him until
he glowed with God's Spirit:

*Oh, that in me the sacred fire might now begin to glow;
Burn up the dross of base desire, and make the mountains
flow.
Thou who at Pentecost didst fall, and all my sins consume;
Come, Holy Ghost, for Thee I call, Spirit of burning, come!*

Can you and I also begin to pray that His Spirit will glow
in us, allowing us to meet the needs of the world today?
Sitting in its precarious position of uncertainty, the world is
waiting for the church to stand up and give its testimony—the
church that God has called out, the church that God has
anointed, the church that God has appointed to bring revival
to a hurting world.

An old Okie proverb says, "There is none so deaf as them that will not hear." Will you hear Him calling to us as a church today?

Will you also say to Him, "Come and burn through every wall of doubt. Come and burn through every obstacle. Come and burn through all the pessimism. Come and burn through negativism. Come and burn through our sins. Burn away all the things that keep us from being the answer to the world's cry. Come and burn Your truth into our minds until we conclude it is 'not by might, nor by power, but by my spirit, saith the Lord of hosts'" (Zechariah 4:6)?

John Fletcher, colleague and successor of John Wesley in the English Methodist Societies, who often spoke of the baptism with the Holy Ghost and with fire and of burning love, wrote, "Let us enter the full dispensation of the Spirit. Till we live in the Pentecostal glory of the church: Till the Spirit of burning and the fire of Divine Love have melted us down."

THE CHURCH AFLAME PERMITS GOD'S SPIRIT TO MOVE

We have our programs and methods in our churches. We have our way of doing things. Maybe we should allow our ways to die and allow Christ to move. Let us allow the Spirit to burn up some of the things we don't need and turn them into ashes. Let us lay them at the feet of Jesus and say, "We are utterly helpless in this ministry without Your Spirit and Your power."

Let's ask Him to burn out those things that have kept us from being victorious, that have left us at the mercy of the Enemy, that have left us beaten down, defeated, and dying. Let's ask Him to come and burn away those things that have hurt us inside the church, that have taken the life out of many of our churches and left them less than triumphant. Let us throw all of our carnal weapons at His feet and catch a new vision. "For the weapons of our warfare are not carnal, but mighty through God to the pulling down of strongholds" (2 Corinthians 10:4). Paul said all of the natural weapons should be laid at the feet of Jesus anyway, for they are no match for Satan.

In our spiritual warfare one of our main concerns should be the fortress that Satan has set up in our minds, where our imaginations and thoughts are. Big battles are won or lost on the battlefield of the mind. Paul tells us in 2 Corinthians 10:5, "Casting down imaginations . . . that exalteth itself against the knowledge of God, and bringing into captivity every thought to the obedience of Christ." As one Bible professor used to say, "The greatest nation is imagination." Satan comes to set himself up in the minds of men. He doesn't have to worry about his other programs as long as he is in control of the mind, for "as . . . [a man] thinketh . . . so is he" (Proverbs 23:7).

There is only one thing that can defeat and destroy the power of Satan in the mind, and that is the spiritual weapon of destruction—the sanctifying, burning power of the Spirit. Our weapons are not natural, human, earthly, physical weapons, but the weapons of the Spirit. As Paul says they are, "divinely potent to demolish strongholds" (2 Corinthians 10:4, *NEB*).

THE CHURCH AFLAME SUBMITS TO HIS POWER

When the church receives that kind of power, it will storm Satan's garrisons and demolish the opposition. Then the church will be the church, as the song says, alive and potent, overthrowing and destroying the strongholds of the Enemy. I pray, "Come, Holy Ghost, for Thee I call, Spirit of burning, come!" Dear God, set the church aflame!

The episode of Elijah on Mt. Carmel in 1 Kings 18 is a clear picture of many of the people in our churches today who would be greatly used of God but cannot be because they have not taken authority over the spiritual enemies of the soul. Elijah said, "The God that answereth by fire, let him be God" (v. 24). The prophets of Baal prayed. They tried, they prayed, they cried, they cut themselves, they screamed! "They prophesied until the time of the offering of the evening sacrifice, that there was neither voice, nor any to answer, nor any that regarded" (v. 29). There was no answer!

The failure of the prophets of Baal was a supreme moment for Elijah. He could have decided to try for an answer by fire with the same methods used by them. How many times have we thought that the human methods used by the world are what we need? And perhaps we've all been at least a little tempted to rely on them. We have tried to scream the fire down or shout the fire down or pay the fire down or sing the fire down. The truth is that none of these will bring the fire of God. They may accompany God's move, but they won't bring the move. The only way to bring an answer by fire is to pray it down. Elijah took preliminary steps that teach us a valuable lesson.

Elijah called the people near to him, and "he repaired the altar of the Lord that was broken down" (v. 30). If there is anything that will bring a blast of fire into our churches, it is the rebuilding of the altars—altars that have been torn down in our home, in our church, in our schools, and in our nation. Our altars represent the place where God dealt with us once, where God moved upon us and the anointing of the Lord fell, and we felt so close to God and had the spirit of victory.

"Then he dug a trench about three feet wide around the altar. He piled wood upon the altar and cut the young bull into pieces and laid the pieces on the wood. 'Fill four barrels with water,' he said, 'and pour the water over the carcass and the wood.' After they had done this he said, 'Do it again.' And they did. 'Now, do it once more!' And they did; And the water ran off the altar and filled the trench" (vv. 32-35, *TLB*).

THE CHURCH AFLAME GETS ANSWERS FROM GOD

Elijah left no room for doubt! He wanted the whole group to know that God would answer by fire. He wanted them to know that God would work through everything that would try to hinder Him. They poured water on the burnt offering. They flooded the altar until the trench was completely full of water, and it looked like God couldn't possibly answer. He wanted no one to be able to say it was a trick. Then with a simple prayer of 63 words, the fire came down and consumed the sacrifice and the stones and licked up the water in the trench. God had given a mighty blast of burning fire that no amount of water could quench to let them know that it is still by the Spirit of God that miracles come. No amount of water, no amount of doubt, no amount of satanic hindrance could keep Him from answering.

The church in our day still has all of its pessimisms, doubts, negative thoughts, and satanic hindrances. One Bible scholar once said, "When a spirit of revival comes, someone will take a bucket of water and pour it on the fire that is burning. One will say, 'I know we can do it!' and another one will pour a bucket of water on it and say, 'It can't be done!' Another one will say, 'The Lord wants to move,' and another will come up with another bucket of water and say, 'But He's never done it like this before!' The anointing may begin to fall, and someone else will come and say, 'It's just not our way of doing it.' So we see the water of doubt and pessimism and negativism go on the altar."

Probably every pastor and every church leader has had to contend with those who doubt, those who constantly carry from the well of doubt a bucket of water to pour on the Spirit, saying, "It can't be done!" or "We don't have the funds!" But when God begins to move, when the real fire of God begins to fall, the flame of the burning Holy Spirit takes care of all the water of doubt, fear, and uncertainty. The church begins to affect the world. The church is then respected, feared, and recognized not as an organization but as an organism. It is not a dead institution but is a living body, alive and well. It is the body of Christ, the Lord of the church, the One who spoke and said, "I will build my church; and the gates of hell shall not prevail against it. And I will give unto thee the keys of the kingdom of heaven: and whatsoever thou shalt bind on earth shall be bound in heaven: and whatsoever thou shalt loose on earth shall be loosed in heaven" (Matthew 16:18, 19).

How do we know that this will work? The next scene on Mount Carmel shows us specifically what happens when the fire falls. There is a lesson for us. When the Spirit of burning from God came, the fire started at the top and worked its way to the bottom. "Then the fire of the Lord fell and consumed the burnt-sacrifice, and the wood, and the stones, and the dust, and licked up the water that was in the trench" (1 Kings 18:38). It was a miracle, and all the people fell on their faces at once declaring that Jehovah was God! Verse 39 says, "And when all the people saw it, they fell on their faces: and

213

they said, The Lord, he is the God; the Lord, he is the God." There was reverence, and there was respect.

When God begins to fall on our altars in our churches, He always works from the top to the bottom. Somebody used to say years ago in our church, "When there's fire in the pew, there will be fire in the pulpit." The Bible teaches us differently. When God begins to move in a church, He moves from the pulpit to the pew, not from the pew to the pulpit. He moves from the preacher to the layman. God still speaks to men today as He did to men of old. If He is going to move on us as church leaders, then we need a blast of the burning power of the Holy Spirit to consume us and burn up all of the impurities that contaminate us. Let Him burn up anything that is wrong—all of our ambitions, all of our selfish desires, any little flaw in our lives, any spot and blemish, all of those things that keep us from ministering in power. We must stand before Almighty God and say, "God, I cannot do this job myself. Only You can do it! God, I want you to anoint me with the power of the Holy Spirit and give me that leadership. Let me depend not upon myself but upon You and Your power. Come and burn all of my talents, my training, and all of the skills that I have. Burn them up and bring forth new weapons which are mighty through God to the pulling down of strongholds."

CONCLUSION

When the fire falls on the pulpit, it will then fall on the pew. The church will begin to recognize that it is called of God, separated from the world, and anointed to carry His message. Ministry will then break forth from the laity. There will be an increased interest in sharing the gospel with a world that is hungry for Christ. Pastors and laymen will join hands to go heal the sick and cast out devils. The church will grow as it did in Acts, and the world around us will recognize that Jesus is Lord.

The church He is purging is the church He is protecting. May we come as Wesley did and pray, "Come, Holy Ghost, for Thee I call, Spirit of burning, come!" Dear God, set the church aflame!

THE SEED ROYAL

Guy BonGiovanni

SCRIPTURE: 2 Chronicles 23

INTRODUCTION

This message is based upon one of the most dramatic coming-out parties recorded in Old Testament history. It is couched in ambition, intertwined with intrigue, vehement with violence, and thrilling in triumph.

Three principal actors dominate the drama: (1) *the anointed one,* Joash, who is the rightful heir to the throne and thus the sovereign human authority in Judah; (2) *the adversary,* Athaliah, his grandmother, who wanted the throne so badly she would and, in fact, did kill her kin for it; (3) *the advocates* of the anointed one, led by Jehoiada, the priest, who protected Joash and worked for his installation as leader of Judah.

In this narrative are some challenging parallels to the installation and the protection of a pastor by his congregation. These parallels are very basic and essential for an effective pastoral ministry. Let us consider them.

THE ADVERSARY'S THREAT

The Death of a Lineage

"She [Athaliah] arose and destroyed all the seed royal of the house of Judah" (2 Chronicles 22:10).

What an inhumane atrocity that a grandmother should seek the death of her own flesh and blood! But Joash was the rightful authority figure in Judah, the heir apparent. And Athaliah could not reign as queen as long as the *seed royal* was alive. So, until she felt assured her insidious mission was complete and her throne secured, she focused her energies on the destruction of Joash.

The Dignity of Leadership

In an assembly of believers, the seed royal is represented by its pastor. Paul makes this clear in his letter to the Ephesians: "And he [Jesus] gave some . . . pastors" (4:11). It is unequivocably clear that pastors are *appointed* by Jesus, the head of the church . . . an awesome thought! They are *selected* and *set apart* by divine mandate to shepherd God's flock.

It easily follows, therefore, that the uniqueness of pastors is not to be found in their *perfection* of character, though they must be examples to the believers (1 Timothy 4:12; 5:19, 20). Nor is the uniqueness of pastors to be found in their *performance skills*, though they must be "apt to teach" and diligent in their study of the Word of God (1 Timothy 3:2; 2 Timothy 2:15). Neither is their uniqueness to be found in the degree of their *popularity*, although one who leads the church must be prepared to be "all things to all men, that . . . [he] might . . . save some" (1 Corinthians 9:22).

Joash was not unique because of his performance, popularity, or perfection. He was really just a child, unlearned and unproven in his abilities. But *he* had been *chosen* by God Almighty as were the true shepherds of the Lord in the New Testament church. They too were the *seed royal* of the Lord. He ordained and set *them* apart. And it is this uniqueness and nothing else that justifies the appeal to church members: "Obey your spiritual leaders and be willing to do what they say" (Hebrews 13:17, *TLB*).

216

The authority of a church is *not* in its eldership, its dea-conate, or its trusteeship. The government, the authority, in God's church has always been and must always remain—if it is to be *God's* church—in the hands of the *ordained* ministry. It must certainly never be in the hands of novices, nor must it be committed to the hands of people who have not *first* been proven (1 Timothy 3:6, 10).

The Deterioration of a Relationship

Athaliah became Joash's chief adversary, even though she was his grandmother. That blood relationship underscores the cruelty of her heart and the madness of her ambition. Not even the special bond of grandparent to grandchild bridled her seething lust for power. So far as she was concerned, she would mount the throne even though the scarlet runner leading to that post of power must be the blood of her grand-son.

It's unfortunate that a close proximity to pastoral authority carries some heavy potential for deteriorating personal relation-ships. Of course, it doesn't have to be, but often it is. The discovery that pastors also have "feet of clay" is disillusioning, and not everybody can cope with it.

Occasionally an associate, observing pastoral performance at close range, concludes, "There isn't much to it . . . I can do it as well or better than he." The Saul-David syndrome is triggered. They become competitors, and the relationship dete-riorates.

Athaliah would have been queen mother, but that wasn't enough! She wanted to be *queen*! And she took advantage of her closeness to the seed royal to improve her own chances at the throne by killing off her competitors. She was close to the *seed*. And that was the problem, because her spirit was wrong.

The Danger of Presumption

In Numbers 16 we read that the princes of Israel enjoyed status and closeness to Moses. But they wanted more! They wanted his authority! They challenged him: "You're not the only one God can use. You're no more holy than the rest of us. God's anointing is on us, too! So why do you put yourself above the congregation?"

Moses' response was really very simple: "This is God's business. He makes the choices. He put you in a special service role among His people. Do you think that position is a small thing? And now do you want the position of the priesthood as well?"

We must give our people opportunity to serve, to lead in worship, to minister the Word of God, to serve as officers in the assembly, to be our group leaders, to be active men and women in the body of Christ. But we must exercise great care lest the Enemy convert their proximity to pastoral authority into positions that can deteriorate the very authority that put them into a place of influence in the first place. Notwithstanding her close relationship, Athaliah became Joash's greatest enemy and most serious threat.

THE ADVOCATE'S TACTICS

Jehoiada, the priest, came on the scene. He mobilized the congregation and led the defense of God's anointed. As one reads this story, he discovers quite readily that four actions were taken to protect the *seed royal*:

Joash Was Concealed

He was hidden in his early years (2 Chronicles 22:11). Joash, indeed, was anointed, but he also was too new and too vulnerable to be allowed full exposure to his role. A newly installed pastor can identify with Joash's plight. Wise leadership in an assembly, therefore, will "hide" their new pastor because of his special vulnerability, and they will try to protect him from the insidious work of the Enemy.

They will hide him, for example, from verbal abuse and from vocational misuse. Church folk need to understand that a critical spirit and a cutting tongue can kill their Joash. Expecting him to be their chauffeur, their repairman, their errand boy, and socialite can be as deadly to him as Athaliah's assault. Guard him against loose tongues and release him to do the things he is called to do rather than consume his valuable time with the mundane.

The People Were Contracted

The people made a covenant with him (23:3). Notice, particularly, that the Scripture points out that *"all the congregation* made a covenant with the king. Isn't that good! They made a commitment to help him make it! One can almost feel the strength of the people's determination as Jehoiada said to them, "Behold, the king's son *shall* reign." You sense the iron in Jehoiada's spirit. He was saying essentially, "Joash, you can make it. We'll see to that!" What a refreshing gift to your pastor to let him hear you say, "Pastor, you can make it. We'll see to that!" There is strength in that commitment, both for him and for you.

The People Organized Care

They organized to protect him (vv. 4, 5). Notice what Jehoiada said: "This is the thing that ye shall do." Nothing was left to chance. They carefully planned Joash's protection and then the leadership acted. One-third of the leadership (priests and Levites) was assigned to keep watch at the doors of the Temple. One-third was assigned to stay at the king's house. One-third was to be on guard at the Foundation Gate. The rest of the men were to be in the courtyard of the Temple. The officers led the way. Then "all the people . . . [gathered] in the courts of the house of the Lord" (v. 5). They had a plan to protect the seed royal.

As he viewed the burden and stress of his pastor, one layman asked, "Who is my pastor's pastor?" And in response to his own question offered himself for whatever service he might be to his pastor. It is this same spirit that has led many churches to organize a Pastoral Concerns Committee. The care and well-being of their seed royal is too important to leave to chance.

Joash Was Circumscribed

They surrounded him (vv. 7, 10). Notice the protective strategy of Joash's advocates. "The Levites [the leaders of Judah] shall *compass the king* round about, every man with his weapons in his hand." Nobody was to be there unless he was prepared to fight. The Levites, in fact, became a *living wall* of protection.

219

Their actions said for Joash what the action of the people of your assembly should be saying for your pastor. "You can't get him without getting us first!" It was that kind of commitment Jehoiada and the Levites made. "You can't get him without getting us first!" Say it to the disagreeable! Say it to the disgruntled! Say it to the devil! It will make a difference in your church.

Joash's advocates put in motion this four-part strategy to protect the king and then had one of the greatest coming-out parties recorded in the Bible. Look at verse 11: "Then they brought out the king's son." And notice the five things they did:

1. They put upon him the crown.

2. They gave him the testimony of the Lord.

3. They made him king.

4. Jehoiada anointed him.

5. Then he announced him saying, "God save the king."

It was a powerful, noisy, exciting, gala celebration. The seed royal was anointed and announced. The seed royal had escaped the adversary's threat. The seed royal had triumphed!

THE ANOINTED ONE'S TRIUMPH

Look at the anointed one's triumph in verse 20. They "brought down the king from the house of the Lord: and they . . . set the king upon the throne of the kingdom." There is something quite significant here. The king's triumph was not in the *celebration* of his installation alone. His triumph was in his *cultivation* of his kingdom.

They Wrote a Contract

This is what happened. First, from verse 16, we are told *they made a covenant.* The significance of this covenant is that it was made not between the people and God, or even between Joash and God. The covenant was made between the people and the king! It is important for pastors to realize, as did Joash, that they, as well as their people, have *terms of contract* they must live up to and that these terms of contract are spelled out quite clearly in Scripture.

Peter is very candid in teaching that a pastor is obligated to Feed, to Lead, and to Oversee the flock of God. If he does that, his ministry will "FLO" with such ease and effectiveness that it will bring refreshing and renewal to the people in his sheepfold (1 Peter 5:1-3). A pastor does not punch a clock; he is plugged into Jesus. He serves the head of the church among the congregation without concern for bloodlines, stage lines, or money lines. Such terms of contract apply to all true pastors. They must be respected even as Joash recognized the terms of contract with his people. As long as he respected them, things went well for him.

They Destroyed the Counterfeit

The second thing to notice in the wake of Joash's triumph is that *they destroyed the symbols of idolatry* (v. 17). They "brake . . . [Baal's] altars and his images in pieces." They granulated the symbols of a different lifestyle. They were determined to so thoroughly clean out Judah that nothing in the land would even suggest an alternate lifestyle. They were committed to Jehovah, the true God.

They Changed Their Companions

Third, *they changed their relationship to the messengers of false religion* (v. 17). "And [they] slew Mattan, the priest of Baal." They didn't coddle him. They didn't say he was a great guy, a noble citizen of the community; that he wasn't hurting anybody; that he is in the minority now, the underdog, so it's safe to let him hang around. "Who knows? . . . Maybe he will even get converted and serve the true God." No! They didn't indulge such fantasy. Instead they took very positive action. They dared to confront Mattan; and they killed him!

They Appointed Only the Contented

Fourth, *they appointed officers to serve* (v. 18). The Scripture makes a very special point that they were appointed to serve "with rejoicing and with singing," a most unusual distinction but important. They were *happily* serving God and the king.

It is significant that in response to Joash's triumph, officers who were happy about things were appointed. They were the

221

kind of people who were saying things like "We're glad you're here as our king. We're happy about the way things are going. We're pleased about the people you are gathering around yourself. We share a spirit of kingship with you. We're moving together with you. We share in your vision. We feel bonded with your spirit."

That's the kind of commitment and relationship that causes a church to grow. And if a member can't have that kind of spirit, wisdom dictates that he should resign from any position he holds in the church. It should also be said if he can't resign and live quietly among the people, he should go one step farther in the interest of peace and take his membership to a sister church.

They Kept Things in Control

Notice the fifth response of Joash to his triumph. *He delegated special agents to make sure that nothing unclean entered the house of God* (v. 19). They were not playing games. They were in spiritual warfare. They had to be certain of the commitment of everybody in leadership. They couldn't afford commitments of convenience. Too much was at stake. And they recognized the subtlety with which the Enemy insidiously attempts to infiltrate the body, create discord and division, and destroy the work of God. So they appointed a corps of security agents to make sure nothing unclean entered the house of God.

This is not to suggest deacons should stand guard as security agents or run off on witch-hunts. They are, nevertheless, responsible, with the pastor, to make sure nothing inappropriate enters the house of God.

CONCLUSION

The grand finale of Joash's installation service is recorded in verse 21: "And all the people of the land rejoiced: and the city was quiet." Such joy mingled with tranquillity can be the legacy of every true man of God and every sensitive flock of God who willingly deny themselves, take up their crosses daily, and follow the Lord (Luke 9:23). Joy and peace are mingled in a magnificent tribute to the shepherd who gives his life for the sheep and a flock that garrisons its shepherd with provision and protection.

AND I SOUGHT FOR A MAN

Adrian L. Varlack Sr.

SCRIPTURE: Ezekiel 22:30

INTRODUCTION

The implication in our text is that if God had found a man to make up the hedge and stand in the gap, the moment of judgment would have been stayed. That God stakes so much on individuals is a biblical fact not well understood by the church in the 20th century. In an age of big-business organizations, multinational corporations, and the phenomenal growth of information and technology, we are apt to lose sight of the individual in the church as much as in the secular world. In a strange way, our inordinate dependence upon the church's vast, organizational infrastructure may be a contributing factor to the serious moral failings in the ministry and to our woeful lack of spiritual power.

MAN IS NOT A WEAKLING IN GOD'S EYES

E.M. Bounds wrote in *Preacher and Prayer*: "We [in the church] are constantly on a stretch, if not on a strain, to devise new methods, new plans, new organizations to advance the church and secure enlargement and efficiency for the gospel. This trend of the day has a tendency to lose sight of the man in the plan or organization. God's plan is to make much of the man, far more of him than of anything else. Men are God's method. The church is looking for better methods; God is looking for better men."

Bounds' idea that "God's plan is to make much of the man" squares with both Scripture and history. Our Lord's actions toward the people of the Bible and His testimony about them attest that He not only holds us in high regard but that we are necessary to His purposes and work in the universe. This is not to suggest an affront to the attributes of God; but in His own sovereign, self-limiting way, He includes us as a part of His eternal purposes.

It is this act of self-limiting that lets God deal with us on an arm's-length basis, permitting love and hate, pleasure and disappointment, joy and grief, faithfulness and failure in our lives. It is this self-limiting that makes true relationship possible between the Creator and His creatures. The other side of this equation, however, is that man is a fully responsible and accountable moral creature within God's plan of redemption. Our ability to will, to choose to be faithful, to have integrity in the face of suffering, and to endure adversity without blaming God is assumed in Scripture. We are without excuse (Romans 2:1).

MAN'S ROLE IS SIGNIFICANT

Since we live in this morally depraved world, it is natural for us to look at ourselves as a lower, helpless victims of circumstance. But God's view, as revealed in Scripture, contends that we are morally and spiritually capable and therefore accountable and responsible. This implies the possibility of reward and the certainty of judgment. It also suggests that individuals who deal in the things of God can cause the success or failure of those things committed to their trust. We can either gain or lose in the way God counts gaining or losing. When we wake up to the awesome reality of this question, we tend to shirk from the responsibility. Heaven gains or loses on the rise or fall of the individuals to whom God entrusts His divine mysteries.

Paul wrote to the Corinthians, "Let a man so account of us, as of the ministers of Christ, and stewards of the mysteries of God. Moreover it is required in stewards, that a man be found faithful" (1 Corinthians 4:1, 2). The thought that God's mysteries could or would be entrusted to us as stewards (in the face of the spiritual and demonic forces at work in "high places") is a humbling testimony of God's confidence in our ability to choose the right and to do right.

A parallel thought is contained in 1 Corinthians 15:21, 22: "For since by man came death, by man came also the resurrection of the dead. For as in Adam all die, even so in Christ shall all be made alive." The key to these two verses is their contrast: "For since by man came . . . by man came also. . . . For as in Adam . . . even so in Christ. . . ." This is indeed a compelling thought that raises the significance of man in the affairs of God.

It appears that despite our fallen nature, God regards us as having the capacity to engage and overcome the devil, even though the devil is regarded as the prince of the power of the air (see Ephesians 2:2). Now we understand that apart from a right relationship with God, we can do nothing righteous. We are dependent on God in a sort of mutually binding relationship. No wonder the Scripture teaches that "we are labourers together with God" (1 Corinthians 3:9).

Yes, our role is significant. That makes us both accountable and responsible.

GOD'S MEN OF THE PAST

Some of our modern preaching tends to try to save God from the straightforward implications of His own Word. Difficult passages tend to present God in irreconcilable paradoxes: He is almighty, yet repented and grieved that He made man (Genesis 6:5, 6). Jesus wept over Jerusalem rather than meeting its terms of showing a sign of His messiahship or using His power to destroy it (Luke 19:41-44). In the same way, His wonderful dealings with man baffle us. Without explaining His purposes to either Job or to us, He entered a "wager" (to use Phil Yancey's word) with Satan that Job's faith could not be shaken. In other words, God permitted the destruction of all that Job had, based on His confidence that Job would not deny Him even if reduced to nothing but a mass of sores (see Job 2:3-7).

At a time when men had no use for God, Enoch went against the tide and "walked with God: and he was not; for God took him" (Genesis 5:24). God's regard for Enoch is not explainable; we can only say that God was pleased with him.

Abraham was called the "Friend of God" (see James 2:21-24). God even confided to him His intended destruction of Sodom and Gomorrah (see Genesis 18:17-19). Not only was Abraham informed, but he was allowed to petition God to change His mind, somewhat suggesting that God could be making a mistake. While such a suggestion is obviously a grave error, it is treated by God as a natural outgrowth of His relationship with Abraham.

We are told that the Lord spoke with Moses face-to-face as a man speaks with a friend. Moses took what seemed to be exceptional liberties with God by requesting that he be allowed to see God's glory and by insisting that he would not enter the Promised Land unless God's presence accompanied him. God's sympathetic treatment of his request was nothing short of remarkable (Exodus 33:11-23).

All these instances (and there are many more) speak of the power and privilege God grants to men, His dependence on their faithfulness, and His regard for their integrity. Hebrews 11:16 teaches, "God is not ashamed to be called their God: for he hath prepared for them a city."

GOD IS STILL SEARCHING

"The effectual fervent prayer of a righteous man availeth much" (James 5:16). James proceeded to tell how Elijah prevailed with God over an entire nation though he was "a man subject to like passions as we are" (v. 17).

In sending Ananias to lay hands on Saul, our Lord confirms His selection of Saul as a chosen vessel separated unto God, chosen for suffering (Acts 9:10-16). When Saul (now called Paul) faltered, God himself encouraged him (23:11). Paul's power with God was such that he was known among the demons (19:15). His prayers changed the outcome of a disastrous voyage (27:10, 20-26); He understood that he was chosen as a pattern to them who would believe (1 Timothy 1:12-16).

Individuals such as Elijah and Paul seem to have had an unusual and very personal acquaintance with God. But God also depended upon quite ordinary men. Ananias of Damascus is referred to simply as a "certain disciple" but he obviously had a very personal acquaintance with his Lord. When his name was called by the Lord, Ananias calmly replied, "Behold I am here, Lord" (Acts 9:5-10). Contrast that response with Saul's—Saul cried out: "Who art thou, Lord?" (v. 5).

It was the angel of the Lord who spoke personally to Philip and sent him to the Gaza area to preach Christ to the Ethiopian eunuch (Acts 8). We could go on and on about God's personal appearances in one form or another, His deliverances of His servants, His personal encouragements to them, and His dependence upon them.

The lack of such personal intimacy with God in our day is certainly not due to some new indifference on God's part. God's desire to fellowship and to commune with us is still as intense as ever. He is indeed searching among us for individuals with whom He can have such a relationship and upon whom He can depend. Perhaps the church, because of the failure of prominent men in the past, tends to diminish the role of men in the affairs of the kingdom of God. Perhaps we have opted to protect institutional integrity from man's potential for moral failure. Perhaps we would prefer that God choose some corporate form of exerting His power in the world instead of risking it on fallible men. Our tendency is to make the institution our primary focus. God's plan, as Bounds says, is to make much of the man.

"Without God, we cannot. Without us, God will not," said Augustine. God and His work is intricately and inextricably bound up with people. The witness of the New Testament is that we can quench, grieve, or resist the Holy Spirit (1 Thessalonians 5:19; Ephesians 4:30; Acts 7:51). It seems as if God has placed upon us the responsibility of the gospel and risked the outcome on our faithfulness. This is truly an incredible thought—a thought that is humbling and sobering at the same time.

CONCLUSION

Where are the individuals whom God has troubled in this

closing period of the 20th century? Where are those who will reecho the commitments of God's men of old? "As for me and my house, we will serve the Lord" (Joshua 24:15). "Though he slay me, yet will I trust in him" (Job 13:15). "How then can I do this great wickedness, and sin against God?" (Genesis 39:9). "Neither count I my life dear unto myself" (Acts 20:24). Where are the individuals who are worthy to be messengers of God because they have "hazarded their lives for the name of our Lord Jesus Christ" (Acts 15:26)?

Are any today worthy to make up the hedge and stand in the gap before God for the land? Can His judgment against His people once again be stayed because righteous men prevail? We believe it can! If the church expected as much from man as God does, better men would be produced. Today we seem content with performers and their performances, when what we really need is God-called, God-committed men of integrity who unsettle us with sound Bible-based preaching, teaching, and praying. God still seeks such individuals today. Will He find you to be one of them?

THE BIGGER THE GIANT, THE GREATER THE VICTORY

William A. Reid

SCRIPTURE: John 10:10

INTRODUCTION

This text is probably one of the most powerful verses in the Bible. Jesus warned His disciples, "The thief cometh not, but for to steal, and to kill, and to destroy." Everyone knows who the thief is! It is the devil!

The devil has a design on each life. The devil's design is to steal, to kill, and to destroy. There is an alarming complacency among Christians today. They serve God from the standpoint that they no longer have to fear what the devil wants to do to them. No matter who you are, the devil's design is still to kill, to steal, and to destroy.

The devil wants to rob young people of their innocence! He is trying to steal our children! He works to destroy our marriages!

The very moment you are lulled into a sense of complacency, thinking you have gone too far for the devil to get to you, then you are in great danger. Whenever you come to the place in life that you think you have arrived, that you no longer have to struggle, battle, and be in conflict with the devil, you are standing on dangerous ground. The devil never gives up!

GOD'S PLAN FOR YOUR LIFE

The beautiful part of verse 10 says, "I am come that they might have life, and that they might have it more abundantly." Jesus' desire for you is that you might have life and have it more abundantly.

So often people think that abundant living means the house they live in, the car they drive, and how much money they have in the bank. That is not what Jesus Christ was speaking of. When Jesus Christ talked about abundant life and abundant living, He was not talking about what kind of car you drive, where you live, or how much money you may have in the bank. He was talking about having the kind of relationship with Him that when all around you is sinking sand, on Jesus Christ, the solid Rock, you stand. Abundant living is dependent upon your relationship with the Lord, not on situations or circumstances in the world. It does not matter how good or how bad things are; if you really have that relationship with the Lord Jesus Christ, you can live the abundant life.

Someone may say, "But you don't understand where I live; you don't understand where I work; you don't understand the relationship I have with my husband, or with my wife; you don't understand the difficulty I am having with my children." It does not matter where you live, where you work, what kind of relationship you have with anybody if your relationship with Jesus Christ is intact.

In 1 Samuel 17 is the story of a young man named David. We will notice three things in the story about David that will help us to have the abundant living that Jesus Christ wants us to have in our lives—God's anointing, God's will, and God's victory.

GOD'S ANOINTING

In chapter 16 God had spoken to Samuel, telling him to go anoint a new king in Israel. All of Jesse's sons came by except David. Finally, when David was brought in, Samuel took the horn of oil, which symbolized the anointing of God, and poured it upon the head of David. When the oil came down upon David's hair, it ran down his face, down his garments, and all the way to the ground.

There was a sweet-smelling savor that went forth from that anointing oil. The Word of God says, "And the Spirit of the Lord came upon David from that day forward" (16:13). From that time, when he was just a ruddy-complexioned teenage boy, the anointing of God came upon him. No matter where David went, he went as God's anointed.

When difficult situations or circumstances come into your life, you have to realize that you too are the anointed of God. Jesus told His disciples in John 15:16,

Ye have not chosen me, but I have chosen you, and ordained you, that ye should go and bring forth fruit, and that your fruit should remain: that whatsoever ye shall ask of the Father in my name, he may give it you.

It is easy to realize you are the anointed of God when you are in a good worship service. It is easy to sit and say, "Oh, praise God! I am the anointed of God!" The next morning when you get out of bed, you are still the anointed of God. When you go to work, you are still the anointed of God. It does not matter where you go, you are still the anointed of God. It is time to stand on your feet, square your shoulders, look the devil in the eye and say, "Devil, you are fighting against an anointed servant of God."

David was God's anointed. Three of David's brothers had been drafted by Saul. One day David's father came to him and said, "Son, I want you to take some provisions over to your brothers—some corn, some cheese, some bread. Take them to your brothers and their commander, and see how your brothers are doing."

David started out toward his brothers. Finally, he came to the valley where the armies of God and the armies of the Philistines were fighting. David was so excited to think he was going to see the armies of God defeat the armies of the Philistines!

While David was talking with his brothers, from across the valley came the booming voice of a giant named Goliath. History tells us that Goliath was at least 9 feet 5 inches tall (maybe as tall as 10 or 11 feet). Goliath stepped out from the Philistines' battle lines and challenged them:

Why are ye come out to set your battle in array? am not I a Philistine, and ye servants to Saul? Choose you a man for you, and let him come down to me. If he be able to fight with me, and to kill me, then will we be your servants: but if I prevail against him, and kill him, then shall ye be our servants, and serve us. And the Philistine said, I defy the armies of Israel this day; give me a man, that we may fight together (1 Samuel 17:8-10).

David was a little taken aback as he looked out and saw Goliath. We can imagine David's first question to his brothers then was, "Hey, what are we going to do?" The armies of Israel had run away at the sight of Goliath and were probably hiding behind the rocks on their side of the valley.

When Saul and all Israel heard those words of the Philistine, they were dismayed, and greatly afraid. . . . And all the men of Israel, when they saw the man, fled from him, and were sore afraid (vv. 11, 24).

This was not the first day Goliath had stood and made this challenge to the armies of God. For 40 days the last thing Israel had heard before going to sleep at night was the booming voice of Goliath as he stood on the other side of the valley saying, "Send me a man to fight against me!" The first thing they heard in the morning was Goliath's repeated challenge: "Send me a man to fight against me!"

Then along came David. "What are we going to do? Who's going to go out and fight against him?" David was probably looking around to see who was getting ready to go out to fight against Goliath. David's oldest brother looked at him and said something like, "Hey kid, what are you doing here? What do you have in your basket? Who's taking care of the few sheep back on the Judean hillside? That's your responsibility, David. We're men of war! We've come out to fight in the armies of Saul! Who is taking care of the little responsibility assigned to you?"

Have you noticed that when you do get enough spiritual courage to do something, there are always those standing around about you to say, "What makes you think you can do that?" There are always those who want to put you down.

The men began to question David's motives. His brother Eliab said, "I know thy pride, and the naughtiness of thine heart; for thou art come down that thou mightest see the battle" (v. 28). It is bad enough to be intimidated by people in the world, but when you decide to do something for God, there are also people in the church who will intimidate you and tell you it cannot be done.

David responded to his brother, "Is there not a cause?" (v. 29). In other words, "Is there not a reason to be angry? Is there not a reason to go out there and fight against this great giant Goliath?" David was first of all God's anointed. When David saw the enemy defying the armies of God, he became angry and said, "We've got to do something! Someone has to fight against Goliath! Someone has to show him that he cannot defy the armies of God and the God of Israel!"

GOD'S WILL

It is time for the people of God to get angry—not at each other but at the devil. It is time to get angry about the over 1 million abortions performed each year, about the drugs flowing in the streets of America, about what the devil is doing in our country. It is time for men and women of God to get angry enough to do something!

It is easy to talk, but it is time for you to act. Being angry at Goliath for defying God is not enough; you have to do something about it! If you are doing it for the Lord Jesus Christ, do not worry about those who question your motives.

David finally got the attention of King Saul. David told the king he would go and fight Goliath. Saul said, "Thou art but a youth, and he a man of war from his youth" (v. 33). David kept insisting, "Somebody has to do something! Something has to happen!"

The church needs to be careful that it does not get lulled into a sense of complacency, letting somebody else do what needs to be done for God. It is time for the people of God to be willing to do what God has instructed them to do. Everyone has a work to do for God.

Saul finally said, "Well, if you are going to go, put on my armour." The Bible says that when Saul was chosen to be king over Israel, he was head and shoulders taller than all the other men of Israel. David said, "I can't go out to fight Goliath like this." Notice his reason: "I have not proved them" (v. 39). What he meant was, "I can't fight the enemy with somebody else's armor. I have to fight the enemy with what I know is right, with what I know is good." There are a lot of people today that want you to fight the enemy using their armor, using their battle gear. What has brought the church this far is what the church needs to continue to use in the fight against the devil—that is, the Word of God, which is the sword of the Spirit.

David said, "I have to use what I know is proven." He took off Saul's armor and started across the valley. He had his shepherd's staff, his sling, and a pouch. He stopped at the brook, took five smooth stones, and put them in the bag.

GOD'S VICTORY

David walked across the valley, and there was Goliath. David had to strain to look up at him. Goliath "disdained him" (v. 42) from the moment he saw him—he hated him. He said, "Am I a dog, that you would send a boy out here to fight me? I'm a man of war, and you sent a boy to fight against me! I am going to feed you to the birds" (see vv. 43, 44). David looked up at Goliath and said,

This day will the Lord deliver thee into mine hand; and I will smite thee, and take thine head from thee; and I will give the carcases of the host of the Philistines this day unto the fouls of the air, and to the wild beasts of the earth; that all the earth may know that there is a God in Israel (v. 46).

Big, brave talk for this inexperienced youth with the ruddy complexion! But there he stood!

Where do you think the armies of Israel were while this was going on? Perhaps, while peering around a rock, one of David's brothers said, "Boy, ole David's sure gonna get a lickin' this time."

David took a stone, put it into the sling, and sent it right into the enemy's forehead! Goliath fell to the ground. Where do you think the armies of God were then—still behind the rocks? David went up and stood right on Goliath's chest—a grand and glorious victory!

The devil's design is to steal, to kill, and to destroy. The devil wants to ruin you, but you can have the same victory David experienced if you will trust God.

CONCLUSION

Many of you have come to church time after time. The man of God has preached, the Spirit of God has moved, and by faith you have reached out. You have even knocked the giant down, but you have not decapitated him! You have not held him up in the face of the devil and said, "Devil, look! The giant is dead!"

You *can* see your giants defeated—giants of unforgiveness, bitterness, rebellion, sickness. God wants to kill those giants.

You may say, "You still don't understand. You don't know how big the giant is!"

It does not matter how big the giant is in your life! The bigger the giant, the greater the victory the Lord Jesus Christ wants to give you! You have to be willing to do as David. Step out and say, "There is a reason! There is a cause! I am not going to allow that giant to live in my life anymore. In the name of Jesus, I am going to take the Word of God, which is the sword of the Spirit, and cut off the head of the giant."

Victory is ours in Jesus Christ!

THE DAY THE LORD HATH MADE

Melvin L. West

SCRIPTURE: Psalm 118:24

INTRODUCTION

How many of us have waited patiently, or perhaps impatiently, for a certain day to arrive? Then when it arrives we're happy because it's the day we've been waiting for, it's "our day."

To a child, it's probably Christmas. To a teenager, it might be the day when he or she is old enough to get a driver's license. Or it could be the day that Mom and Dad allow that first unchaperoned date. Graduation day is always a time we look forward to with great anticipation.

To the church there are several special days during the year we look forward to. There is Christmas, a day to honor the virgin birth of our Lord Jesus Christ; Palm Sunday, a day to remember the triumphal entry of Christ into Jerusalem; Good Friday, the day our Lord was crucified; then Easter, which has been called the "Day of days" in the life of Christ and the Christian church.

All of these are wonderful days on our calendar, and they give us reasons to rejoice and be glad. However, we do not have to interpret the psalmist to mean some special day or holiday, and neither should we limit our joy and gladness to Sunday or other special days.

As we remember God's works and wonders of old, while at the same time acknowledging the value of the present and the promise of the future, we can say with the psalmist, "This is the day which the Lord hath made; we will rejoice and be glad in it" (Psalm 118:24). Now let's look at some things that can help us to rejoice daily.

REMEMBER THE WORKS OF THE LORD

Let us say with the psalmist: "I will remember the works of the Lord: surely I will remember thy wonders of old. . . . That they might set their hope in God, and not forget the works of God, but keep his commandments" (Psalms 77:11; 78:7). Shouldn't this make us rejoice?

Each of us is responsible not only for *what* we remember but also for *how* we remember it. This means that we are responsible to train and educate our memory not merely for the purpose of remembering facts but for practical and spiritual purposes.

It is important that our memory be consecrated to God that we may have a mental record of what God has done for us. But will we remember?

1. *We should remember the Lord's mercies.* He has led us these many years in the wilderness of this world (see Deuteronomy 8:2). For this we should be thankful, praising God in the darkness and the storm, as well as in the light and the calm.

Some of us are like people who, when they get better of their sickness, grudge the doctor's bill. It is sometimes said, "We forget the mercies as soon as they are past, because we only enjoyed the sweetness of them while it is in our mouth."

2. *We should remember the distresses that have prompted us to pray.* The psalmist said, "In my distress I cried unto the Lord, and he heard me" (Psalm 120:1). Stephen Alford in his book *Heart Cry for Revival* says:

It is my conviction that we are never going to have revival until God has brought the church of Jesus Christ to a point of desperation. As long as Christian people can trust religious organization, material wealth, popular preaching, shallow evangelistic crusades, and promotional drives, there will never be a real revival. But when confidence in the flesh is smashed and the church comes to the realization of her desperate wretchedness, blindness, and nakedness before God, then and only then will God break in.

3. *We should remember the prayers God has answered.* In the latter part of Psalm 118:5, the writer states, "The Lord answered me, and set me in a large place." This is the same Lord who says in Jeremiah 33:3, "Call unto me, and I will answer thee, and shew thee great and mighty things, which thou knowest not." In fact, the Lord said to Isaiah, "Before they call, I will answer; and while they are yet speaking, I will hear" (65:24).

Evan Roberts, who was so greatly used in the 1904 revival in Wales, bowed himself over a church pew and prayed, "O God, bend me, bend me, bend me." God answered his longing heart and met him in a revival blessing that influenced the whole area.

4. *We should remember God's Word, wonders, and His doings.* Psalm 77:10-12 states:

And I said, This is my infirmity: but I will remember the years of the right hand of the most High. I will remember the works of the Lord: surely I will remember thy wonders of old. I will meditate also of all thy work, and talk of thy doings.

The first nine verses of Psalm 77 reveal a troubled soul crying out to God. In fact, verse 3 reveals that the psalmist was troubled at his remembrance of God. He complained and was overwhelmed. This is always the result of preoccupation with self. But in verses 10-12, the psalmist got his memory in gear.

5. *Remember that the Lord is on your side.* Or as *The Living Bible* puts it, "He is for me!" (Psalm 118:6).

6. *Remember to learn from your past.* Know your limitations. Identify your weaknesses; accept the counsels of prudence from your failures, and control your ambitions by remembering where you broke down. "And Joseph called the name of the firstborn Manasseh: For God, said he, hath

made me forget all my toil, and all my father's house" (Genesis 41:51).

W.E. Sangster said:

We often read advertisements in the newspapers for systems of mind and memory training. We regard it as a great natural endowment if anybody has the gift for recalling a face, a fact, a name, just when he wants to. We say, "He has a good memory," and we feel that he is a man to be envied. Nevertheless, I want to convince you that precious though a good memory is, the power to forget is hardly less precious.

He further stated:

If I were a teacher of mental efficiency and giving all my time to the training of minds, I should make it a close concern not only to teach people how to remember but also how to forget.

Joseph was made to forget. He looked back over his past: He was put into a pit, sold by his brothers, slandered by a lascivious woman, thrust into prison, and forgotten by the chief butler. Despite these horrible experiences, Joseph said, "God has made me forget."

We, too, must be made to forget some things. We must not look back and see only ourselves, our victories, our successes. To do so is to show how conceited we are. It is foolishness, so forget it.

On the other hand, we must not dwell upon our failures either. Let us never say, "I have tried and failed over and over again. I might as well give up and accept inevitable defeat." Nonsense! Learn your lesson well. Forget it and say, "I can do all things through Christ who strengthens me" (Philippians 4:13, *NKJV*).

Alexander Maclaren said, "If my memory weakens me for present work, either because it depresses my hope of success or because it saddens me with the remembrance of departed blessings, then it is a curse and not a good."

We must forget the hurtful things that have been done against us. In the Lord's Prayer we say, "Forgive us our debts, as we forgive our debtors" (Matthew 6:12). Do you need forgiveness? Remember, "With what measure ye mete, it shall be measured to you" (Mark 4:24). Have you been hurt? Have you been sinned against? Has somebody slandered you or done you the deepest injury? Forget it! For your soul's sake, get that poison out of your system.

The following poem sums up well those times we need to forget the past.

What to Forget

If you see a tall fellow ahead of a crowd,
A leader of men marching fearless and proud,
And you know of a tale whose mere telling aloud
Would mean that his head must in anguish be bowed,
It's a pretty good plan to forget it.

If you know of a skeleton hidden away
In a closet, and guarded and kept from the day
In the dark; and whose showing, whose sudden display,
Would cause grief and sorrow and lifelong dismay,
It's a pretty good plan to forget it.

If you know of a thing that will darken the joy
Of a man or a woman, a girl or a boy,
That will wipe out a smile, or the least way annoy
A fellow, or cause gladness to cloy,
It's a pretty good plan to forget it.

—One Thousand New Illustrations

REMEMBER TO RECOGNIZE OPPORTUNITY

To rejoice and be glad, we must recognize not only what the Lord has done, but also what He is doing today. The psalmist declared, "This is the Lord's doing; it is marvellous in our eyes" (Psalm 118:23).

Maclaren said, "Opportunity is amongst us and even within us." God has given us the faculty of perception, of observation, of intuition; we can see what is before us—our interest, our duty, our possibilities.

To neglect God-given opportunity is most definitely a very serious sin. It is the same as hiding our talent in the earth—a sin that calls forth strong condemnation (Matthew 25:24-26).

It is said that if we should take one of a migratory flock of birds out of the line of flight, which the God-given instinct has formed to guide it to its distant home, and cage it behind iron bars, it will beat its wings against the cage in frantic efforts to rise and go on its journey. But let the season pass in which birds migrate, then open the cage, and the bird will not go. Though we might take it in our hands and toss it high into the air, it will be of no use. The instinct for motion has passed, and the bird will return heavily to the same spot.

Today is our "day of migration." So let us not cage up our times of opportunity. Wise use of the opportunities before us will give us calmness in the face of death, even as it did to Peter, Paul, and others.

Now take a look at a wise man as described by Maclaren:

The wise man is he who makes the most and the best he can of that which is within his reach, and that which is before his face. He does not spend his time in looking and longing for that which is at the ends of the earth; he sets himself to cultivate the patch of ground, however small or poor, that is just outside his door. He works his capital, however small it may be. He reads well his books, however limited his library may be. He serves others, however narrow his sphere may be.

It has been said, "The discernment of the day of opportunity is an important step toward its improvement." A large insurance company invited all its agents throughout the country to a business conference in New York. While in attendance, one of the agents from the West insured a barber, an elevator man, and a restaurant waiter—all of whom were employed by the insurance company in its home office building. No one else had thought to offer policies to these people in the home office building.

The apostle Paul said, "For a great door and effectual is opened unto me, and there are many adversaries" (1 Corinthians 16:9). Another translation puts it like this: "For a wide door for effective service has opened to me, and there are many adversaries" (*NASB*). And Jesus said it like this: "I must work the works of him that sent me, while it is day: the night cometh, when no man can work" (John 9:4).

Charles L. Allen, in his book *All things Are Possible Through Prayer*, tells about a man who put his keys into one of his shoes each night before going to bed. The next morning when he dressed to begin a new day, that shoe was the last thing he would put on. He would take out those keys, hold them in his hand, and then say something like this:

Lord, this day I will come to certain doors that are locked, but I shall use these keys to open those doors. And may I remember this day that there is a key to every situation, a solution to every problem. May I never surrender to one of life's locked doors. Instead, may I use the keys on the key ring of prayer until I find the right key and the door is opened.

CONCLUSION

Once again let us be reminded that it doesn't have to be a special day, a holiday, or a Sunday for us to rejoice and be glad. One day at a time, let us declare what the psalmist said centuries ago, "This is the day which the Lord hath made; we will rejoice and be glad in it."

DESERT PETE

Leon Stewart

SCRIPTURE: Revelation 22:17

INTRODUCTION

Imagine with me a person traveling out across a barren, burning, sandy desert—dehydrated, needing water, can't go much farther. Suddenly that person staggers upon a rusty water pump. Tied to the water pump is an old Clabber Girl baking-powder can. The person opens it and finds a note in it that reads something like this: "October 31, 1938, I fixed this pump, cleaned it out, repaired the points, put in new leathers. It should be good for five years. Under the white rock is a bottle of water. I put it there to keep it from evaporating. Get it, pour one-fourth of it into the pump, let it set five minutes so that the leathers may soak, pour the rest of the water in the pump, and then pump like crazy. There will be plenty of water for you to drink. Refill the bottle, put it under the white rock, and leave it for the next stranger who passes this way." Signed: "Desert Pete."

If you should happen upon a situation like that, you have a choice. You could just drink the water from the bottle and go your way. You could prime the pump, get excited about having plenty of water to drink, toss the empty bottle away, and finish your journey, or you could refill the bottle as instructed for the next traveler.

I submit to you that we are all traveling across life's troubled, sandy, barren, sometimes hostile desert. All of us come to that place and time when we need a drink of water. We all know that Jesus is that needed drink—the Water of Life.

YOU MUST HAVE FAITH

If you were the traveler who found the note, what would you do? First of all, if you do what this note says, you will need to have faith in somebody. You have to believe in Desert Pete if you pour that bottle of water into that pump. You have to believe in someone who has passed this way.

And hasn't Jesus passed our way? The difference in Christianity and all other major religions is simple. Man is in a box. All other religions, save Christianity, say to man, "With works, achievements, disciplines, and systems, get out of the box, and you will find your God." But in Christianity, God saw man in his despair, left the ivory palaces above, came into a world of woe, and burst into that box, saying, "Here I am, living among you."

Jesus is the Water of Life. Can we have faith in Him?

Years ago the Chaldeans were overrunning the land of Palestine, and Habakkuk said in essence, "Oh, God, what do You mean by letting Your own people suffer?" (see Habakkuk 1).

And God could have answered something like this: "Habakkuk, you are not going to like the answer, but here it is. It doesn't matter, Habakkuk, what might happen. It doesn't matter what the external circumstances may appear to be. The just, the righteous, are going to survive." God did say explicitly in Habakkuk 2:4, "The just shall live by his faith."

You are taking a tremendous risk to pour that water into the pump. Man's situation is really a case of life and death. Putting your faith and confidence in Jesus Christ is a tremendous risk. You see, there are millions of Muslims out there today who say you are not right. There are multitudes with other religious persuasions who say you are mistaken. Can you believe in the Virgin Birth, the Crucifixion, the Resurrection, the Ascension and exaltation? Do you really believe Jesus fulfilled the teaching of the Word in these events? We must risk putting our faith in Jesus.

I know that in these days we are being told we must have a triangle of faith with the Word of God, the Bible, at one point, at another point the interpretation of the church fathers, and down here at the third point human reasoning. You must have it all to make it complete, we are told. Maybe so. If you want to accept that, it is OK with me. But don't go too far with me in either interpretation or human reason. Bring me back to the Bible that brought me from the quagmire of sin and set me on the way of holiness.

You ask, "Do you really believe that Book?" I sure do. Three hundred years ago Voltaire, that French infidel, said of the Word, "The Bible! Why, with these bare hands I will destroy the edifice built by those 12 apostles." What happened? Voltaire is dead, and the Geneva Bible Society bought the house where he lived when he made that statement and installed printing presses for the purpose of printing Bibles. In the room where he made his threat, the society stacked Bibles from the floor to the ceiling. Out of that house and around the world has gone Bible after Bible carrying the life-giving Word of Jesus Christ. The Bible is still the everlasting Word of God.

YOU MUST FOLLOW THE DIRECTIONS

Now, not only do you have to have faith in somebody, you have to follow the instructions. We Pentecostals are not too good at following the written instructions. We want God to speak to us every day and tell us exactly what to do—some kind of special revelation, you know. In fact, we are getting so carried away nowadays that some of our people believe God should pour their corn flakes every morning and tell them what to do that day.

If you want to know what makes the pump work, read the note! Read the Word of God if you want to know what will bring life to this barren world of ours. Read the Book and follow the instructions. You are taking a tremendous risk by simply following the instructions in the Bible, the Word of God. We want all these revelations and confirmations because we have so little knowledge of God's eternal Word. We like to say, "Well, I am just going to do what the Spirit tells me to do." OK, as long as it harmonizes with the Book. We can rest assured that if what we "feel led" to do does not harmonize with the Scripture, it is not the Spirit telling us to do it. "I have been doing it this way for 40 years, and I am going to keep on doing it." But you have never gotten any water out of the pump in 40 years. Do something different, for heaven's sake! We don't need you to preserve the tradition of what you have been doing. We need water!

Read the Book! It will help you understand what Jesus meant when He said, "I do always those things that please him" (John 8:29). We are so susceptible to being deceived in our times because of a lack of knowledge of the Word of God. You see, if the Antichrist came along today, he wouldn't have to call fire down from heaven to deceive most of us. All he would have to do is speak in tongues. I wish you would get back into the Book, read what it says, and do what it says in your everyday life.

YOU MUST REFILL THE BOTTLE

The third thing you must do before you leave the pump and go on your way is to refill the bottle. Folks, America is no longer a Christian nation. I would probably debate the issue whether or not it ever was. There is no trace of the Bible Belt. There are 80 to 90 million people who do not know Jesus Christ in our land and 40 million more who seldom ever go to church. The church, an institution of bureaucracy, is no longer interested in meeting the needs of people. The church is interested in perpetuating itself and on Sunday morning doing its little performance that it calls worship—having a good time, living with a "bless me" attitude, and going on its merry way. We need to repent for such an attitude.

As a church we pay a tremendous price for going our own way. We have lost our children to the sands of the desert. We have lost our grandchildren to the winds of that blighted land. For, you see, when we came to the pump, we were interested in ourselves. (I am convinced that the greatest sin of today is selfishness. There is more of it in the church than I like to admit.) We didn't take time to prime the pump. We were a little too busy for that. We had to hurry on our way to beat the noon crowd to the cafeteria on Sundays. We just drank the water.

246

Some of us decided that we should follow the instructions to the point that we got the pump primed, and it was really giving water. We drank and we drank, and we got so excited that we started dancing and worshiping and clapping our hands. Then leaving the empty bottle in the desert sand, we walked off into the sunset feeling good.

A generation of young people walked up to that pump, found the baking-powder can, the note, and a dry, dusty bottle lying close to it. They had no choice but to turn away from what should have been help and hope. There go their tracks, leading off toward the horizon that says, "We are the masters of our own destiny. We will do our own thing." There they go in another direction, saying, "Out here we will find affluence, and *things* will become the greatest part of our value system." And there is yet another trail of steps, tracks of our young people and children who should have been in our churches but who instead are walking out to a pleasure-seeking world that is saying, "Whatever feels good, do it. Live for today."

CONCLUSION

We have been on the barren desert, but I believe God has brought us back to the pump in the desert today. I believe the pump is there, the baking-powder can with the directions intact, and a full bottle of water under the white rock. The Holy Spirit has brought us to this good hour to take positive steps to bring our children and grandchildren home. They don't have to seek after secular humanism or materialism or pleasure any longer. They can find what they need at the pump, the Water of Life.

Lord, thank You for that Water. May we never walk away again without leaving the bottle for the next stranger who will pass this way. In Jesus' name I pray. Amen.

GIVE ME THAT OLD-TIME RELIGION

David M. Griffis

SCRIPTURE: Jude 3

INTRODUCTION

The apostle Jude, in his concise but powerful epistle, explained to his readers the urgent need to return to the foundations of their Christian faith lest they fall into the mire of apostasy. He explained that he was writing because it was "needful." The obvious answer to their need, according to Jude, was for them to "earnestly contend [fight for, strive for, work] for the faith which was once delivered unto the saints" (v. 3).

Only a great victory is worth a great battle, and the fact that this faith was "once delivered" simply means that it can be delivered again, providing that the seeker contends for it.

A favorite song in Evangelical and Pentecostal circles for many years, dating back to the revival fervor that swept across this country in the early years of this century, was "The Old-Time Religion." Verses were often added by those singing it until certain verses became a part of its tradition. The message of some of those verses gives ample reason to the true believer to "contend" for the faith once delivered to the saints.

THIS FAITH MAKES US LOVE EVERYBODY

Christ said that love is the chief identifying trait of a disciple. "By this shall all men know that ye are my disciples, if ye have love one to another" (John 13:35). John's reminder to us is "If God so loved us, we ought also to love one another" (1 John 4:11). Paul declared that faith, giving, miracles, knowledge, spiritual gifts, and all other virtues are secondary to the attribute of godly love (1 Corinthians 13). Love is the nature of God for "God is love" (1 John 4:16). Old-time religion, real salvation, makes you love everybody, for you take on the nature of Christ. When compelled to go a mile, you go two miles. When asked for your coat, you give a cloak also.

You render good for evil and pray for those who despitefully use you. You forgive because you cannot escape the memory of your own forgiveness. You love not only those who love you, which is easy, but also those who show you no love. You know that all the drunkard needs is the new wine of the Spirit. You know that liars need the Truth. You know the hungry need the Bread of Life. You know the immoral need the acquaintance of Him who is altogether pure and holy. In short, you love others because you are loved.

THIS FAITH WAS GOOD FOR PAUL AND SILAS

The testimony of this particular verse of the old song is evident when you read the account of Paul and Silas' Philippian imprisonment and deliverance in Acts 16. Here we're reminded that the Christian faith is not always easy, that it has adversity as well as advantage. Sometimes doing good brings our greatest trial. Paul and Silas, while preaching the gospel, bringing revival to a pagan city, and delivering a demon-possessed damsel, were beaten unmercifully and imprisoned. Their only crime was doing good, and their sentence would have been severe for even the most diabolical felony. Lonely, in a darkened dungeon, with no balm for their wounds, they prayed and sang praises to God in the darkness. God then turned dilemma into deliverance. They were not only set free, but a revival ensued and apologies were given by their tormentors. Yes, old-time religion was indeed good for Paul and Silas.

THIS FAITH WILL TAKE US ALL TO HEAVEN

Salvation through faith in Christ is the only way. The Scripture plainly declares, "Neither is there salvation in any other" (Acts 4:12). The Scripture labels anyone trying to enter any other way "a thief and a robber" (John 10:1). God is not bribed with gold; He walks on it. Real estate doesn't get His attention, for "the earth is the Lord's and the fulness thereof" (Psalm 24:1). The power of the mighty doesn't sway His opinion, for He said, "All power is given unto me in heaven and in earth" (Matthew 28:18). Our own goodness and philanthropic deeds do not merit salvation, "for all have sinned, and come short of the glory of God" (Romans 3:23). Salvation is free, bought and paid for with God's "unspeakable gift" (2 Corinthians 9:15). Salvation and salvation alone will take us all to heaven.

THIS FAITH WILL DO WHEN WE ARE DYING

One verse of the old melody says old-time religion "will do when I am dying." That's when the bottom line is written. That's when we can no longer fake anything. Death brings the end to all chances, the finality of all opportunities, and the reality that we are, after all, mortal. At the door to the unknown we must have an experience with God or we cannot smile as we enter our sleep. Acquaintances cannot go with us; friends must let go of our hand; companions must stay behind; children must linger. Christ in us is our only hope of glory (see Colossians 1:27). Money, power, houses and land, influence, and knowledge will not "do when I am dying." But the fact that "ye are complete in him" (Colossians 2:10) makes death a simple passage into His eternal presence.

CONCLUSION

May our understanding of the "faith once delivered unto the saints" be such that we will strive to know Him, love Him, and serve Him till He "takes us all to heaven."

JESUS CHRIST, YOUR ANSWER

Raymond E. Crowley

SCRIPTURE: John 1:1, 2

INTRODUCTION

The word *beginning* (the Greek word *arche*) means the first, before everything, before time began. Jesus Christ is eternal, as are the other persons of the divine Trinity. The divine Trinity always has been and always will be. Verse 3 says, "All things were made by him; and without him was not any thing made that was made." When we think of Creation, we think of God the Father. Jesus was there with God when everything was made. The fact that Jesus came and became incarnate in the flesh, born of a woman, and took upon Himself the sins of the world does not lessen His deity in any degree. Hebrews 13:8 assures, "Jesus Christ the same yesterday, and to day, and for ever." All hope of humankind depends on the eternity of Jesus Christ.

Jesus Christ came because He loved us and because God the Father loved us. "For God so loved the world, that he gave his only begotten Son, that whosoever believeth in him should not perish, but have everlasting life" (John 3:16). His death brought salvation to all who will accept Him. His resurrection brought eternal life.

THE PROMISE OF JESUS CHRIST

For unto us a child is born, unto us a son is given: and the government shall be upon his shoulder: and his name shall be called Wonderful, Counsellor, The mighty God, The everlasting Father, The Prince of Peace. Of the increase of his government and peace there shall be no end, upon the throne of David, and upon his kingdom, to order it, and to establish it with judgment and with justice from henceforth even for ever (Isaiah 9:6, 7).

Here Isaiah prophesied of the coming Messiah in the form of a child and of the extent of His reign and His kingdom. I am sure many have doubted the eternal victory of the church and the kingdom of God. There have been brutal attacks on the work of the Lord down through the years. Don't ever doubt! His kingdom will never come to an end—"Of the increase of his government and peace there shall be no end."

"And there shall come forth a rod out of the stem of Jesse, and a Branch shall grow out of his roots" (Isaiah 11:1). Here we have another prophetic and victorious promise of the coming of the Messiah. "And the spirit of the Lord shall rest upon him, the spirit of wisdom and understanding, the spirit of counsel and might, the spirit of knowledge and of the fear of the Lord" (v. 2). Notice the promise of a sevenfold anointing of the Messiah.

In verse 10 Isaiah gave another glorious promise: "And in that day there shall be a root of Jesse, which shall stand for an ensign of the people; to it shall the Gentiles seek: and his rest shall be glorious."

THE COMING OF JESUS CHRIST

Now the birth of Jesus Christ was on this wise: When as his mother Mary was espoused to Joseph, before they came together, she was found with child of the Holy Ghost. . . . That which is conceived in her is of the Holy Ghost. And she shall bring forth a son, and thou shalt call his name JESUS: for he shall save his people from their sins (Matthew 1:18, 20, 21).

The word *Jesus* is used 979 times in the New Testament. It is the earthly name of God's Son. As God He was not called Jesus or Christ. *Jesus* is the Greek form of the Hebrew *Yehoshua*, rendered *Joshua* 215 times, meaning "savior" or "God is salvation."

"Behold, a virgin shall be with child, and shall bring forth a son, and they shall call his name Emmanuel, which being interpreted is, God with us" (Matthew 1:23). This child, Jesus, was not just another baby. He was conceived of the Holy Ghost. He was both God and man.

Luke 2:8-12 records the angelic announcement to the shepherds. Verse 10 says, "And the angel said unto them, Fear not: for, behold, I bring you good tidings of great joy, which shall be to all people." His coming brought joy, not sadness. The angelic host worshiped God and Jesus. "And suddenly there was with the angel a multitude of the heavenly host praising God, and saying, Glory to God in the highest, and on earth peace, good will toward men" (vv. 13, 14). Not only was there joy on the occasion of His birth, but throughout His life He continued to bring joy.

After the angel's annunciation to Mary, she "arose . . . and went into the hill country with haste, into a city of Juda" (Luke 1:39). When she entered into the house of Zacharias and greeted Elizabeth, the baby leaped in Elizabeth's womb, and she was filled with the Holy Ghost (vv. 40, 41). In verse 44 Elizabeth said, "For, lo, as soon as the voice of thy salutation sounded in mine ears, the babe leaped in my womb for joy."

Luke 2:25-32 records the encounter of Simeon and the coming of the Christ. Simeon was waiting for His coming. It had been revealed to him by the Holy Spirit that he would live to see the Messiah. When Jesus was brought to the Temple, as the custom was, Simeon took Him up in his arms and said, "Lord, now lettest thou thy servant depart in peace, according to thy word: for mine eyes have seen thy salvation, which thou hast prepared before the face of all people; a light to lighten the Gentiles, and the glory of thy people Israel" (Luke 2:29-32).

Jesus is the salvation not only of Israel but of all who will receive Him. "He came unto his own, and his own received him not. But as many as received him, to them gave he power to become the sons of God" (John 1:11, 12). He is not just salvation to the Jews but to every nation on earth. Let all the earth rejoice because He came! Because of His visit to this earth, there is salvation for the lost, help for the troubled, healing for the sick, freedom for those held captive by evil powers, and a hope that reaches beyond this life!

THE AUTHORITY OF JESUS CHRIST

When Jesus came to this earth, He did not relinquish His authority. Matthew 4:2-11 relates the temptation of Jesus by Satan. "And when he had fasted forty days and forty nights, he was afterward an hungred." The tempter came to him. Notice the devil's approach. He did not address Him as the Son of God. He said instead, "If thou be the Son of God, command that these stones be made bread." Jesus answered, "Man shall not live by bread alone, but by every word that proceedeth out of the mouth of God." Then the devil said, "If thou be the Son of God, cast thyself down." Jesus answered, "It is written again, Thou shalt not tempt the Lord thy God." But Satan still had not finished his tempting. "Again, the devil taketh him up into an exceeding high mountain, and sheweth him all the kingdoms of the world, and the glory of them; and saith unto him, All these things will I give thee, if thou wilt fall down and worship me." Again, Jesus answered, "It is written, Thou shalt worship the Lord thy God, and him only shalt thou serve." Only then did the devil leave Him, "and, behold, angels came and ministered unto him." He maintained His divine authority over Satan, sin, and all manner of disease.

After His powerful Sermon on the Mount in Matthew 5—7, Jesus commanded divine authority over Satan and disease. In chapter 8, Jesus healed a leper, a centurion's servant, and Peter's mother-in-law. He cast out devils and healed all who were sick.

"Jesus went about all the cities and villages, teaching in their synagogues, and preaching the gospel of the kingdom, and healing every sickness and every disease among the people" (Matthew 9:35). He also healed a man with a withered hand (12:13). "Great multitudes followed him, and he healed them all" (v. 15). "Then was brought unto him one possessed with a devil, blind, and dumb: and he healed him, insomuch that the blind and dumb both spake and saw" (v. 22).

When they were gone over, they came into the land of Gennesaret. And when the men of that place had knowledge of him, they sent out into all that country round about, and brought unto him all that were diseased; and besought him that they might only touch the hem of his garment: and as many as touched were made perfectly whole (Matthew 14:34-36).

Great multitudes came unto him, having with them those that were lame, blind, dumb, maimed, and many others, and cast them down at Jesus' feet; and he healed them (Matthew 15:30).

The same thing happened in Matthew 19:2, and in Matthew 20:34 Jesus also healed two blind men.

These are a few of the examples of the authority of Jesus over Satan and disease. Isaiah wrote, "But he was wounded for our transgressions, he was bruised for our iniquities: the chastisement of our peace was upon him; and with his stripes we are healed" (53:5). A scourge was a Roman implement for severe bodily punishment. It consisted of a handle with about a dozen leather cords with jagged pieces of bone or metal at each end to make the blow more painful and effective. The victim was tied to a post, and the blows were applied to the bare back and loins. Often the victim fainted and sometimes died. If the scourge used on Jesus had 12 thongs and He was beaten 39 times, this would make 468 stripes. Isaiah 52:14 says, "As many were astonied at thee; his visage was so marred more than any man, and his form more than the sons of men."

By His blood we are saved from sin; by His stripes we are healed. Surely the Lord is concerned about our healing or He would not have suffered as He did. Hebrews 11:1 tells us, "Now faith is the substance of things hoped for, the evidence of things not seen." Simple faith brings healing. So often those who are newly saved have simple believing faith and are healed.

During the first General Assembly my wife and I attended after we were married, she became violently ill with ptomaine poisoning. I have never seen her in more pain. I called for

R.P. Johnson and her uncle, Fred B. Marine. These men were two giants in the Lord and in faith. They came into the room. One knelt on one side of the bed and one on the other side. I shall never forget those powerful prayers of faith. God healed her instantly!

THE HOPE OF JESUS CHRIST

Happy is he that hath the God of Jacob for his help, whose hope is in the Lord his God: which made heaven, and earth, the sea, and all that therein is: which keepeth truth for ever (Psalm 146:5, 6).

By whom also we have access by faith into this grace wherein we stand, and rejoice in hope of the glory of God. (Romans 5:2).

Knowing that everything around us will pass away, that everything material will decay, deteriorate, rot, rust, or wear out, we have no lasting hope in the carnal and material. These will all pass away.

"If in this life only we have hope in Christ, we are of all men most miserable" (1 Corinthians 15:19). So many people today are miserable, depressed, and unhappy. Great numbers are dependent on chemicals and medication. People are trying to find hope and assurance in this life and in the material world. Many times after people have given their time and talent in pursuit of materialism and the things that this world offers, they realize how empty it all is. Their disappointment is more than they can handle. Too often they wind up on drugs or alcohol or even become suicidal.

Jesus promised, "Peace I leave with you, my peace I give unto you: not as the world giveth, give I unto you. Let not your heart be troubled, neither let it be afraid" (John 14:27). Lasting hope and meaningful peace depend on Jesus Christ, our Lord and Savior. Those who base their hope on secular humanism will be disappointed. Those who deny Him and reject Him as Savior and Lord will not find peace. The Jewish people are proof of this fact. They denied Him as Messiah, rejected Him as Savior, and have been scattered and persecuted beyond measure. Today they are in constant war, fighting, and turmoil. The Arab world rejected Him and are a group of nations entangled in hatred, fighting, and war not only with other people but also among themselves.

The hope of tomorrow hinges on the Resurrection morning. If Jesus had remained in the grave, all hope would have been gone. He alone is the conqueror of death, hell, and the grave. After His resurrection and glorification, He gave the glorious promise of returning again.

And when he had spoken these things, while they beheld, he was taken up; and a cloud received him out of their sight. And while they looked stedfastly toward heaven as he went up, behold, two men stood by them in white apparel; which also said, Ye men of Galilee, why stand ye gazing up into heaven? This same Jesus, which is taken up from you into heaven, shall so come in like manner as ye have seen him go into heaven (Acts 1:9-11).

CONCLUSION

Regardless of what many of the world's cults say and teach, He is coming again! Regardless of what the liberal theologians say and teach, He is coming again!

For if we believe that Jesus died and rose again, even so them also which sleep in Jesus will God bring with him. For this we say unto you by the word of the Lord, that we which are alive and remain unto the coming of the Lord shall not prevent them which are asleep. For the Lord himself shall descend from heaven with a shout, with the voice of the archangel, and with the trump of God: and the dead in Christ shall rise first: Then we which are alive and remain shall be caught up together with them in the clouds, to meet the Lord in the air: and so shall we ever be with the Lord. Wherefore comfort one another with these words. (1 Thessalonians 4:14-18).

CAUSES AND CURES FOR SPIRITUAL STALENESS

Carl Richardson

SCRIPTURE: Job 7:3-7

INTRODUCTION

In America he was a well-known sports figure—on television regularly. He was the brilliant young coach of the Oakland Raiders football team, perennially in the divisional play-offs, perennially a winner, always a fierce competitor.

He was a leader, an innovator, a creative and fiery coach. Suddenly, at the end of the 1978 football season, John Madden announced that he was quitting as a head coach—forever. At the top of his profession, he had had it with football. He said he was burned out. He said he was stale.

Remember when 6-foot-8-inch Dave Cowens of pro basketball's Boston Celtics walked off the court and announced he was quitting? He said playing ball just wasn't fun anymore. He said the excitement was gone—that's all, just gone. He said that life had gone stale and he just had to get a handle on life again.

If we are honest, none of us are exempt from going stale. All of us have felt the dulling emptiness of spiritual staleness. Most of us can identify with Job when he says:

Wearisome nights are appointed to me. When I lie down, I say, When shall I arise, and the night be gone? and I am full of tossings to and fro until the dawning of the day. . . . My days are swifter than a weaver's shuttle, and are spent without hope. . . . Mine eye shall no more see good (Job 7:3, 4, 6, 7).

For Job, obviously life had grown stale. He was infected and infested with staleness and cynicism. He looked forward to nothing—not even to death. He seemed to be saying, "I've had it with life. I've come to the end of my rope. I can't sleep. I can't eat. I don't enjoy life. I'm wiped out as a person. All hope is gone that things will ever get any better."

Stale living, like stale bread, is disappointing and distasteful, but living does have its peaks and valleys. When staleness sets in, we become ingrown and locked into our own lives. Consequently, we are overwhelmed with pessimism. We are no longer in control of our lives. We take hold of the future with the handle of fear and not with faith. It's true—almost all of us have experienced staleness. Some of us are going through it right now. Something inside us goes limp. Something inside us dies. We feel trapped. We see no hope. We seek no help. We just wait powerlessly for that elusive thing called fate to somehow change things. But the longer we wait, the deeper our cynicism becomes entrenched as a part of our lives.

I have to be honest. It bothers me to ever feel stale. It disturbs me to realize that all my goals may not be achieved. We face it at every level of our living, and it affects each of us in a different way.

My friend and colleague Dr. Paul L. Walker tells of a young man who had all his dreams ahead of him. He had made big plans and was going to achieve greatness; but every time he pressed on the accelerator, there just wasn't enough power. He never quite made it. One day in his 40s he had to face the fact that he would never compose the music, never paint the picture, never build the skyscraper, never own his own business, and never be the president of the company. And so he feels disappointed in himself as life, for him, loses its vitality and drive. Life becomes dull, pale, uninteresting. Living is drudgery, a duty instead of a privilege. His body becomes saturated with tension. His soul dries up with neglect. Deep inside he feels the dull ache of monotony and mediocrity. And for one so young, life has gone stale.

The truth is, most shadows are caused by standing in our own sunshine.

Spiritual staleness has definite causes and definite cures.

UNKNOWN OR UNCONFESSED SIN

When did we quit caring? When did we quit taking sin seriously? We've become so coolly cynical and so hard and so hip anymore that we seem almost oblivious to every one of life's darkest possibilities. What we thought would be temporary moral numbness has grown into a large dead spot inside us. Somewhere along the road to broad-mindedness and permissiveness, the last remains of innocence got stomped to death.

The biggest change of all that has taken place deep inside us is our inability to work up any feeling about what is going on between us and God.

In this era of materialism, the catch-all religious con men and hucksters teach and preach that anything a man does is OK . . . just as long as he's sincere. If you think positive thoughts and send your money into his coffers, you are promised (even guaranteed) that you will experience incredible prosperity and health. What hogwash that is! The fact of personal sin must be taken into account, and we, as individuals, will be held accountable for our own sins. "Every one of us shall give account of himself to God" (Romans 14:12).

Sin! One can't even say the word without hearing the hiss of the serpent. Sin writes wrinkles on your brow, slows your step, stoops your shoulders, and makes your hand unsteady. Sin clouds your visage, dims your eye, dashes your hopes, and weakens your heart. Sin darkens the morning and clouds the evening. Sin—God help us to see it as He sees it!

Some people feel that for sin to be counted as sin, it must be a public sin that causes a scandal and dishonors the cause of Christ through its bad publicity. But sin doesn't have to make the headlines for it to be sin in the sight of God. Sin doesn't have to become a public issue before it causes spiritual staleness. On the contrary, it is unknown and unconfessed sin that devastates the soul and numbs our sensitivities.

All unconfessed sin is unforgiven sin.

What about you? If everyone knew you as God knows you, would your friends still respect you? The issue is not what others think about you; it is what God knows about you that counts most.

Often we may wonder why great causes fail or slacken, why so little real good comes of various programs of doing good. It all looks so promising, so good on the surface. But without a doubt, failure is there. We see whole churches that were at one time beacons of hope to a dying community leave their first love and lose their power and passion. They are stale. Their worship is stale. The singing is stale. The preaching is stale. The praying is stale! It could be that there is sin in the camp! People who pray will stop sinning. And people who sin will stop praying. Spiritual staleness sets in, and a musty stench replaces the fragrant aroma of forgiveness.

In the early church the people believed in the forgiveness of sin. And so do I! The stench of life's sordidness and the mustiness of spiritual staleness can never blot out the fragrance of God's pardon. His pardon is full and complete.

ATTENTION TO SPIRITUAL BASICS

When we ignore the spiritual basics of the Bible, will reap the consequences.

Prayer is a spiritual basic. Prayer is to the soul what breath is to the body. Prayer grasps the omnipotent hand. When that grasp is strong, the whole life is strong. When that grasp is weak, the whole life is weak.

Bible reading is also a spiritual basic. David the king was a man who battled spiritual staleness and constantly battled with the presence of sin in his own life. It is therefore noteworthy that he shares with us a secret we need to learn: "Thy word have I hid in mine heart, that I might not sin against thee" (Psalm 119:11).

Staleness will disappear when we repent of sin—all sin. Staleness will disappear when we pray and when we attend to other spiritual basics such as Bible reading and regular worship in the house of God.

Faith will then replace doubt as surely as the sunrise follows the darkness. Staleness will be replaced with freshness when we live in the Spirit, talk in the Spirit, walk in the Spirit, pray in the Spirit, and worship in the Spirit.

Priority to our spiritual relationship with God is at the heart of what can be called "spiritual basics." Misplaced business scrambles our priorities. Churchly work becomes a substitute for spiritual relationship. Our values become distorted. We become spiritually numb and want to feel again. We want to feel hope again. We want to feel peace again.

Two artists each painted a picture to illustrate his own conception of peace. The first chose for his scene a still, lone lake among the far-off mountains.

The second threw on his canvas a thundering waterfall, with a fragile birch tree bending over the foam. At the fork of the branch, almost wet with the spray, sat a robin on the nest.

The first scene indicated stagnation; the last scene was peace.

The life of Jesus Christ outwardly was one of the most troubled lives in history—tempest and tumult, tumult and tempest, the waves breaking over it all the time until the worn body was laid in the grave. But the inner life was a sea of glass. The great calm was always there.

POSITIVE ATTITUDES AND STATEMENTS

Spiritual staleness makes us live a life of pieces rather than peace. Wholeness seems unattainable. Maturity seems a foolish quest. Order seems always out of reach. Fulfillment seems always impossible. Satisfaction is forever elusive.

Cultivating negative attitudes and making negative statements seems understandable. In the name of candor, we often whine. When we should be singing in the rain, we are whimpering in the sunshine.

As with the nursery rhyme character Chicken Little, our sky always seems to be falling. "Out of the abundance of the heart the mouth speaketh" (Matthew 12:34) is of primary importance when we really want to find some answers.

Negative attitudes and negative statements are declarations of Satan's power. Constantly thinking and talking about how the devil is hindering you, how he is keeping you from success, how you always seem to be plagued by spiritual staleness, is an admission of defeat.

The Bible teaches that we should not "give place to the devil" (Ephesians 4:27). Negative attitudes and negative statements are spiritually draining. They drain your faith. They drain your hope. They drain your joy. They drain your peace.

By your attitude and by your conversation, you are either going to give God absolute dominion over you or you are going to give Satan dominion over you.

To be saved from sin, you must first confess the lordship of Jesus Christ (Romans 10:9).

Spiritual staleness is never welcome. Staleness is an unwelcome intruder. It does not belong in the life of a child of God. But it may become resident within you by an unconscious consent.

So often we accept the testimony of our physical and emotional circumstances instead of accepting the testimony of God's Word.

What does the Bible say? Ask that question on any subject. And then stand on that truth—the truth of God's Word—rather than any negative circumstance.

No, faith doesn't stick its head in the sand like an ostrich. Faith is aware of the negative circumstances. Faith, however, believes that God is abundantly able to deliver in spite of any negative circumstances.

What should we think? What attitudes should fill our minds? How should we pray? We should cultivate those attitudes and pray those prayers that are purely "Word-centered" and not experience-centered or circumstance-centered.

Practice it; it works! You may have been going in the wrong direction for so long that it seems difficult, but eventually you will start cultivating those attitudes and making those statements that will be Word-centered. Staleness will evaporate. Freshness will flow.

CONCLUSION

Here are some positive steps to whipping staleness:

1. Change your walk. Renounce the presence of unknown or unconfessed sin in your own life.

2. Change your talk. Declare the truth of God's Word rather than the illusions of your own feelings. Quote God's Word often and aloud—even to yourself when you first feel spiritual staleness setting in.

3. Change your values. Put first things first. Your own spiritual relationship with God can bring you "times of refreshing . . . from the presence of the Lord" (Acts 3:19).

To receive Christ is to receive a new spirit (see Ezekiel 11:19).

To receive Christ is to receive a new heart (see Psalms 51:10).

To receive Christ is to receive a new language (see Ephesians 4:29).

To receive Christ is to receive a new love (see 1 John 4:7).

To receive Christ is to receive a new mind (see Romans 12:2).

To receive Christ is to receive a new inner power (see 2 Corinthians 4:16).

To receive Christ is to receive a new song (see Revelation 15:3).

To receive Christ is to receive a new name (see Revelation 3:12).

To receive Christ is to receive a new life (see 2 Corinthians 5:17).

CALLED TO BE SAINTS

James A. Cross

SCRIPTURE: Romans 1:7; 1 Corinthians 1:2

INTRODUCTION

Saints are real, living, everyday people who are separated, dedicated, and blood-cleansed Christians. Alexander Maclaren said, "Saints are not an eminent sort of Christian, but all Christians are saints; and he who is not a saint is not a Christian." One little boy said, "A saint is a dead Christian." Not so. The Word of God makes living saints. This is our calling.

DEFINITION OF SAINTS

A. They are a people immersed in everyday work of the world but separated from the world (John 17:15).

B. They are a people dedicated to God's cause and work.

C. They are a people devoted to worship and service of God.

SAINTS ARE REFERRED TO AS

A. Sun, stars, light

B. Treasures, jewels, gold, silver

C. Lively stones, little children, obedient children

D. Trees planted by rivers

E. Vines, figs, fatted calves in a stall

F. Sometimes the persecuted ones

THE DESTINATION OF SAINTS

A. There is a day appointed for the saints' coronation.

"Be thou faithful unto death, and I will give thee a crown of life" (Revelation 2:10).

1. A crown of righteousness (2 Timothy 4:8)

   "And they had on their heads crowns of gold" (Revelation 4:4).

2. A crown of glory (1 Peter 5:4)

B. They shall reign with Christ.

C. They shall forever be with the Lord.

CONCLUSION

If a letter were sent to the saints in your town, would the letter be delivered to your address? God has some real-life saints dwelling everywhere upon the face of the earth. Continue being faithful and you will rejoice with the holy saints forever in the presence of God.

BY MY SPIRIT, SAITH THE LORD

Daniel Greenlee

SCRIPTURE: Zechariah 4:6-9

INTRODUCTION

After 70 years of captivity a remnant of the Israelites had returned under Zerubbabel's leadership and began to rebuild the Temple in Jerusalem. They had faced tremendous opposition, and after 16 years the Temple was still unfinished. In the midst of discouragement, God sent two prophets to stir up the people—Haggai to rebuke them for their apathy and Zechariah to encourage them to complete the task.

HISTORICAL BACKGROUND OF THE TIMES

HAGGAI, THE FIERY PREACHER (Haggai 1:1-9)

A. His rebuke for their materialism and loss of vision

B. His appeal to consider their ways

C. His challenge to build the Temple again

D. The people's response (v. 14)

ZECHARIAH, THE ENCOURAGER (Zechariah 4:6-9)

A. They shall succeed through God's Spirit.

B. Their obstacles shall be removed.

C. The task shall be completed.

D. The Temple will be completed by the grace of God.

E. Zerubbabel and the people responded (Ezra 5:1, 2).

APPLICATIONS

A. The church of Jesus Christ (Matthew 16:13-19)

B. The people of God (Philippians 1:6)

CONCLUSION

God's grace will continue to persist in the lives of His people to fulfill His will. Success for the things of the Kingdom is dependent upon the flow of His enabling Spirit, which is working in us and through us. As always, when the task is completed, there is a sense of understanding that it is by grace—not our own efforts but His ability which has been provided for us.

PURIFIED FOR A PURPOSE

Kenneth E. Hall

SCRIPTURE: John 15:3

INTRODUCTION

All too often in Christian circles, we tend to sidestep the importance of purity in our lives.

Obviously, in Jesus' eyes, being cleansed, or purity, was not unobtainable, but rather it was essential to His call to go into the harvest. We cannot reap a bountiful harvest for the Lord until we have been cleansed of our old man and made more like Christ. Purity is the personhood of God in our lives, and as such, it is essential to our very existence as Christians.

PURIFICATION BECOMES A PART OF OUR LIVES ONLY THROUGH A RELATIONSHIP WITH JESUS

A. Isaiah

B. Malachi

C. Jesus

PURIFICATION IS A NATURAL PROCESS THAT GOD PERFORMS IN OUR LIVES

A. By this transaction God can work in us and through us.

B. This does not mean perfection but cleansing.

C. It is for the glory of God.

PURIFICATION IS TO MAKE US PLIABLE FOR SERVICE

A. Hebrews 9:14 — to serve the living God

B. 1 Peter 1:22 — to love others

PURIFICATION KEEPS GOD'S PURPOSE FOR OUR LIVES FRESH AND NEW

A. We must renew our lives daily.

B. We must maintain a constant and continual relationship with Christ.

PURIFICATION WILL KEEP OUR LIVES BALANCED AND OUR FOCUS CLEAR

A. It gives purpose and meaning to our lives.

B. It brings a purified lifestyle.

CONCLUSION

Without purification, we cannot fulfill the purpose to which we have been called. There is no way we can grasp the true impact of purification without a committed life. Purification is not how a person acts; it is what he is. We are to allow God to purify our lives so that His Spirit may abound in us and flow out to a hurting, dying world.

A RIGHT-SIDE-UP MESSAGE FOR AN UPSIDE-DOWN WORLD

Doug Beacham

SCRIPTURE: 1 Thessalonians 1:1-10

INTRODUCTION

Use Acts 17:1-9 to show how the gospel preaching of Paul revealed the fundamental conflict between the kingdom of Christ and the kingdoms of the world. Show how the kingdoms of the world create an upside-down world when they fail to stand under the order of God's authority: Hitler's Nazism; Assyria's arrogance (Isaiah 10; 14:23-27); Babylonian arrogance (Daniel 5, 7).

RIGHT-SIDE-UP DISCIPLESHIP (1 Thessalonians 1:3)

A. Energizing faith

B. Loving service

C. Hope that stabilizes life

PROVING THE PRESENCE OF THE SPIRIT (1 Thessalonians 1:4-10)

A. Effects of Christian preaching

1. The Word

2. Power

      3. The Holy Spirit

      4. Deep conviction

  B. God's people respond to God's messengers.

      1. Learning to model (imitate) faithful Christians (Illustrate with Jesus, Paul, contemporary examples.)

        a. Affliction does not hinder receiving the Word.

        b. Affliction results in joy through the Holy Spirit.

      2. Willing to be a model for others

  C. God's people respond to God's message.

      1. Turn from idols to serve God (v. 9)

      2. Applications of the Lord's return (v. 10)

        a. The reality that He is risen

        b. Salvation in Christ gives us a changed status —from wrath to grace.

CONCLUSION

Use the "changed status" theme to show the changing from "upside-down" to "right-side-up" as we witness to the world through effective discipleship and life in the Spirit.

A DESTRUCTIVE FORCE

Elwood Matthews

SCRIPTURE: Proverbs 15:4; 18:21

INTRODUCTION

The little saying "Sticks and stones may break my bones, but words can never hurt me" sounds good enough, but many people have been destroyed by the words of others. You see, the tongue is a creative force, but it is also a destructive force.

THE TONGUE IS DESTRUCTIVE TO FAITH

Negative speech creates negative thinking.

    A. Israel at Kadesh-barnea (Numbers 13, 14)

        1. They are too strong.

        2. We saw the children of Anak.

        3. We are not able.

    B. Jews at Antioch in Pisidia (Acts 13)

        1. Paul preached Christ in the synagogue.

        2. Jews stirred up devout and honorable women.

        3. Paul and Barnabas were expelled from them.

THE TONGUE IS DESTRUCTIVE TO REPUTATION

A. Jewish leaders slandered Jesus.

   1. Sabbath breaker

   2. Coequal with God

   3. Beelzebub

B. Paul slandered by legalizing Jews

   1. Not an apostle

   2. Too liberal

THE TONGUE IS DESTRUCTIVE TO THE CHURCH

A. The Corinthian church (2 Corinthians 12:19-21)

   1. Paul had sent others when he couldn't come.

   2. He feared he might find debatings, envyings, wraths, backbitings, whisperings.

B. The Ephesian church (Ephesians 5:4)

   1. Foolish talking—idle or stupid talk

   2. Jesting—obscene and offensive conversation

C. The modern-day church

   1. Cliques

   2. Talebearing

   3. Critical of fellow members

   4. Matthew 12:37—"For by thy words thou shalt be justified, and by thy words thou shalt be condemned."

   Proverbs 18:6-8—"A fool's lips enter into contention, and his mouth calleth for strokes. A fool's mouth is his destruction, and his lips are the snare of his soul. The words of a talebearer are as wounds, and they go down into the innermost parts of the belly."

THE GLORY OF THE KING'S BIRTHDAY

H. Lynn Stone

SCRIPTURE: Luke 2:1-20

INTRODUCTION

It is a common custom of mankind worldwide to remember the day of one's birth. Furthermore, we generally count our age for an entire year from our birthday. From the time of one's 21st birthday he is 21 years old until his 22nd birthday. However, there is only one birthday that every nation on earth acknowledges, and that is the birthday of the King of Kings, Jesus of Nazareth. When one says, "This is the year 1990," that is a testimony of the 1990th year the birth of the King. It was a glorious birth that is universally celebrated even by nonbelievers.

THE GLORY OF THE ANNOUNCEMENT OF THE KING'S BIRTH

A. The glory of nature's announcement

1. The star of Bethlehem (Matthew 2:1-12)

2. The Dayspring from on high (Luke 1:78)

3. The day star (2 Peter 1:19-21)

B. The glory of the angelic announcement

1. To Zacharias (Luke 1:8-17)
2. To Mary (Luke 1:30-33)
3. To Joseph (Matthew 1:20-23)
4. To the shepherds (Luke 2:10-14)

THE GLORY OF THE PRAISE AT HIS BIRTH

A. Zacharias praised God for the Dayspring (Luke 1:67-79).

B. The shepherds praised God for the Savior (Luke 2:20).

C. The wise men praised God for the King (Matthew 2:2, 11).

D. Simeon praised God for the Light of the World (Luke 2:28-32).

E. Elizabeth praised God for the birth (Luke 1:41-45).

F. Mary praised God for mercy (Luke 1:46-55).

THE GLORY OF HIS NAME GIVEN AT BIRTH

A. The glory of His heavenly name, *Emmanuel*
   1. Its meaning—"God with us"
   2. Its prophecy (Isaiah 7:14)
   3. Its fulfillment (Matthew 1:18-25)

B. The glory of His earthly name, *Jesus*
   1. *Jesus* is the Lord's personal name.
   2. Its meaning—"The Lord is salvation."
   3. The reason (Matthew 1:21)
   4. The only Savior (Acts 4:12)

C. The glory of His title name, *Christ* (Messiah)
   1. Its meaning—"The Anointed One"
   2. He is anointed as prophet.
   3. He is anointed as priest.
   4. He is anointed as king.

CONCLUSION

The celebration of the King's birthday continues 1,990 years later. The list of guests has registered celebrities from every nation and culture in every year since His birth. All those who profess His name also participate in the glory of His birth.

I HAVE A SECRET

Sandra Goodwin Clopine

SCRIPTURE: Psalm 25:14; 91:1; Matthew 6:33; Romans 3:23

INTRODUCTION

In the "secret place" with God we find "our place" of service. Our intimacy with the King of Kings and Lord of Lords determines our sensitivity to all that concerns Him. I have a secret for a happy, abundant Christian life that He has shared with me. I want to share it with you.

DON'T KEEP SCORE (Psalm 91:1)

A. Make it a habit to give without expecting returns.

   1. Let God keep the record.

   2. "God loves us the way we are, but He loves us too much to leave us that way" (Leighton Ford).

B. Maintain your relationship with the Lord.

   1. Live in His abiding presence.

   2. Be active in the service of Christ, but don't forget to love Him.

DO NOT FORGET YOUR RIGHTS (Romans 3:23)

    A. Only God is just.

        1. He will never disappoint us.

        2. His Word shows true equality—*all* have sinned and *all* have come short.

    B. Only heaven is perfect.

        1. Some folks view life with the attitude, "Is that all there is?"

        2. Others praise God for their future hope.

DETERMINE TO CENTER ON CHRIST (Matthew 6:33)

    A. For confidence

        1. Someone said, "I asked God for all things that I might enjoy life: God gave me life that I might enjoy all things."

        2. We can focus our attention on everything that goes wrong, or we can rejoice in the strength God gives.

    B. For fearlessness

        1. Inner peace replaces doubt.

        2. One writer penned, "Courage is fear which has said its prayer."

CONCLUSION

"A dew drop does the will of God as much as a thunderstorm" (anonymous). The Lord does not always manifest Himself in great actions. Sometimes His greatest activity is expressed in those secret moments we spend with Him.

ESSENCE OF DELIVERANCE

Roy H. Hicks

SCRIPTURE: 2 Corinthians 1:10

INTRODUCTION

In one verse of Scripture we have the story of God's power to deliver us. It is a complete delivery—from the cradle to the grave.

PAST DELIVERANCE

A. From our sins (Isaiah 53:4-6)

B. From sickness (1 Peter 2:24)

We need only to believe to receive. It is already finished for us.

PRESENT DELIVERANCE

A. In temptations (Hebrews 4:14-16)

B. In trials (Hebrews 7:25)

He, as our high priest, is yet involved with our deliverance. This present-tense work of our Lord Jesus is constant.

FUTURE DELIVERANCE

A. From death (1 Corinthians 15:51-57)

B. From destruction (1 Thessalonians 5:1-10)

Jesus, as our prophet, delivered us from sin and sickness. As our high priest He is now delivering us from temptation and trials. Now, as our coming king, He will yet deliver us from death and destruction.

CONCLUSION

The Bible does not teach that we are destroyed for lack of worship, praise, or enthusiasm. It does teach that we are destroyed for lack of knowledge. Christians must know what belongs to them through the finished work of our Lord Jesus on the cross. What He has done as our prophet, what He is now doing as our high priest, and what He is yet to do as our coming king must be recognized and acted upon.

WITH CHRIST IN THE UPPER ROOM

(First in a Series of Six)

Joel Hobbs

SCRIPTURE: John 13-17

INTRODUCTION

John 13 introduces us to an extended series of discourses, all given on Thursday of Holy Week, containing some of the most profound statements that ever passed our Lord's lips and spoken only to His disciples. These words, including the High Priestly Prayer in chapter 17, thus embracing five chapters, compose almost one-fourth of John's Gospel. While the other three Gospels give us an account of the institution of the Lord's Supper (and John does not), the apostle does give us the story of Christ's washing the disciples' feet, which is omitted by the other Gospels.

These five chapters of this Gospel (13-17) are marked off as a distinct section of the book, first by their historical setting and second by their special character. The importance of this special portion of our Lord's ministry is evident by the space it occupies, being little less than a fourth of the whole Gospel. The 12 previous chapters cover a period of nearly three years; these chapters are the record of a single evening. The previous 12 chapters rang through Judea, Samaria, and Galilee in places such as the wilderness, on the seaboard, in the streets, in the synagogue, and most often in the Temple itself. The events in these five chapters take place in a single chamber of a private house. In the previous chapters we are aware of the presence of the multitudes, all classes of disciples, hearers, observers, opponents; in these only the smaller circle of the disciples are present, which may be called the Lord's own family.

In every great biography you will find that the last few days and the death of the character are passed over in a few pages, or at least in a single chapter. In John's account of the life of Christ this is reversed. Thus the entire section from John 12:12-20:25 is devoted exclusively to a record of the last eight days of our Lord's life on earth.

HIS BEQUEST—What Christ Left Us When He Went Away

HE LEFT US AN EXAMPLE OF TRUE SERVANT-LEADERSHIP (John 13:1-17)

    A. The mind of Christ (John 13:1-3)

        1. The knowledge of Christ (vv. 1-3)

            a. He knew that His hour was come (v. 1).

            (Note the use of the word *hour* in John's Gospel: John 4:21, 23; 7:30; 12:23; 13:1; 17:1)

            b. He knew He was going to depart out of the world unto the Father (v. 1).

        2. His love for His own (v. 1)

            a. What were His thoughts concerning them?

            Peter . . . John . . . James . . . Judas . . .

            b. He was to express this later.

        3. Other factors in the knowledge of Christ (v. 3)

            a. That the Father had given all things into His hands —*authority*

            b. That He came forth from God—*procession*

            c. That He was going to God—*ascension*

    B. The act of Christ (John 13:4-11)

        1. The dissension of the disciples

        Luke's account of dissension during the passover —"And there was also a strife among them, which of them should be accounted the greatest" (Luke 22:24; see also vv. 25-30).

2. The custom of washing feet

3. The action of Jesus (vv. 4-11)

    a. He riseth . . . laid aside . . . took . . . poured . . . began to wash . . . to wipe . . . clothed Himself . . . sat down (*cf.*, Philippians 2:1-11).

    b. Jesus had taught humility by

        (1) *Precept*—"He that shall humble himself shall be exalted" (Matthew 23:12).

        (2) *Parable* as in the story of the Pharisee and the publican (Luke 18:9-14).

        (3) *Example* as when He took a child in His arms (Luke 9:46-48).

        (4) And now *condescension* (John 13:4, 5).

        (5) Peter and Jesus (John 13:6-9)

C. The instruction of Christ (John 13:12-17)

    1. "Know ye what I have done to you?" (v. 12).

      a. He acknowledged that He was their Lord and Master (v. 13).

      b. He demonstrated their love duty to wash one another's feet (v. 14).

      c. "I have given you an example" (v. 15).

      d. A principle: "The servant is not greater than his lord" (v. 16).

    2. *A comment*: William Barclay says, "When we are tempted to think of our dignity, our prestige, our place, our rights . . . let us see again the picture of the Son of God, girt with a towel, and kneeling at His disciples feet."

HE LEFT US A NEW LOVE COMMANDMENT (John 13:34, 35)

"A new commandment I give unto you, That ye love one another; as I have loved you, that ye also love one another. By this shall all men know that ye are my disciples, if ye have love one to another."

A. As a commandment love was not new.

1. The old commandment was "Love thy neighbour *as thyself*."

2. The new commandment is "Love one another *as I have loved you*."

B. The use of the word *new* in the Scriptures.

1. Contrast the two Greek words *kainos* and *neos*, both translated "new" in the King James Version.

2. The measure of our love for one another is set by Christ's love for us.

C. How did Christ love His disciples?

1. He loved them unselfishly.

2. He loved them sacrificially.

3. He loved them understandingly.

4. He loved them forgivingly.

HE LEFT US THE PROMISE OF SHARING THE FATHER'S HOUSE (John 14:2, 3)

"In my Father's house are many mansions: if it were not so, I would have told you. I go to prepare a place for you. And if I go and prepare a place for you, I will come again, and receive you unto myself; that where I am, there ye may be also."

A. Heaven is God's dwelling place (1 Kings 8:30; Matthew 6:9).

1. There He is Lord of heaven (Daniel 5:23; Matthew 11:25).

2. He reigns in heaven (Psalm 11:4; 135:6; Daniel 4:35).

3. He answers His people from heaven (1 Chronicles 21:26; 2 Chronicles 7:14; Nehemiah 9:27; Psalm 20:6).

4. He sends His judgment from heaven (Genesis 19:24; 1 Samuel 2:10; Daniel 4:13, 14; Romans 1:18).

B. Saints have a link with heaven.

1. Their names are written there (Luke 10:20; Hebrews 12:23).

2. They lay up treasures there (Matthew 6:20; Luke 12:33).

3. They will be rewarded there (Matthew 5:12; 1 Peter 1:4).

C. The conditions of heaven are described.

1. There will be no sorrow (Revelation 7:17; 21:4).

No curse (22:3)

No pain (21:4)

No night (22:5)

No death (21:4)

No corruption (1 Corinthians 15:42, 50)

2. *But* there will be joy in heaven (Psalm 16:11; Luke 15:7, 10), treasures (Matthew 6:20; 19:21) and, right-eousness (2 Peter 3:13).

HE LEFT US HIS NAME AND ITS AUTHORITY (John 14:13, 14)

"And whatsoever ye shall ask in my name, that will I do, that the Father may be glorified in the Son. If ye shall ask any thing in my name, I will do it" (cf. 16:23, 24).

A. The power and authority of the name of Jesus is shown.

1. The Father's bestowal (Philippians 2:9-11).

2. By His achievements

3. By virtue of His deity

B. Believers are to use the name of Jesus in salvation (Matthew 1:21; Acts 4:12); in baptism (Matthew 28:19); in healing (Acts 3:6, 7, 16); in preaching (Luke 24:47; Acts 8:12); in miracles (Acts 3:16; 4:30); in judgment (1 Corinthians 5:1-5); in appeals to others (1 Corinthians 1:10); in prayer (John 14:12-15; 16:23-26); in all gatherings (Matthew 18:20); in singing (Romans 15:9); in combat (Mark 16:17; Luke 10:17; Ephesians 6:10-18); and in all things (Ephesians 5:20; Colossians 3:17).

HE LEFT US THE PROMISE OF THE HOLY SPIRIT (John 14:16, 17)

"And I will pray the Father, and he shall give you another Comforter, that he may abide with you for ever; Even the Spirit of truth; whom the world cannot receive, because it seeth him not, neither knoweth him: but ye know him; for he dwelleth with you, and shall be in you."

A. Christ will intercede for the Spirit to be sent. "I will pray the Father . . . " (v. 16).

B. The Spirit will be the Father's gift. "I will pray the Father, and he shall give you another Comforter" (v. 16).

　　1. The use of the word *Comforter*

　　　　a. One called to the side of another for help or counsel.

　　　　b. The word is used by John 14:16, 26; 15:26; 16:7, and 1 John 2:1, where it is rendered "advocate."

　　2. The use of the word *another*—from the Greek word *allos*—expresses a numerical difference and denotes another of the same sort or kind.

C. The work of the Holy Spirit is revealed by Christ to His disciples.

　　1. He will be an abiding and indwelling Spirit (John 14:16).

　　2. He will be a teaching Spirit (14:26).

　　3. He will be a reminding Spirit (14:26).

　　4. He will be a testifying Spirit (15:26).

　　5. He will be a reproving Spirit (16:8).

　　6. He will be a guiding Spirit into all truth (16:13).

　　7. He will be a revealing Spirit (16:13).

　　8. He will be a glorifying Spirit (16:14).

CONCLUSION

Our greatest need is a deeper disclosure of Jesus Christ —who He is, the power of His atoning death, and the strength that can come from His indwelling. The Holy Spirit can make this known to us as He glorifies Christ in our hearts.

CHRIST'S HIGH-PRIESTLY PRAYER
(Second in a Series of Six)

Joel Hobbs

SCRIPTURE: John 17:1-26

INTRODUCTION

There are a number of the prayers of Christ recorded in the New Testament. Among all the prayers of Christ, this prayer stands by itself. In the prayer He solemnly presents Himself, His work and His people to the Father.

CHRIST'S PRAYER FOR HIMSELF (John 17:1-8)

A. The request to be glorified by the Father (v. 1)
  1. "The hour is come"—an hour fixed by God, the supreme hour of the world's history, the hour to which all other dispensations were preparatory.
  2. "Glorify thy Son"—by enthroning Him at Your right hand, by sending down the Holy Spirit, by putting all enemies under His feet.
  3. "That thy Son may glorify thee" (see also 1 Corinthians 15:24-28).

B. The Father's gift of authority to the Son (vv. 2, 3)
  1. Authority over all flesh

2. That He should give eternal life

3. Christ's definition of eternal life

C. His declarations to His Father (vv. 4-8)

1. "I have glorified thee on the earth" (v. 4).

2. "I have finished the work which thou gavest me to do" (v. 4).

3. "I have manifested thy name" (v. 6).

4. "I have given unto them the words which thou gavest me" (v. 8).

CHRIST'S PRAYER FOR ALL BELIEVERS: THE PETITIONS (John 17:9-24)

A. He prays that they might be kept by the Father's name (vv. 11, 12).

1. They are in the world.

2. "Holy Father, keep . . ."

B. He prays that they might have His joy fulfilled in them (v. 13).

C. He prays that they might be kept from the Evil One (vv. 14-16).

D. He prays that they might be sanctified through the truth (vv. 17-19).

E. He prays for their unity and oneness (vv. 20-23).

F. He prays that they might behold His glory (v. 24).

CHRIST'S CONCLUDING REASSERTION OF HIS PURPOSE FOR HIS OWN (John 17:25, 26)

A. They believe Christ was sent by the Father (v. 25).

B. Christ has declared unto them the Father's name (v. 26).

C. The purpose of all this is that the love of the Father and the Son might abide in them (v. 26).

CONCLUSION

What should be our response to this prayer?

1. We should know we can have confidence in the Father's power to keep us.

2. We should appropriate Christ's joy.

3. We should strive for the unity that Christ so earnestly prayed for.

4. We should anticipate sharing His glory.

THE HOLY SPIRIT:
HIS PERSONALITY AND DEITY
(Third in a Series of Six)

Joel Hobbs

SCRIPTURE: John 14:16; 15:26

INTRODUCTION

It is vital to an understanding of the Holy Spirit that we clearly see the truth of His personality and deity.

THE HOLY SPIRIT—HIS PERSONALITY

The first question that confronts us is, Who is the Holy Spirit? The Holy Spirit is a divine person coequal and coexistent with the Father and the Son (or the eternal Word).

A. The Holy Spirit is a person.

Three things are combined in personality; namely, intelligence, emotion, and volition (intellect, sensibility, and will). The Holy Spirit is a person possessed of intelligence, emotion, and volition in an infinite degree.

B. The personality of the Holy Spirit is set forth in the following biblical facts:

1. Personal names are given to the Holy Spirit.

a. The Comforter (John 14:16; 15:26; 16:7)

b. The Holy Ghost or Holy Spirit (Matthew 28:19; Acts 2:4)

2. Personal pronouns are used of Him (see John 14:16-26; 15:26; 16:7-15).

3. Personal association with the Father and the Son indicate personality.

   a. The baptismal formula (Matthew 28:19)

   b. The apostolic benediction (2 Corinthians 13:14)

4. Personal attributes and works are ascribed to Him.

   These are personal activities: He speaks, searches, wills; reveals, commands, guides, makes intercession, chooses church leaders, orders the affairs of the church. (See Acts 13; 20:28; Romans 8:26, 27; 1 Corinthians 2:10, 11; 12:8-11).

5. Personal treatment is ascribed to Him.

   He can be blasphemed (Matthew 12:31, 32); lied to (Acts 5:3, 4); tempted (Acts 5:9); resisted (Acts 7:51); grieved (Ephesians 4:30); quenched (1 Thessalonians 5:19).

THE HOLY SPIRIT—HIS DEITY

The deity of the Holy Spirit is set forth in the following manner:

A. He is spoken of as God (see Acts 5:3, 4; 1 Corinthians 3:16; 6:19; 12:4-6).

B. Divine attributes are ascribed to Him.

   1. Eternity (Hebrews 9:14)

   2. Omnipotence (Luke 1:35; Acts 10:38)

   3. Omniscience (John 14:26; 16:12, 13; 1 Corinthians 2:10, 11)

   4. Omnipresence (Psalm 139:7-10)

C. Divine works are ascribed to Him.

   1. Creation (Job 33:4; Psalm 104:30)

   2. Regeneration (John 3:5-8)

   3. Resurrection (Romans 8:11)

D. Association with the Father and the Son

   1. In the Great Commission (Matthew 28:19, 20)

2. In the apostolic benediction (2 Corinthians 13:14)

3. In administration of the church (1 Corinthians 12:4-6)

THE HOLY SPIRIT IN HIS RELATIONSHIP TO BELIEVERS
(Fourth in a Series of Six)

Joel Hobbs

SCRIPTURE: John 16:13, 14; Acts 13:2

INTRODUCTION

So often we have a tendency to depersonalize the Holy Spirit without realizing that in so doing we miss something of is tender touch upon our lives.

The Holy Spirit is personally interested and involved in bringing each of us into a true living relationship with the Lord Jesus Christ.

Note His personal activities in relation to us.

HE REGENERATES US, ATTENDING OUR SPIRIT-BIRTH AND STARTING US ON THIS NEW LIFE ADVENTURE

    A. John 3:3—"Jesus answered him, I assure you, most solemnly I tell you, that unless a person is born again (anew, from above), he cannot ever see—know, be acquainted with [and experience]—the kingdom of God" (*Amp.*)

    B. How is this accomplished?

John 3:5—"Except a man be born of water and (even) the Spirit, he cannot [ever] enter the kingdom of God" (*Amp.*).

Titus 3:5, 6—"He saved us, not because of any works of righteousness that we had done, but because of His own pity and mercy, by [the] cleansing (bath) of the new birth (regeneration) and renewing of the Holy Spirit, which He poured out [so] richly upon us through Jesus Christ our Savior" (*Amp.*).

HE FILLS OUR LIVES WITH JOY, PEACE, AND HOPE

Romans 15:13—"Now the God of hope fill you with all joy and peace in believing, that ye may abound in hope, through the power of the Holy Ghost."

Three great words are presented here: We are filled with *joy, peace, hope.*

HE SHEDS HIS LOVE IN OUR HEARTS

A. Romans 5:5—"God's love has been poured out in our hearts through the Holy Spirit Who has been given to us" (*Amp.*).

B. Romans 15:30—"I appeal to you—I entreat you—brethren, for the sake of our Lord Jesus Christ and by the love [given by] the Spirit, to unite with me in earnest wrestling in prayer to God in my behalf" (*Amp.*).

C. Colossians 1:8—"Who also declared unto us your love in the [Holy] Spirit" (*Amp.*).

Summary note: The four great blessings that come to those who are in Christ are (1) joy, (2) peace, (3) hope, and (4) love. These are four things no man can have in their fullness while living in sin and rebellion against the Lord.

HE GIVES DIVINE UTTERANCE TO THOSE WHO WISH TO SING, PRAY, AND WORSHIP IN THE SPIRIT (John 4:24)

The Father's search of worshipers:

A. Acts 2:4—"They were all filled with the Holy Ghost, and

began to speak with other tongues, as the Spirit gave them gave them utterance."

B. Acts 10:45, 46—"The free gift of the Holy Spirit had been bestowed and poured out largely even on the Gentiles. For they heard them talking in [unknown] languages and extolling and magnifying God" (*Amp.*).

C. 1 Corinthians 14:15—"Then what am I to do? I will pray with my spirit—by the Holy Spirit that is within me; but I will also pray intelligently—with my mind and understanding; I will sing with my spirit—by the Holy Spirit that is within me; but I will sing (intelligently) with my mind and understanding also" (*Amp.*).

D. Ephesians 6:18—"Pray at all times—on every occasion, in in every season—in the Spirit, with all [manner of] prayer and entreaty. To that end keep alert and watch with strong purpose and perseverance, interceding in behalf of all the saints (God's consecrated people)" (*Amp.*).

E. Jude 20—"But you, beloved, build yourselves up [founded] on your most holy faith—make progress, rise like an edifice higher and higher—praying in the Holy Spirit" (*Amp.*).

F. Ephesians 5:18, 19—"And be not drunk with wine, wherein is excess; but be filled with the Spirit; Speaking to yourselves in psalms and hymns and spiritual songs, singing and making melody in your heart to the Lord."

The Amplified Bible: "But ever be filled and stimulated with the (Holy) Spirit. . . . Speak out to one another in psalms and hymns and spiritual songs, offering praise with voices [and instruments], and making melody with all your heart to the Lord."

HE LIBERATES OUR LIVES FROM SIN AND SPIRITUAL BONDAGE

A. Romans 8:2—"For the law of the Spirit of life [which is] in Christ Jesus [the law of our new being], has freed me from the law of sin and death" (*Amp.*).

B. 2 Corinthians 3:17—"Now the Lord is the Spirit, and where the Spirit of the Lord is, there is liberty—emancipation from bondage, freedom" (*Amp.*).

C. Isaiah 61:1—"The Spirit of the Lord God is upon me,

because the Lord has anointed and qualified me to preach the Gospel of good tidings to the meek, the poor and afflicted; He has sent me to bind up and heal the brokenhearted, to proclaim liberty to the [physical and spiritual] captives, and the opening of the prison and of the eyes to those that are bound" (*Amp.*).

Note: Believers in bondage need the delivering liberty that the Spirit gives. So many believers are bound by fear, doubt, bitterness, and inability to worship God freely, but the Holy Spirit releases us to true freedom and trust.

HE STRENGTHENS US IN THE INNER MAN AND CAUSES US TO WALK IN GOD'S WAYS

A. The strengthening of the inner man:

Ephesians 3:16—"May He grant you out of the rich treasury of His glory to be strengthened and reinforced with mighty power in the inner man by the (Holy) Spirit [Himself]—indwelling your innermost being and personality" (*Amp.*).

B. It is by His power and leadership that we are able to overcome the flesh:

Galatians 5:16—"But I say, walk and live habitually in the (Holy) Spirit—responsive to and controlled and guided by the Spirit; then you will certainly not gratify the cravings and desires of the flesh—of human nature without God" (*Amp.*).

Note: These works of the flesh are mentioned in verses 19-21.

HE PROTECTS US FROM THE ENEMY

A. Isaiah 59:19—"When the enemy shall come in like a flood, the Spirit of the Lord will lift up a standard against him and put him to flight—for He will come like a rushing stream which the breath of the Lord drives" (*Amp.*).

B. Our enemy is Satan:

1 Peter 5:8—"That enemy of yours, the devil, roams around like a lion roaring [in fierce hunger], seeking someone to seize upon and devour" (*Amp.*).

C. The Holy Spirit gives us power and lifts up a standard against him.

HE REFRESHES THE THIRSTY AND GIVES REST TO THE WEARY

A. John 7:37-39—"Out from His innermost being springs and rivers of living water shall flow (continuously)" (v. 38, *Amp.*).

B. Isaiah 63:14—"As the cattle that go down into the valley [to find better pasturage, refuge and rest], the Spirit of the Lord caused them to rest" (*Amp.*).

C. Release in the Spirit refreshes:

Isaiah 28:11, 12—"For with stammering lips and another tongue will he speak to this people. To whom he said, This is the rest wherewith ye may cause the weary to rest; and this is the refreshing: yet they would not hear."

THE GIFTS OF THE HOLY SPIRIT

(Fifth in a Series of Six)

Joel Hobbs

SCRIPTURE: 1 Corinthians 12, 13, 14 (An Overview)

INTRODUCTION

Note the significance of the number *three*.

THREE CHAPTERS

A. 1 Corinthians 12—gifts of the Spirit and the body of Christ

B. 1 Corinthians 13—the motivation of spiritual gifts

C. 1 Corinthians 14—the explanation of gifts and their reputation

THREE DIVINE PERSONS (1 Corinthians 12:4-6)

A. Spirit—gifts (v. 4)

B. Lord—administrations (v. 5)

C. God—operations (v. 6)

THERE IS THE MANIFESTATION OF THREE ATTRIBUTES OF THE HOLY SPIRIT (1 Corinthians 12:7-11)

A. Omniscience—revelation gifts

B. Omnipotence—power gifts

C. Omnipresence—inspiration gifts

THREE CATEGORIES OF GIFTS (1 Corinthians 12:7-11)

A. Revelation gifts (mind gifts)

1. Word of wisdom (v. 8)

2. Word of knowledge (v. 8)

3. Discerning of spirits (v. 10)

B. Power gifts (hand)

1. Faith (v. 9)

2. Gifts of healing (v. 9)

3. Working of miracles (v. 10)

C. Inspiration gifts (tongue)

1. Prophecy (v. 10)

2. Divers kings of tongues (v. 10)

3. Interpretation of tongues (v. 10)

A THREEFOLD RELATIONSHIP OF THE MEMBERS OF THE BODY

A. Organically related

B. Cooperatively related

C. Sympathetically related

CONCLUSION

The number *three* has been recognized as the number of Divinity. These three chapters of 1 Corinthians have all the marks of supernatural life stamped on them.

Let us seek the best gifts (12:31).

SPEAKING IN TONGUES
(Sixth in a Series of Six)

Joel Hobbs

SCRIPTURE: 1 Corinthians 14

INTRODUCTION

The apostle Paul wrote and spoke much about the subject of speaking in other tongues. Speaking in tongues was a vital part of his spiritual life, for he stated, "I thank my God, I speak with tongues more than ye all" (1 Corinthians 14:18).

The purpose of this study is to set forth major reasons why all believers should speak in tongues and to help them see the blessings which can be theirs through appropriating the power and inspiration of the Holy Spirit daily.

Chapter 14 is used by many to negate the value of speaking in tongues and to exalt prophecy above tongues. However, a careful reading of this chapter will reveal many positive and instructive truths about speaking in tongues.

Consider the following positive statements.

"HE THAT SPEAKETH IN AN UNKNOWN TONGUE SPEAKETH . . . UNTO GOD" (1 Corinthians 14:2)

A. Tongues are addressed to God.

B. Prophecy is addressed to men for their edification, exhortation, and comfort (v. 3).

"HE THAT SPEAKETH IN AN UNKNOWN TONGUE SPEAKETH MYSTERIES" (1 Corinthians 14:2)

The *Amplified Bible* reads, "In the (Holy) Spirit he utters secret truths and hidden things [not obvious to the understanding]."

"HE THAT SPEAKETH IN AN UNKNOWN TONGUE EDIFIETH HIMSELF" (1 Corinthians 14:4)

A. 1 Corinthians 14:4—"He who speaks in a [strange tongue] edifies and improves himself" (*Amp.*).

B. Jude 20—"But ye, beloved, building up yourselves on your most holy faith, praying in the Holy Ghost."

C. Isaiah 28:11, 12—Isaiah speaks of this as a refreshing: "For with stammering lips and another tongue will he speak to this people. To whom he said, This is the rest wherewith ye may cause the weary to rest; and this is the refreshing: yet they would not hear."

D. This edification does not involve the mind since the speaker does not understand what he has said. It is a personal edification in the area of the emotions, of deepening conviction, of fuller commitment and greater love.

HE THAT SPEAKS IN TONGUES PRAYS WITH HIS SPIRIT

A. 1 Corinthians 14:14—"For if I pray in an unknown tongue, my spirit prayeth, but my understanding is unfruitful."

B. 1 Corinthians 14:15—"I will pray with the spirit."

C. Man is body, soul, and spirit (1 Thessalonians 5:23; Hebrews 4:12).

D. The Holy Spirit can transcend our thought processes and make intercession for us (see Romans 8:26, 27).

HE THAT SPEAKS IN TONGUES GIVES THANKS WELL

This is the highest form of praise.

A. 1 Corinthians 14:15, 16—"I will sing with the Spirit. . . . Bless with the spirit."

B. Luke 1:46, 47—"And Mary said, My soul doth magnify the Lord, and my spirit hath rejoiced in God my Saviour."

C. Acts 10:46—"They heard them speak with tongues, and magnify God."

HE THAT SPEAKS IN TONGUES EDIFIES THE CHURCH WHEN THE TONGUES ARE INTERPRETED

A. The interpretation of tongues becomes prophecy or its equivalent.

1 Corinthians 14:5—"For greater is he that prophesieth than he that speaketh with tongues, *except* he interpret, *that the church may receive edifying.*"

1 Corinthians 14:13—"Wherefore let him that speaketh in an unknown tongue pray that he may interpret."

B. In its notes on 1 Corinthians 14:5, the *New International Version Study Bible* says, *"He who prophesies is greater.* Because he serves the common good more effectively since what he says can be understood and thus edifies the church. *Unless he interprets.* If the tongues-speaker also has the gift of interpretation, his speaking is as beneficial as prophecy, for then it can be understood" (see v. 13).

CONCLUSION

This is a limited overview of speaking in tongues but is sufficient to point out that the experience is one of great joy to the believer, assuring him of the presence of the Holy Spirit in his life.

HOLINESS

R. Edward Davenport

SCRIPTURE: Hebrews 12:14

INTRODUCTION

The word *holiness* is found 43 times in the Bible. *Holy* and its derivatives and *sanctify* and its derivatives come from the same root in both Greek and Hebrew. Our Declaration of Faith states, "Holiness . . . [is] God's standard of living for His people."

Holiness is not (1) a denomination, (2) a movement, (3) a certain social order, (4) a certain dress code, or (5) a man-made theology. It is a divine attribute of God.

WHAT HOLINESS IS NOT

To understand what it is, let us look first at what it is not.

    A. It is not eradication of sin.

        1. Sin nature is not totally removed.

        2. If so,

           a. No more death

           b. Children not born fallen

        3. This is contrary to life experience.

4. It is unscriptural (1 John 1:8).

B. It is not legalism.
1. It is not just keeping rules and regulations.
2. We can't *do* enough to be holy.
3. Law fails to sanctify (Romans 6).
4. Paul says in Romans 8:3 . . . .
5. Paul illustrates this in Romans 9:31.

C. It is not asceticism.
1. This means self-denial.
2. This is human attempt to subdue flesh.
3. It comes from ancient heathenism.
4. Paul illustrates Israel's attempt in Romans 10:2, 3.

THE TRUE NATURE OF HOLINESS

Now we see the qualities and true nature of holiness.

A. Separation
1. Holiness separates God from all else.
2. Man can experience holiness.
3. God separates man from sin.
4. God sanctifies him.
5. This is divine deliverance.

B. Dedication
1. This is a commitment to.
2. Holy people are committed to
   a. God
   b. Jesus Christ
   c. Holy Spirit
   d. Home
   e. Church
   f. Community
3. This commitment makes us willing to suffer (Acts 20:24).

C. Purification
1. A condition of holiness
2. A partaking of divine nature

      3. Paul says in Hebrews 9:13, 14 . . . .

      4. Also read 2 Corinthians 6:14—7:1.

  D. Consecration

      1. This means to "fill one's hands for service."

      2. It means to live out the holy life.

      3. The Word tells us we are

        a. Called to holiness (1 Peter 1:14, 15).

        b. To follow holiness (Hebrews 12:14).

        c. To mature in holiness (2 Corinthians 7:1).

  E. Service

      1. It prepares us for holy service.

      2. We will desire to labor for the Lord.

      3. Scripture says we are to

        a. Offer spiritual gifts (1 Peter 2:5).

        b. Give sacrifice of praise (Hebrews 13:15).

        c. Be a living sacrifice (Romans 12:1).

      4. This is "reasonable" service.

WHEN ARE WE SANCTIFIED?

There has long been a great debate.

  A. Is it instant and complete or progressive?

  B. Four terms describe it.

      1. Instantaneous: at new birth

      2. Positional: in Christ

      3. Progressive: lifelong experience

      4. Practical: perfected daily

HOW IS IT OBTAINED?

Three essential ways:

  A. The blood

      1. Gives us eternal sanctification

      2. 1 John 1:7-10

      3. Hebrews 10:14

  B. The Holy Spirit

      1. Gives us internal sanctification

    2. 2 Thessalonians 2:13

    3. 1 Peter 1:2

C. The Word

    1. Gives us external sanctification

    2. John 15:3

    3. John 17:17

    4. Ephesians 5:25, 26

    5. Psalm 119:9

CONCLUSION

Our holiness is a gift of God through His Son, Jesus Christ, and has its spiritual and literal application through the blood, the Spirit, and the Word of God!

MAN ON THE RUN

Edgar R. Lee

SCRIPTURE: Genesis 28:10-22

INTRODUCTION

A few years ago the media reported that in metropolitan Atlanta, with a population at that time of less than 1.5 million people, there were over 1 million auto trips daily which did not go out of the area. How illustrative of the fact that we Americans are constantly on the run. Many of these trips are necessary for our modern lifestyles. But at the same time, our frenetic travel may well betray an inner restlessness traceable to our alienation from God, others, and our true selves. So it was with Jacob in this passage!

RUNNING FROM THE PAST

A. Jacob sinned against his father, Isaac, and his brother, Esau, by deceiving them to gain prematurely the blessing of the oldest son (Genesis 27:1-29), although God had already promised that the elder would serve the younger (25:23).

B. When we sin against God and others, we sow the seeds

of our own destruction. Esau banked his flaming anger and plotted to kill Jacob for cheating him (27:41).

C. Sin results in broken hearts. Rebekah was forced to send her favorite son, Jacob, away for 20 years, never to see him again.

D. So in this text we see Jacob running from the consequences of his sins.

Instead of happiness and satisfaction, his sin brought flight, loneliness, sorrow, and insecurity. His life was a shambles.

HOPING FOR A FUTURE

A. Though a fugitive, Jacob, like all of us, hoped for someone to love. His father commanded, "'Take a wife . . . from among the daughters of Laban'" (28:2, *NIV*).

B. Fearful in that lonely place, Jacob soon expressed his desire for security: "'. . . watch over me . . . so that I return safely'" (vv. 20, 21, *NIV*).

C. Bereft of the abundant supply of his affluent home, Jacob now coveted an adequate livelihood: "'. . . give me food to eat and clothes to wear'" (v. 20, *NIV*).

D. Already homesick, he prayed to "'. . . return safely to my father's house'" (v. 21, *NIV*).

Lying there alone under the stars, Jacob must have realized how precarious were all his dreams, given the unexpected consequences of his sins.

ENCOUNTER IN THE PRESENT

A. Caught in a lonely place between a ruined past and a doubtful future, Jacob for the first time was a candidate, emotionally and spiritually, for an encounter with the living God.

B. During Jacob's troubled sleep, God took the initiative and in a powerful dream gave the suffering deceiver a glorious, transforming vision of Himself (vv. 12, 13).

C. Revealing Himself as the God of Jacob's grandfather, Abraham, and father, Isaac, God then promised the covenant blessings to the newly sensitive wanderer and assured him of his return home (vv. 13-15).

D. Upon awakening, Jacob made a heartfelt, binding response:

"'If God will be with me . . . then the Lord will be my God. . . . I will give you a tenth'" (vv. 20-22, *NIV*).

Jacob awoke the next morning with a second chance at the future because of his transforming encounter with the living God. Beginning at Bethel, God blessed Jacob and led him to greatness.

CONCLUSION

Though we may be in headlong flight from our guilt and despair, knowing that we too have ruined our past and endangered our future, God desires to reveal Himself to us, forgive our sins, and guarantee our future.

RECIPE FOR ENDURANCE

Joaquin Garrison

SCRIPTURE: Matthew 24:13; James 5:11

INTRODUCTION

If one is to live an overcoming Christian life, he must have the biblical character trait of endurance. A clear difference exists between the world's interpretation of endurance and the Scriptures'. The world says, "What can't be cured must be endured," but this is scarcely the endurance of the Scriptures. The world's type of endurance provides no joy at all; it is forced submission to necessity. The endurance of the Bible is of a happier character.

The imprisonment of Paul and Silas at Philippi is a good example of Christian endurance. Their situation was not accepted in a joyless manner. They had no choice in what came their way, only in their response to the given circumstances.

Endurance is a character trait all Christians must add to their faith. Three ingredients make up the recipe for this endurance. Let us examine them carefully.

FAITH

A. The shield of faith—"Take unto you the whole armour of God. . . . Above all, taking the shield of faith, wherewith ye shall be able to quench all the fiery darts of the wicked" (Ephesians 6:13, 16). Without the protection of this shield, one would find endurance impossible.

1. A shield is not a weapon.

2. A shield is a protective item of armor, guarding the soldier amid blows and buffetings. We have no control over what comes our way while under Satan's attacks, only in how we respond.

B. This shield enables us to "take a licking and keep on ticking." "This is the victory that overcometh the world, even our faith" (1 John 5:4). Remember our text: "He that shall endure unto the end . . . shall be saved" (Matthew 24:13).

LOVE

A. Love "endureth all things" (1 Corinthians 13:7).

1. This love enables us to love, accept, and forgive without limitations.

2. "Charity [love] shall cover the multitude of sins" (1 Peter 4:8).

3. This love "beareth all things" (1 Corinthians 13:7).

B. Our Lord empowers His children to endure by this love He kindles in their heart. Where *agape* love is present, power to endure is present. (Love is also one of the fruit of the Spirit.)

INNER VISION

A. Moses "endured, as seeing him who is invisible" (Hebrews 11:27).

Note: What you are and what you become in life largely depends on what you see, and what you see depends on whether your vision is high or low.

B. Moses endured because of his inner vision—not sight but *insight.*

1. If you are to endure, you must be able to see above circumstances.

2. Job endured, saying, "[Though I can't see or feel God], I know that my redeemer liveth" (Job 19:25).

C. To see the invisible when the circumstances are against us is to have the power to win. Elisha prayed for his servant: "Lord . . . open his eyes, that he may see" (2 Kings 6:17).

D. Jesus, the Master, demonstrated an endurance like none other.

1. He did not falter even in Gethsemane; His ability to endure was equal to the agony of Calvary.

2. The unclouded vision of His Father's face kept Him going.

3. Our key for endurance is: "looking unto Jesus" (Hebrews 12:2).

CONCLUSION

If a recipe is to be successful, all the ingredients must be included. This is true with *endurance.* All three of these basic ingredients—*faith, love, inner vision*—are needed to bring the end result. If you plan to live an overcoming life, you must endure to the end.

LET THE ROCKS BE SILENT

G. Earl Beatty

SCRIPTURE: Luke 19:32-40

INTRODUCTION

The largest public address system in the world is installed at the Ontario Speedway in California. It draws nearly 31,000 watts and is connectible to 355 horn speaker systems. It is capable of communicating the spoken word to 230,000 people above the noise of 50 screaming race cars (*Encyclopedia of 7,000 Illustrations*).

Within our lifetime, reflector satellites have been deposited in space. Television pictures, telephone messages, and voice transmission by radio can be heard around the world in a matter of seconds. The world has developed a system of communication that would seem to counteract what occurred at Babel. We can almost speak with one voice again. Yet we know that is not true. As important as techniques of communication are, the content of what we communicate is vital. Jesus stood looking back toward Jericho from the mountain and reflected on the events of yesterday. Bartimaeus had been healed, and Zacchaeus had been converted. The good news of the Kingdom had been heard and had changed lives.

NO SENSITIVITY WITHOUT COMPASSION

Jesus was making His triumphal entry into Jerusalem. Throngs of people accompanied Him from the hill down the Mount of Olives. They shouted, "Hosanna; Blessed is he that cometh in the name of the Lord" (Mark 11:9). Compassion flooded His heart and brought with it a sensitivity for the city. His cry of anguish should be echoed by our own.

A. Vision opens the door to compassion. While the world suffers in poverty, hunger, disease, and despair, we are distracted with affluence and financial security by a steady bombardment of Madison Avenue commercials. Their message is "You deserve better." But the Lord of the harvest is saying, "Look on the fields."

    1. John Knox had a vision of the deplorable spiritual condition of his country and prayed, "Give me Scotland, or I die."

    2. Until our vision is expanded to see the contrast of what God requires and how far away we are from meeting those requirements, we aren't likely to have compassion.

B. Compassion opens the door to sensitivity.

    1. Sensitivity leads to action. Until we look into the eyes of a child starving for food or starving for love, we may be void of sensitivity.

    2. Action begins when we match our efforts with our words.

NO SERVICE WITHOUT COMMITMENT

A. Jesus said, "For the Son of Man also came not to be served, but to serve" (Mark 10:45, *RSV*).

    1. Jesus is not only a model for our service, He is also a model for our commitment. He could say to the rich young ruler without hesitation, "Sell all you have, give the money to the poor . . . and come follow me" (Mark 10:21, *TLB*).

    2. He had washed His disciples feet before He charged them, "If I then, your Lord and Teacher, have washed your feet, you also ought to wash one another's feet" (John 13:14, *NKJV*).

B. Our responsibilities are equivalent to our call.

1. The Pharisees in the text reproved Jesus for allowing the public disturbance. Jesus said, "If these were silent, the very stones would cry out" (Luke 19:40, *RSV*).

2. We were born to serve the Lord. Our commitment to Him includes worship. All creation stands in judgment against us when we fail to do so.

NO SACRIFICE WITHOUT COST

A. In 1 Chronicles 21 David had numbered Israel in violation of the covenant. He was faced with an ultimatum:

1. Three years of famine
2. Three months of warfare with Israel being defeated
3. Three days of pestilence administered by the angel of the Lord.

He chose the latter. Seventy thousand died as a result. David saw the angel of the Lord ready to strike Jerusalem and fell down before the Lord requesting that his sin be administered upon his own head and that the city be spared. He was told to set up an altar of sacrifice on Ornan's threshing floor. Ornan offered it to him free of charge. David spoke forceful words that should challenge us, "I will not sacrifice to the Lord, that which cost me nothing" (see v. 24).

B. God asks only that we offer ourselves as a sacrifice holy and acceptable to Him (Romans 12:1).

1. It is not without cost.
2. It is not without pain.
3. It is not without commitment.

CONCLUSION

The Triumphal Entry into Jerusalem was not just a half-mile morning stroll. It was the march of the Son of God before a throng of rejoicing people. They were to learn that there can be no sensitivity without compassion, no service without commitment, and no sacrifice without cost. When we have learned those three lessons, never again will the rocks cry out. We will have learned that sensitivity, service, and sacrifice will bring rejoicing to our hearts and praise to our lips.

CHURCH AFLAME

John E. Hedgepeth

SCRIPTURE: Isaiah 4:4, 5

INTRODUCTION

"Produce your credentials. Let us see what you really are. Are you really alive as you claim to be, or are you dead? Do you have the goods to back up your doctrine and your widespread claims, or is the church just another institution that preaches one thing and practices another?"

THE CHURCH IS UNDER ATTACK

A. The church can be alive and on fire.

B. The Holy Spirit gives a blast of power and fire.

1. He cleanses His people.

2. He baptizes His people.

3. He consumes His people.

THE CHURCH IS NOT BUILDINGS

A. The church is people.

B. Our ways should die so Christ can move.

C. Satan has set up fortresses in our minds.

    1. Satan wants to control man's mind.

    2. The sanctifying power of the Spirit can destroy Satan's hold.

WHEN GOD'S PEOPLE RECEIVE HIS "BURNING," THEY RECEIVE POWER

A. Elijah is a prime example.

    1. He took authority over spiritual enemies.

    2. He did not rely on human methods.

    3. He prayed down the fire.

B. Our spiritual altars must be rebuilt.

HINDRANCES TO AN ALIVE CHURCH

A. Pessimism

B. Doubt

C. Tradition

WHEN GOD BEGINS TO MOVE, HE WORKS FROM TOP TO BOTTOM

A. The Holy Spirit removes doubt and uncertainty.

B. The church begins to affect the world.

    1. It is recognized as a living body, alive and well.

    2. It is the body of Christ.

C. Church leaders need the Holy Spirit to burn out impurities.

D. When fire falls on the pulpit, it will then fall on the pew.

    1. The Spirit will move from preacher to layman.

    2. Ministry will break forth from laity.

    3. The church will grow.

CONCLUSION

A church on fire is a church that impacts the world and makes a difference.

WHERE THE GOSPEL IS

Roy D. King

SCRIPTURE: Hebrews 2:3, 4

INTRODUCTION

At the burial of the famed Scottish reformer John Knox, the Earl of Morton stated, "Here lies one man who never feared the face of man." From exile, Knox's fiery exposition breathed new life into his countrymen. He provoked monarchs and moved nations back to righteousness. He was a dynamic preacher!

We need a rebirth of powerful preaching, modern-day John the Baptists crying in the wilderness to prepare the way of the Lord and make His paths straight.

THE PREACHER'S HERITAGE

    A. Preachers of the Reformation

       1. John Wycliffe—the Bible for Britain

       2. John Hus—the martyr of Bohemia

       3. Martin Luther—"The just shall live by faith" (Romans 1:17).

    B. Preachers of the early church/apostolic era

1. Simon Peter—Pentecostal preacher
2. Paul—Persevering apostle
3. John Chrysostom—"Golden-mouthed"

C. The Ministry of Jesus Christ

1. An uncompromised mission to redeem man
2. An authoritative message to convict man
3. An anointed ministry to preserve man

THE PREACHER'S CONTENT

A. A simple but profound gospel

1. The truths of God's character
2. The woeful condition of humanity
3. The efficacy of Christ's sacrifice
4. The challenge to live as His ambassadors

B. A gospel devoid of error

1. Untainted by vain philosophy
2. Unedited and filled with power

THE PREACHER'S EXPECTATION

The faithfulness of God to honor His Word

A. Signs and wonders

B. Divers miracles

C. Gifts of the Holy Ghost

CONCLUSION

The intellectual may scoff and the self-righteous may balk, but where the gospel truly is, we will witness the dynamic power of the Holy Spirit. Lives will be transformed, the bride of Christ will be strengthened, and God will receive glory.

TIME: THE FAMILY TREASURE

Paul L. Walker

SCRIPTURE: Ecclesiastes 3:1-14

INTRODUCTION

There is an old saying, "Time waits for no one." As old as it is and as many times as it has been used, this saying still conveys a relevant message: time management and happiness go hand in hand. Or to put it another way, the way we use our time is a barometer for the level of our joy. We are what we do, and doing obviously involves the utilization of time.

The writer of Ecclesiastes—the teacher—wrote, "To everything there is a season, a time for every purpose under heaven?" (Ecclesiastes 3:1, *NKJV*). This passage reminds us of the importance of treasuring our time, because the joy of life is directly correlated to the investment of our time.

Happiness in families is to a large degree dependent on application of biblical principles of time management.

THE CONCERN

A. The biblical message is concerned with the brevity of time (Psalm 90:12; Ecclesiastes 12:1; 1 Corinthians 7:29).

B. The apostle Paul was concerned about the utilization of time in the most productive way (Ephesians 5:15, 16; Colossians 4:5).

C. If we want balance, meaning, order, tranquillity, congruence, peace, and joy in our lives, it is important for us to share this biblical concern so that we too as families redeem the time.

THE CONTROL

A. The secret for treasuring our time is control, not only in setting our schedules but in disciplining ourselves to keep our commitments (see Ecclesiastes 3:11).

B. No one can find out the work that God does from beginning to end (see Ecclesiastes 3:11).

C. Every man should eat and drink and enjoy the good of all his labor—it is the gift of God (see Ecclesiastes 3:12, 13).

D. We are to use time in such a way that we can rejoice and do good, because we all want to eat, drink, and find enjoyment in our life's work.

E. The control of our time has at its base the reverence of God and respect for the gift of life.

THE CONTEXT

A. With this scriptural basis for treasuring our time before us, it is necessary to live our lives in the context of God's will for the use of our time (Ecclesiastes 12:1-7).

B. We recognize that we have a duty to God and are responsible for the use of the resources He gives us (Ecclesiastes 12:13).

C. The point is that each family needs a biblical philosophy of time that delivers it from the tyranny of the world's rat race.

  1. The family strives to arrange priorities with God first, others second, and the self last.

EVERY GOOD GIFT COMES FROM GOD

A. We are to live our lives in such a way that we see every good gift as a blessing from God.

B. Moses had to constantly remind Israel of this (Deuteronomy 8:18).

C. Time and time again the prophets reminded Israel of the same theme (Haggai 2:8).

D. In the New Testament (James 1:17)

E. We get caught in the Nebuchadnezzar syndrome—we forget the source of our blessings (Daniel 4).

F. We are suffering from the same kind of selfishness as Nebuchadnezzar.

   1. High blood pressure

   2. Urban decay

   3. Absence of community

   4. Absence of integrity in relationships

G. We experience the results of selfishness in the erosion of quality in almost every area of life, work, and service —a me-first worldview.

H. Whatever we have accomplished in establishing our high level of affluence, we have accomplished because we were founded on the knowledge that every good gift comes from God and is to be used to its most productive form.

 I. We keep our joy when we use God's gifts to the best advantage for His glory, the ministry to others, and our own highest good.

APPROPRIATE USE OF GOD'S GIFTS YIELDS SPIRITUAL BENEFITS

A. The gifts of God properly appropriated result in happiness, goodness, prosperity, and satisfaction.

B. Once we establish a time philosophy on the premise that every good gift comes from God and then are able to utilize our time to appropriate these gifts according to God's Word, the results are astounding.

   1. Psalm 37.4

   2. Proverbs 3:9, 10

   3. Luke 6:38

C. The process is not only to view time as a gift of God but to schedule the appropriate sharing and utilization of all our resources as a sacrifice of praise (see Hebrews 13:15, 16).

D. In this regard the Bible talks about four levels of giving:
   1. Proportionate giving (Deuteronomy 16:17)
   2. Systematic giving (1 Corinthians 16:2)
   3. Sacrificial giving (2 Corinthians 9:7)
   4. Expectant giving (Malachi 3:10)

E. Using God's resources is directly connected to our scheduling, and the way we schedule determines the level of our joy.

ASSUME ACCOUNTABILITY

A. A biblical philosophy of time demands a sense of accountability.

B. We are accountable to God to use our resources as individuals who have been trusted with "the mysteries of God" (1 Corinthians 4:1, 2).
   1. 2 Corinthians 9:6
   2. 2 Corinthians 9:11

THE BOTTOM LINE

A. The bottom line is that we must use our time in such a way that will make the biblical philosophy work.

B. We treasure our time when we
   1. Analyze—check out our committed time and wasted time, and then decide how much time to use—to treasure for its highest good.
   2. Synchronize—share the family priorities and then decide what events are necessary, determine when these events can be attended, and make scheduling in advance an important priority.
   3. Spiritualize—make devotional time a regular part of daily activities.
   4. Programize—take the seven spiritual vitamins consistently to live in the grooves of grace in the church and the home.
   5. Personalize—set aside individual time for private relaxation and activity.

C. If we want to keep our joy, we must treasure our time with a biblical philosophy that recognizes that

1. Every gift comes from God.

2. The appropriate use of God's gifts yields spiritual benefits.

3. We are accountable for the way these gifts are used in our lives.

BECOMING FRUITFUL CHRISTIANS

Robert P. Frazier

SCRIPTURE: Matthew 13:3-8

INTRODUCTION

We are colaborers with God (1 Corinthians 3:9). If you aren't concerned about being prosperous, God certainly is. An industrious man took a weed-covered vacant lot and transformed it into a lovely garden. A passerby remarked to him, "God has certainly made a lovely garden here." The man replied, "You should have seen it when God had it all by Himself."

In light of the parable from Matthew 13:3-8, consider the following problems in becoming a fruitful Christian.

THE WAYSIDE

   A. Literally "beaten pathways" through the field and represents a *hard-hearted Christian.*

   B. What "beats a pathway" through our lives and makes us unproductive?

      1. Wrong friends

      2. Pet sins

3. Deliberate ignorance

THE STONY PLACES

A. The soil was so shallow the seed could not properly root.

B. This represents the *shallow Christian* who operates at an emotional level and never firmly "roots."

GOD'S REMEDY—PLOWING

A. General information in plowing

B. The beaten path necessitates *longer plowing.*

Our objection is our own impatience.

C. For the shallow place, God's remedy is *deeper plowing.*

Our objection is our own pain.

CONCLUSION

If we would become productive Christians (bringing forth a hundredfold, sixtyfold, or thirtyfold), we must submit to God's method of cultivating us as His field.

A SPECIAL ANOINTING FOR A SPECIAL HOUR

William A. Reid

SCRIPTURE: Acts 19:11, 12

INTRODUCTION

Paul was on his third missionary journey. For three months he had preached and the people had worshiped in other quarters. Tyrannus, who operated a school in the city, offered his facilities to the Christians. In one old account of this period, it is recorded that Paul used the school from 11 a.m. to 4 p.m. each day.

During Paul's long ministry in Ephesus, about two years, his influence spread throughout Asia. The Bible records that "God wrought special miracles by the hands of Paul" (v. 11).

PAUL WAS A SPECIAL PERSON FOR A SPECIAL HOUR

A. His calling was sure.

1. Damascus road experience (Acts 9)

2. He accepted and fulfilled his call as an apostle of Jesus Christ (Romans 1:1; 11:13; Ephesians 1:1).

B. His commitment was focused on Jesus Christ.

1. In thought—"Finally, brethren, whatsoever things are

true, whatsoever things are honest, whatsoever things are just, whatsoever things are pure, whatsoever things are lovely, whatsoever things are of good report; if there be any virtue, and if there be any praise, think on these things" (Philippians 4:8).

2. In action—"But refuse profane and old wives' fables, and exercise thyself rather unto godliness" (1 Timothy 4:7).

3. In example—"Not because we have not power, but to make ourselves an ensample unto you to follow us" (2 Thessalonians 3:9).

C. His challenge was great.

1. Paul did the most marvelous work of his life in Ephesus.

2. Ephesus:

a. A magnificent city of 250,000 population at the center of the Imperial Highway from Rome to the East—the backbone of the Roman Empire

b. Vast multitudes of Diana worshipers became Christians. Churches were founded in cities for a hundred miles.

c. The Temple of Diana was one of the seven wonders of the world. It took 220 years to build.

d. Ephesus became the leading center of the Christian world.

3. His anointing was "special."

a. "And God wrought special miracles by the hands of Paul" (Acts 19:11).

b. "Special" is derived from the same Greek word as used in Acts 1:8—*dunamis*, meaning "power." The words translated "special miracles" in the King James Version are literally "powerful deeds, not ordinary ones."

c. His anointing broke the power of Satan at Ephesus.

YOU ARE SPECIAL PEOPLE LIVING IN A SPECIAL HOUR

A. Jesus calls you to be special: "Ye have not chosen me, but I have chosen you, and ordained you, that ye should go and bring forth fruit, and that your fruit should remain: that whatsoever ye shall ask of the Father in my name, he may give it to you" (John 15:16).

1. Chosen by the Lord Jesus Christ
2. Commissioned to the harvest
3. Confident of fruitfulness

B. The church ministry at this special hour
1. "Go ye therefore, and teach all nations, baptizing them in the name of the Father, and of the Son, and of the Holy Ghost" (Matthew 28:19).
2. "Say not ye, There are yet four months, and then cometh harvest? behold, I say unto you, Lift up your eyes, and look on the fields; for they are white already to harvest" (John 4:35).
3. "Therefore said he unto them, The harvest truly is great, but the labourers are few: pray ye therefore the Lord of the harvest, that he would send forth labourers into his harvest" (Luke 10:2).

C. The challenge of the '90s
1. Social issues
a. Drugs and alcohol
b. Morality
c. Many other issues
2. Stresses
a. Economical
b. Financial
c. Global
3. Spiritual conditions
a. Mysticism, cults, occult, and so forth
b. Carelessness, indifference
c. A form of godliness

YOU HAVE A SPECIAL ANOINTING FOR THIS HOUR

A. Jesus' promise
1. I will send you another Comforter (John 16:7).
2. "Ye shall receive power" (Acts 1:8).
3. "Greater works . . . shall he [you] do" (John 14:12).

B. Jesus' provisions

1. "They were all filled with the Holy Ghost" (Acts 2:4).

2. "Greater is he that is in you" (1 John 4:4).

3. "The weapons of our warfare" (2 Corinthians 10:4, 5)

C. Our proof

1. Mark 16:20

2. Acts 3:1-7

3. Acts 16

4. Acts 19:11, 12

5. Acts 20:9-12

CONCLUSION

We *do* have a special, powerful anointing for this hour!

THE FOUR GREATEST WORDS IN THE ENGLISH LANGUAGE

D. Chris Thompson

SCRIPTURE: Jeremiah 29:11 (Supplemental readings: Jeremiah 29:10-14; Matthew 5:1-16; Hebrews 13:5, 6)

INTRODUCTION

Last year for a Christmas gift my sons received a Nintendo video game. The game with its many available cartridges is amazing but also expensive. The boys love it. In fact, they love it so much they had to be put on a schedule for playing.

The purpose of the game is to "do in" the player. This means to kill all your men, cause you to miss all the ducks, or put Mario down the tubes.

Life may seem much like a Nintendo game. But God is not playing. God is on our side! He sent His Son to die for us that we might be saved. The believer is promised in Romans 8:28, "And we know that all things work together for good to them that love God, to them who are the called according to his purpose." God is for *us*!

The Old and New Testaments are filled with God's expressions of His support for mankind. It is as if the Lord is speaking over and over the four greatest words in the English language—"*I believe in you!*"

JEHOVAH BELIEVED IN ISRAEL (Jeremiah 29:10-14)

A. Context—Jehovah God (spelled with capital letters —*LORD*) was writing a letter of encouragement to exiled Israel.

B. Heart of the passage—" 'For I know the plans I have for you,' declares the LORD, 'plans to prosper you and not to harm you, plans to give you hope and a future' " (Jeremiah 29:11, *NIV*).

C. Beautiful promises of the Lord (vv. 12-14)

D. What was the LORD really saying to Israel?—"I believe in you!"

JESUS BELIEVED IN HIS DISCIPLES (Matthew 5:1-16)

A. Context—Jesus spoke beautiful words to the Jews in this opening passage of the Sermon on the Mount. Perhaps His closest disciples became discouraged at the beautiful promises of blessing, thinking they would have to carry them out by their own abilities.

B. Jesus spoke encouragement directly to the disciples.

   1. Verse 13—You already are the salt of the earth. You can make a difference. You can pervade, permeate, purify, and preserve society.

   2. Verse 14—You are already the light of the world. You can cause darkness to flee away at 186,000 miles per second.

C. Jesus reminded the disciples that their success was dependent on obedience.

   1. Verse 13—Salt having lost its savor

   2. Verse 15—Light under a bushel

D. What was Jesus really saying to His disciples?—"I believe in you."

GOD'S VOICE OF PROMISE FOR TODAY (Hebrews 13:5, 6)

A. The promise—"I will never leave thee, nor forsake thee."

B. The Christian's right to receive the promise (2 Corinthians 1:20)

C. The promise is a double pledge.

1. *Leave*—to withdraw a sustaining hand from a tottering fence; literally to drop

2. *Forsake*—to abandon or desert; to leave in a lurch

D. The writer to the Hebrews is saying that *God believes in His children.*

CONCLUSION

There is nothing more beneficial to a child than to know his parents love and believe in him. With that kind of assurance he can take on the world. So it should be with God's children.

The believer is able to boldly say, as in Hebrews 13:6, "The Lord is my helper." The idea behind the word *helper* that God, like a runner who is poised and ready to run, is ready to come to our assistance as soon as He hears our cry for help.

The Lord believes in His children!

"WHEN THINGS LOOK BAD, GOD LOOKS GOOD"

David M. Griffis

SCRIPTURE: Romans 8:35-39

INTRODUCTION

In this text, the apostle Paul poses a question that defies the devil and enrages hell, for hell and the devil cannot answer it successfully. "Who shall separate us from the love of Christ?" Is there anything in existence that can destroy the household of faith, that can mean God no longer loves us?

God's answer is found in verse 37: "Nay."

PAUL'S LIST OF ANSWERS THAT SOME WOULD OFFER TO HIS QUESTION

    A. Tribulation

        1. Tribulation is trouble from this world.

        2. Jesus said, "And the world hath hated them, because they are not of the world, even as I am not of the world" (John 17:14).

        3. He declared, "In the world ye shall have tribulation: but be of good cheer; I have overcome the world" (John 16:33).

B. Distress

   1. Distress is that place where no answers are in sight.

   2. Paul said, "We are troubled on every side, yet not distressed" (2 Corinthians 4:8).

   3. As long as He is on the throne, as long as He answers prayer, as long as the Word is true, as long as Christ intercedes, and as long as we walk by faith and not by sight, we have the answer.

C. Persecution

   1. Persecution is trouble from people.

   2. Paul said, "Yea, and all that will live godly in Christ Jesus shall suffer persecution" (2 Timothy 3:12).

   3. A blessing comes with persecution according to Christ's Sermon on the Mount. He said, "For great is your reward in heaven" (Matthew 5:12). The Christian prays for his enemies, renders good for evil, gives up the coat and cloak, and walks the second mile, while offering the second cheek for smiting.

D. Famine or nakedness

   1. This means lack of material prosperity.

   2. God always supplies the need. He has promised to be sufficient. There can be no greater promise.

   3. "Things" should never dictate our spiritual temperature, whether we lack or have abundance.

E. Peril or sword

   1. When there is imminent danger to our body, whether through disaster or sickness, has God quit loving us? Absolutely not.

   2. Paul said, "Whether we live therefore, or die, we are the Lords'" (Romans 14:8).

   3. "To live is Christ, and to die is gain" (Philippians 1:21).

   4. Death is the last enemy to be destroyed (1 Corinthians 15:26).

   5. The death of saints is precious in God's sight (Psalm 116:15).

WHEN THINGS LOOK BAD, GOD LOOKS GOOD

A. He is able to keep us.

   1. Jude 24

   2. 2 Timothy 1:12

B. He is always at the right place at the right time with the right answer.

   1. He gave Daniel security in a lions' den (Daniel 6).

   2. He gave the three Hebrew children a miracle in the fiery furnace (Danicl 3).

   3. He gave Paul and Silas a song in their bondage that led to freedom and revival (Acts 16).

   4. He gave a dying thief the promise of passage to paradise (Luke 23:43).

CONCLUSION

"God is our refuge and strength, a very present help in trouble" (Psalm 46:1).

THE DISCIPLINED LEADER

Melvin L. West

SCRIPTURE: 1 Corinthians 9:24-27; Hebrews 12:1

INTRODUCTION

The word *discipline* should be synonymous with *leadership*. Unfortunately, it isn't. The term actually means different things to different people:

To the child, discipline means being compelled to do something. To the soldier, discipline means conformity to regulations. To the athlete, discipline means hours upon hours of self-restraint and practice. And to the Christian leader, discipline means self-denial and taking up the cross daily.

There are at least three basic laws or principles for becoming a disciplined leader.

THE LAW OF TRAINING

    A. Training requires rigid self-control.

    B. Training is very severe.

    C. The athlete in training is required to avoid excesses in eating, drinking, and fleshly indulgence.

    D. God applies the law of training in the preparation of His servants for their work.

THE LAW OF TEMPERANCE

Temperance: Habitual moderation in the indulgence of the appetites and passions—one of the cardinal virtues, according to Webster.

According to 2 Peter 1:5, 6, temperance is to be added as a Christian virtue to help us be fruitful.

A. Leaders must avoid haste.

B. Leaders must learn to say no.

    1. Leaders must sometimes say no to some apparently good things.

    2. Leaders must learn to put first things first.

C. Leaders must adopt Paul's view in 1 Corinthians 6:12.

THE LAW OF SELF-MASTERY

A. The leader must be slow to anger and a good ruler of his spirit (Proverbs 16:32).

B. The leader must be teachable, with a restrained tongue and lots of self-control (James 1:19).

C. In developing self-mastery, we must work on such areas as our emotions, moods, and speech.

HOW TO BECOME A DISCIPLINED LEADER

A. We must acknowledge our need of discipline.

B. We must tackle difficult areas first.

C. Complete the task.

    1. Don't expect to have butter without churning the cream.

    2. See 2 Timothy 2:15 and 1 Timothy 4:12, 16.

D. Don't let a twist of events ruin your plans.

    1. Don't spend your time fretting over events.

    2. Thank God for hidden providence.

    3. Learn in prayer how to turn your frustration into fulfillment.

DANGERS OF DISCIPLINE

A. Thinking that discipline is the supreme accomplishment of life.

338

B. The danger of becoming like the Pharisee who said, "God, I thank thee, that I am not as other men are" (Luke 18:11).

CONCLUSION

Read 2 Timothy 2.

THIS IS MY CHURCH

Raymond M. Pruitt

SCRIPTURE: Psalm 122:1

INTRODUCTION

When a young Army recruit came to the question on the application form "What is your church preference"? he wet the end of his pencil by placing it in his mouth, then wrote, "Red Brick." The church means many things to many people. It may be seen as a redbrick building or a congregation of people, or it may be seen from a variety of perspectives. Only by proper usage can any place be called the house of the Lord. And when it is a house of the Lord, its worth is beyond measure. My church is

A DOOR (which gives me entry)

    A. An opportunity for service to God and man (Mark 10:43, 44).

        "God frees our souls, not from service, not from duty, but into service and into duty; and he who mistakes the purpose of his freedom mistakes the character of his freedom. He who thinks that he is being released from the work, and not set free in order that he may accomplish that work, mistakes the condition into which his soul is invited to enter" (Phillips Brooks).

B. The most meaningful life (John 5:24; Philippians 1:21).

"The Scriptures teach us the best way of living, the noblest way of suffering, and the most comfortable way of dying" (Flavel).

"Let us think often that our only business in this life is to please God" (Brother Lawrence).

The church teaches me that the answer to the question "What is the purpose of life?" is not a *what*, but a *who*. We cannot look at the Cross and still think that our lives are of no account to God.

C. The best of life's experiences (Ephesians 3:17-19).

"Life is currently described in one of four ways: a journey, a battle, a pilgrimage, or a race. Select your own metaphors, but the necessity of finishing is all the same. For if life is a journey, it must be completed. If life is a battle, it must be finished. If life is a pilgrimage, it must be concluded. And if life is a race, it must be won" (*The War Cry*).

"The great use of life is to spend it for something that outlasts it" (William James).

D. Certain hope for the future (1 Peter 1:3, 4).

AN ARMORY (which supplies me with the right stuff)

A. For fighting evil in the world (2 Corinthians 10:4; Ephesians 6:11).

The church is a house of service, not a dormitory for members only. The church is not a tomb with a steeple; it is a place of action.

B. For inspiration to keep the faith and do right (Romans 15:14).

C. To learn how to use spiritual weapons (Ephesians 6:11-17).

D. To have a clearer vision of Christ (2 Corinthians 4:5, 6).

AN ANCHOR (to support me in the storm)

A. It steadies me in the storm (Isaiah 30:20, 21).

B. It keeps me from the breakers (Proverbs 11:14).

A PILOT (to give me direction and bring me safely into the harbor)

A. It guides me through the difficult places (Hebrews 13:17).

B. In the hour of temptation, it keeps me from drifting away from God (Hebrews 6:19).

C. It guides me safely into the harbor (Philippians 3:20, 21).

CONCLUSION

With regard to the world, the church is responsible to preach the gospel to every creature. With regard to its members, the church provides ministries, support, and guidance for Christian service and for living.

A NEW COMMANDMENT

R. Lamar Vest

SCRIPTURE: John 13:33-35

INTRODUCTION

Jesus spent three and one-half years with His disciples. He attempted to open to them the mysteries of the Kingdom. He shared with them His most intimate thoughts and plans. He attempted to synchronize their spirits with His so that they would be able to carry on His work when He returned to His Father.

It was on this occasion, celebrating the Passover Feast with His disciples in a borrowed room, that Jesus demonstrated His love in a way each disciple could understand. When the supper was ended, Jesus arose from the table, laid aside His garment, draped Himself with a towel—the badge of a servant —and began washing His disciples' feet.

From this graphic demonstration of love, Jesus moved on to give a statement that was to become the true mark of discipleship: "A new commandment I give unto you, That ye love one another; as I have loved you, that ye also love one another. By this shall all men know that ye are my disciples, if ye have love one to another" (vv. 34, 35).

Let's take a closer look at this powerful statement.

A NEW COMMANDMENT ("That ye love one another")

A. The old commandment: the law

1. There is no justification in the law (Galatians 3:11).

2. The law is a teacher (Galatians 3:24).

3. The law points us to Jesus (Galatians 3:24).

B. The new commandment: love

1. Love is the true test of discipleship.

2. We are to love everyone—especially fellow believers (Galatians 6:10).

3. Love is a commandment—not an option.

THE STANDARD OF QUALITY ("As I have loved you")

A. The word *love* is abused in our society.

1. Popular music distorts love.

2. T.V. and movies cheapen love.

3. Modern religion speaks of sentimental love rather than holy love.

B. Jesus speaks of self-abandoning love.

1. Jesus never clung to the prerogative as God's Son (Philippians 2:5-7).

2. Jesus loved His disciples to the utmost (John 13:1).

3. A clear definition of Christian love is given (1 Corinthians 13).

THE CONTEXT OF OUR LOVE (before a watching world)

A. The world is invited to watch the church.

1. "By this shall all men know" (v. 35).

2. Love is evidence of our new birth (1 John 3:14).

B. Jesus prayed for the oneness of the church (John 17).

1. If we are not one in the Lord, the world will not believe in Jesus (John 17:21).

2. A shattered body cannot present a true image of Christ (1 John 4:20).

CONCLUSION

A lot of people are never going to believe that God sent Jesus if we who are in the body do not love one another.

WHEN WORSHIP IS REAL

B.L. Kelley

SCRIPTURE: Psalm 150

INTRODUCTION

The closing of another year brings mixed feelings of sadness and joy, victories won, and lost opportunities. The future is yet unspoiled; the new year provides a brand-new start. There is only one problem with going into a brand-new, unspoiled year. I must take myself with my weaknesses into the new year. But I can resolve to make my worship more meaningful and real than ever before. When worship is real, it will manifest itself in three ways: (1) in a vertical aspect, (2) in a horizontal aspect, and (3) through an inward aspect.

THE VERTICAL ASPECT

  A. The primary reason for worship is to minister to the Lord.

   1. The posture of worship is "I will bless the Lord," not "Lord, bless me" (see Psalm 103:2).

   2. The purpose of worship is to lift our attention from ourselves to the Lord.

  B. We are to realize the manifest presence of God in our

midst. God is omnipresent, yet He manifests Himself in different degrees.

  1. "Where two or three are gathered" (Matthew 18:20)
  2. When a group of God's people praise, He inhabits the praises of His people (Psalm 22:3).

C. God said to Moses, " 'My Presence will go with you.' " Moses responded, " 'If your Presence does not go with us, do not send us up from here' " (Exodus 33:14, 15, *NIV*). If we do not have the presence of God in our midst, we are no better than the local civic clubs.

D. Our worship service provides an opportunity for the power of God to be released.

  1. To heal (Luke 5:17)
  2. To lift the discouraged (Matthew 11:28)
  3. To provide a seedbed for the gifts of the Spirit
  4. Worship opens the channels of communication between us and God.

THE HORIZONTAL ASPECT

A. We worship in order to enhance the feeling of unity within the body of believers.

B. We worship in order to provide believers with an opportunity to confess and profess their faith before others.

C. We worship that we might declare the glories of God before unbelievers (Psalm 108:3).

THE INWARD ASPECT

Let us look at the ways in which worship changes the worshiper within.

A. When we worship, it releases each person to an uninhibited expression of praise and worship.

B. Worship services teach and reinforce spiritual truth (see Colossians 3:16).

C. Our songs of worship provide the worshiper with the means to express heartfelt attitudes otherwise difficult to express. Singing gives us an opportunity to express our love to the Lord in words of someone who knows how to say it just right.

D. We bear the resemblance of what we worship (2 Corinthians 3:18).

CONCLUSION

Worship can be an intensely real and rewarding experience. It requires an upward look with devotion, a horizontal concern that touches our fellowman, and an inward soul-searching with the desire to be holy before God.

FORGIVENESS

R.B. Thomas

SCRIPTURE: Matthew 18:21-35

INTRODUCTION

The Greek word for *forgiveness* means remission or a setting free from guilt and debt.

Two things seem especially hard to do at times: to *give* and to *forgive*. The latter is the topic for the message today. It has been well stated that "forgiveness cannot change the past, but it can and does change the future." To this could be added that an unwillingness to forgive can also change your future.

These three aspects of forgiveness will be considered: (1) Forgiveness as a Christian duty, (2) the consequences of failure to forgive, (3) how you can know you have forgiven.

FORGIVENESS AS A CHRISTIAN DUTY

A. God commanded that we forgive: "Be ye kind one to another, tenderhearted, forgiving one another, even as God for Christ's sake hath forgiven you" (Ephesians 4:32).

B. Jesus set the example for forgiving. From the cross,

He prayed for the Father to forgive of His enemies. God has forgiven us. God does not belittle forgiveness, and neither should we.

C. We have needed, do need, and will need forgiveness. We have sinned against God, and He has forgiven us. We have no doubt sinned against others, and they have forgiven us. Don't be like the hardened man in our text who received forgiveness but demanded the letter of the law for those under him.

D. Ultimately our own forgiveness depends upon our willingness to forgive others. "For if we forgive men their trespasses, your heavenly Father will also forgive you: but if ye forgive not men their trespasses, neither will your Father forgive your trespasses" (Matthew 6:14, 15).

E. Forgiveness is a dictate of Christian love; therefore, not to forgive is inconsistent with the ethical code of Christianity.

CONSEQUENCES OF FAILURE TO FORGIVE

A. Failure to forgive destroys your own peace of mind. You feel knotted up inside and dirty when you know that all is not well between yourself and others. If you don't feel this way, you aren't a disciple of Jesus.

B. Failure to forgive destroys your usefulness and productivity. You spend all your time plotting, scheming, looking for opportunities to gain revenge.

C. Failure to forgive can destroy your physical life. Ahithophel, the grandfather of Bathsheba, would not forgive David for seducing his granddaughter. He dedicated his life to getting even. His plot backfired, and he ended his own life by hanging himself (2 Samuel 17:23).

D. Failure to forgive can destroy your soul. When you face eternity in need of forgiveness, you may find that because you locked out forgiveness from your heart, forgiveness will be denied you.

HOW YOU CAN KNOW YOU HAVE FORGIVEN

"Even as Christ forgave you, so also do ye" (Colossians 3:13).

A. True forgiveness is *unsolicited*. Forgiveness for us was in the heart of God long before we asked for it. "While we were yet sinners, Christ died for us" (Romans 5:8).

B. Forgive *completely*. When Christ forgives, He does it all the way. There is no such thing as halfway forgiveness.

C. Forgive *continuously*. Christ has forgiven us, He does forgive us, and He will continue to forgive us. "Whoso confesseth and forsaketh . . . [his sins] shall have mercy" (Proverbs 28:13). Jesus explained that we should forgive "until seventy times seven" (Matthew 18:22).

D. Forgive *graciously*. Some people act as though forgiving belittles them. Jesus does not feel that way about it. He gladly and happily forgives.

E. *Communicate* your forgiveness. Jesus never leaves us in the dark. By His Holy Spirit He communicates His forgiveness to us. By His helping hand He lets us know that we are forgiven.

F. You know you have forgiven when there is *no one* for whom you could not pray God's choice blessings and mean it!

THE MAN, CHRIST JESUS

R.L. Brandt

SCRIPTURE: 1 Timothy 2:5

INTRODUCTION

How can the exalted, Almighty God of the universe relate to us, mere earthbound humans? How can He, whose thoughts are as high as the heavens above our thoughts, relate to us? How can the God of eternity relate to us poor creatures of time? How can God, who cannot be tempted, relate to us in our temptations? How can He, who is life itself, relate to us mortals who are destined to die?

There is only one way. He must descend to our level. This He did in the incarnation of His Son, Jesus Christ.

HE WAS BORN AT OUR LEVEL

    A. Conceived in His mother's womb (Luke 1:35)

    B. Took on Himself flesh and blood (Hebrews 2:14)

    C. Born as a son of Abraham (Matthew 1:1-16)

    D. Was made in the likeness of men (Philippians 2:6, 7)

HE DEVELOPED AT OUR LEVEL

A. Nursed at His mother's breast

B. Had to learn to walk and talk

C. Went to school

D. Experienced adolescence, entered manhood

E. Was a carpenter's apprentice

HE WAS TEMPTED AT OUR LEVEL

A. Was tempted in all points as we are (Hebrews 4:15)

B. Was tempted more than once (Luke 4:13)

HE GREW SPIRITUALLY AT OUR LEVEL

A. Baptized by immersion in Jordan (Matthew 3:13-16)

B. Baptized in the Holy Spirit at our level (Matthew 3:16)

    1. In His case, the sign was a dove.

    2. In our case, the sign is tongues.

HE MINISTERED BY THE POWER OF THE SPIRIT AT OUR LEVEL

His public ministry was that of a man full of the Holy Ghost (Luke 4:18).

HE SUFFERED REJECTION AT OUR LEVEL

A. "His own received him not" (John 1:11).

B. "He . . . [was] despised and rejected of men" (Isaiah 53:3).

HE SUFFERED AND DIED AT OUR LEVEL

A. Not a sinner, but was made to be sin for us (2 Corinthians 5:21)

B. "Found in fashion [condition] as a man" (Philippians 2:8)

C. Suffered the full penalty of sin (James 1:15)

HE SITS AT THE RIGHT HAND OF GOD AT OUR LEVEL—AS A MAN

"For there is . . . one mediator between God and men, the man Christ Jesus" (1 Timothy 2:5).

CONCLUSION

Wherever you are in life's experience, Jesus Christ has been there. He is your mediator.

EVIDENCES OF ONE'S SPIRITUAL PATERNITY

Cullen L. Hicks

SCRIPTURE: 1 John 3:10

INTRODUCTION

Although we live in a highly civilized and enlightened society, many people are of the opinion that everything is relative and that there are no absolutes. Because of the permissiveness of the times, many seem to have lost the ability to discern between what is right and what is wrong. This is particularly true of the younger generation. Yet every Christian, and especially every preacher, should be able to define and declare the difference between right and wrong in an understandable way. They should without reluctance speak openly and boldly of the difference between the righteous and the wicked.

It was, no doubt, with such a motive that the apostle John penned the words of our text. However, while we should be able to distinguish between the children of God and the children of the devil, let us be sure to examine and scrutinize our own conduct, thereby obeying the admonition of Paul, who said, "Let every man prove his own work, and then shall he have rejoicing in himself alone, and not in another" (Galatians 6:4).

THE DEVIL IS THE FATHER AND AUTHOR OF EVIL

In Scripture when a group of people derive a particular quality or likeness of disposition from an individual, it is common for those people to be called the children of the one from whom that quality or likeness was received!

A. "Jabal . . . was the father of such as dwell in tents, and of such as have cattle" (Genesis 4:20).

B. "Jubal . . . was the father of all such as handle the harp and organ" (Genesis 4:21).

C. "He that committeth sin is of the devil; for the devil sinneth from the beginning" (1 John 3:8).

D. Jesus said to the Jews, "Ye do the deeds of your father. . . . If God were your Father, ye would love me. . . . Ye are of your father the devil, and the lusts of your father ye will do" (John 8:41, 42, 44).

E. The sinner's master is the devil, and he obeys his master.

GOD IS THE FATHER AND AUTHOR OF GOODNESS

Scripture teaches us that Christians are born of God and are partakers of His divine nature.

A. "Be ye therefore followers of God, as dear children" (Ephesians 5:1).

B. God is a God of holiness, so His children are to "follow peace with all men, and holiness" (Hebrews 12:14).

C. God is righteous and loves righteousness, therefore His children love and do righteousness (1 John 3:7).

D. God is truth, so His children "walk in truth" (3 John 4).

E. God hates sin, therefore His children hate sin (see Habakkuk 1:13; Psalm 97:10).

F. The Christian's master is Christ, and he obeys his master.

ONE'S DEEDS REVEAL ANCESTRY

Is it possible to distinguish between the children of God and the children of the devil? Our Scripture text states that the children of God and the children of the devil *are* manifest.

Notice it does not say *will be* in the future, but *are* presently revealed. Then by what are they made manifest?

A. Not by their material success, for God sends His rain on the just and on the unjust. He causes the sun to shine on saint and sinner alike. Financial prosperity and physical well-being are given to man without discrimination and is not a distinguishing factor.

B. Not by one's religious profession. As a young convert I used to think so, but I discovered that Judas and Demas both professed to be followers of Christ. There have always been those with a reputation of being alive but were dead and those who had a form of godliness but denied its power.

C. Not by one's doctrine or creed. One may be right and sound in doctrine and creed, saying the right words with the lips; but this is not the way to determine the difference between the children of God and the children of the devil.

D. Then by what are they distinguished and known? "In this the children of God are manifest, and the children of the devil: whosoever doeth not righteousness is not of God, neither he that loveth not his brother" (1 John 3:10). In other words, they are known by whether or not they practice righteousness and exercise love to their fellowman.

THOSE TO WHOM DEEDS ARE MANIFEST

We know that there is coming a time of separation when the tares shall be separated from the wheat. But according to our text, even now the two can be recognized and known —perhaps not perfectly or sufficiently for mere humans to pass judgment, but the deeds are distinguishable and manifest. To whom are the deeds manifest?

A. To God (Proverbs 15:3; 2 Timothy 2:19; Hebrews 4:13)

B. To others (Matthew 5:16; 7:16-20; 12:35)

C. To themselves (1 John 3:14; 24; 5:19)

CONCLUSION

Can a man be wicked and not know it? Can a man practice sin, love darkness, and hate light without knowing it?

Even a fly knows the difference between light and darkness. On the other hand, can a man be godly and claim God's promises if he cannot determine he is in the faith? Can one take advantage of the privileges of the gospel if he cannot know himself? Of course not.

Salvation is not something that comes into a person's life unrecognized, having no impact upon that person, and leaving no evidence of its happening. Salvation is Christ coming into one's heart, transforming and changing one's conduct, affections, and desires (2 Corinthians 5:17). Pleasing and serving God becomes the chief ambition. When this happens, heaven is made to rejoice; the devil himself is made angry, for he has lost a soul he thought he would destroy; and others will see visible evidence of the changes in such a life.

Yes, there is a standard by which God's children and Satan's children are made manifest and known. There is a criterion by which we may judge the reality of salvation in our own lives as well as in the lives of others. When one lies, cheats, steals, and curses, we know that person is only doing the deeds of his or her father, the devil. When one loves and practices righteousness, loves his fellowman, speaks the truth, visits the fatherless and the widows in their afflictions, and keeps himself unspotted from the world, we know that person, too, is doing the deeds of his or her Father, which is God.

Now who is your father? To whom do you belong? Can you bow your knees before God and truly pray, "Our Father which art in heaven . . ."?

COMMISSIONED

Bennie Triplett

SCRIPTURE: John 20:21; Matthew 28:19, 20; Mark 16:15

INTRODUCTION

The strongest amplification of the Great Commission is found in John 20:21. It is one of the most power-packed utterances that ever fell from the lips of Jesus. The Great Commission is found in Matthew 28:19, 20 and in Mark 16:15. Christ was commissioning the disciples as representatives to the uttermost parts of the world. By the anointing of the Holy Spirit, no one will ever be the same after receiving those powerful words of Jesus.

The following three points will be emphasized: (1) We *are* commissioned; (2) we are commissioned *by Jesus*; and (3) we are commissioned *as Jesus*.

WE ARE COMMISSIONED

Let us consider five levels of Kingdom involvement:

A. Spectator

A spectator is one who passes by, looks on, and is attracted by the crowd. Many spectators were present at Christ's triumphant entry into Jerusalem. Even more attended His trial and crucifixion. To a spectator, a crowd is a social event, something interesting and entertaining. To thousands, Christianity is only a spectator sport.

B. Admirer

An admirer is one who holds himself personally aloof from that which he admires. He does not discern or admit that the object of his admiration is making a claim upon his life. Secretly, he strives to be like the one whom he admires, but he is not quite willing to make any sacrifices—to give up any previous attachments, to reconstruct his life, to inconvenience himself, or to assume any responsibility in order to be what he admires. He only verbalizes his feelings.

C. Follower

One who strives to be like that which he admires can be called a follower. No man is so humble that he cannot bear God's image. When one becomes a follower, he is no longer a spectator or an admirer.

D. Disciple

The designation *disciple* means a learner, a student, a scholar, an apprentice, or a carbon copy of the teacher. Accepting discipleship entails discipline and requires submission to His lordship and leadership. To be a disciple is the minimal requirement Christ desires.

E. Apostle

The word *apostle* is from the Greek word *apostolos*, which means, "messenger" or "one that is sent forth." Jesus does not send a spectator, an admirer, or even a follower. He only sends disciples who are ready and willing to be sent. A *commission* is a royal decree. It means to be sent with legal, as well as regal, authority. The one who is sent becomes an agent in divine affairs and is given full power of attorney—that legal, written right to transact business for another, with the same power and authority as the one who gave it. *We are commissioned!*

WE ARE COMMISSIONED BY JESUS

A. "I, Myself, am sending you." Every Christian is sent by Jesus. Whoever possesses His peace, has heard His voice and received His Word, has felt His touch, and has had his heart made glad by His presence is included in Christ's directive. All of us are sent! All of us are under orders! On this earth we are all on an errand bearing eternal consequences!

B. Those He selected were fishermen, tax collectors, and physicians—people just like you and me. He is not reaching for a certain class; He is searching for those He can trust to go in His stead and do the same work the Father called and sent Christ to do.

WE ARE COMMISSIONED AS JESUS

A. The unchanging commandment of Christ

"As my Father hath sent me, *even so* send I you." Note these words: Exactly "*as* my Father hath sent me, even so"—no difference, no variance, no alteration, no dilution, but a precise parallelism. Jesus is saying, "I, Myself, am sending you."

B. The example of Christ

We are to duplicate His attitude, His actions, His intensity, and His work. We have received the same call. We are to feel the same urgency. His commission is now our commission. John 9:4 says, "I must work the works of him that sent me, while it is day: the night cometh, when no man can work."

C. The continuing commission of Christ

Jesus declared, "As my Father hath sent me." Hath sent means that He not only has sent but is presently sending and will continue to send. The work continues; nothing stops it. If He was sent to seek and to save that which was lost, so too are we to "go out into the highways and hedges, and compel them to come in, that my house may be filled" (Luke 14:23). He came not to do His own will but His Father's will, and the same instructions He received, we are to receive today.

D. Acceptance of Christ's commission

Christ was God incarnate. Christ was the embodiment of God. Christ was an extension of God to mankind. Even so, the church is the body of Christ and an extension of the Lord Jesus Christ to all men in all the world.

CONCLUSION

We *are* commissioned! We are commissioned *by Jesus*, and we are commissioned *as Jesus* was commissioned! Total surrender to the call for Kingdom involvement requires that we not be spectators or admirers. As we accept the Great Commission, we become a disciple, an apostle, an agent of Christ committed to preaching the gospel throughout the earth!

CONTRIBUTORS

Beacham, Doug; Senior Pastor, Franklin Springs Pentecostal Holiness Church; Franklin Springs, Georgia

Beatty, G. Earl; Academic Dean, Instructor—Pastoral Theology, Emmanuel College School of Christian Ministries; Pentecostal Holiness Church; Franklin Springs, Georgia

BonGiovanni, Guy; General Overseer, Christian Church of North America; Hermitage, Pennsylvania

Brandt, R.L.; Executive Presbyter, Assemblies of God; Billings, Montana

Carlson, G. Raymond; General Superintendent, Assemblies of God; Springfield, Missouri

Cline, George W.; Pastor, Greeley Foursquare Church; Greeley, Colorado

Clopine, Sandra Goodwin; Secretary, Women's Ministries Department; Editor, *Woman's Touch*; Assemblies of God; Springfield, Missouri

Cross, James A.; Member of Executive Council, Church of God; Valrico, Florida

Crowley, Raymond E.; General Overseer, Church of God International Offices; Cleveland, Tennessee

Davenport, R. Edward; Pastor, Buford Church of God; Buford, Georgia

Frazier, Robert P.; Senior Pastor, Aurora Church of God; Aurora, Colorado

Garrison, Joaquin; Pastor, Pentecostal Holiness Church; Memphis, Tennessee

Gillum, Perry; Public Relations Director, Church of God of Prophecy; Cleveland, Tennessee

Greenlee, Daniel; Pastor/Conference Superintendent, Pentecostal Holiness Church; San Jose, California

Griffis, David M.; State Youth and Christian Education Director, Church of God; Mauldin, South Carolina

Hall, Kenneth E.; State Youth and Christian Education Director, Church of God; Tampa, Florida

Hedgepeth, John E.; Pastor, Northwood Temple Church; Pentecostal Holiness Church; Fayetteville, North Carolina

Hicks, Cullen L.; General Superintendent; Congregationalist Holiness Church Inc.; Griffin, Georgia

Hicks, Roy H.; Retired General Overseer, International Church of the Foursquare Gospel; Los Angeles, California

Hobbs, Joel; Pastor, West Ashley Church of God; Charleston, South Carolina

Hughes, Ray H.; First Assistant General Overseer, Church of God International Offices; Cleveland, Tennessee

Jackson, Gene; Superintendent, Tennessee District; Assemblies of God; Madison, Tennessee

Johnson, Bobby; Pastor, Praise Cathedral Church of God; Greer, South Carolina

Kelley, B.L.; State Overseer, Eastern North Carolina; Church of God; Kenly, North Carolina

King, Roy D.; General Superintendent, Pentecostal Assemblies of Newfoundland; St. John's, Newfoundland

Lawhon, Floyd H.; Pastor, The Upper Room Church of God; Westminster, California

Lee, Edgar R.; Academic Dean, Assemblies of God Theological Seminary; Springfield, Missouri

MacKnight, James M.; General Superintendent, The Pentecostal Assemblies of Canada; Toronto, Ontario

Matthews, Elwood; Radio/TV Speaker, Voice of Salvation; Church of God of Prophecy; Cleveland, Tennessee

May, Danny L.; Senior Pastor, North Cleveland Church of God; Cleveland, Tennessee

Pruitt, Raymond M.; Minister, Church of God Prophecy, Cleveland, Tennessee

Reid, William A.; State Youth and Christian Education Director, Church of God; Simpsonville, Maryland

Richardson, Carl; President, Carl Richardson Ministries International Inc.; Church of God; Brandon, Florida

Stewart, Leon; General Superintendent, International Pentecostal Holiness Church Inc.; Oklahoma City, Oklahoma

Stone, H. Lynn; Coordinator, Ministerial Development; Church of God; Cleveland, Tennessee

Thomas, R.B.; Director of Admissions and Research, School of Theology; Church of God; Cleveland, Tennessee

Thompson, D. Chris; Conference Evangelism Director, North Carolina Conference; Pentecostal Holiness Church; Falcon, Virginia

Triplett, Bennie; State Overseer, Southern Ohio; Church of God; Lebanon, Ohio

Underwood, B.E.; Executive Director, World Missions Department, Pentecostal Holiness Church; Oklahoma City, Oklahoma

Varlack, Adrian L. Sr.; World Missions Secretary, Church of God of Prophecy; Cleveland, Tennessee

Vest, R. Lamar; Second Assistant General Overseer, Church of God International Offices; Cleveland, Tennessee

Walker, Paul L.; Senior Pastor, Mount Paran Church of God; Atlanta, Georgia

Ward, C.M.; Evangelist, Assemblies of God; Stockton, California

West, Melvin L.; District Superintendent, Pentecostal Church of God; Danville, Virginia

Williams, Ronald D.; Editor, *Foursquare World ADVANCE*; International Church of the Foursquare Gospel; Los Angeles, California

INDEX

Manuscript Sermons

Outline Sermons